# HUGGING
# THE
# THIRD RAIL

Plans for Reforming Washington

and

Renewing America

with

Family Friendly Solutions

For 2016 and Beyond

Michael J. Rogers

ISBN:

ISBN-13: 978-1537077659
ISBN-10: 1537077651

# DEDICATION

To my children. I have failed you many times in the past. I have tried to become someone you could be proud of. I love you greatly and dedicate this book to each of you in the hope that you will have a better future because of the implementation of the ideas included here.

# CONTENTS

# ACKNOWLEDGMENTS

**"As iron sharpens iron, so one person sharpens another."**
**Proverbs 27:17**

There are parts of many solutions in here that come from others and ideas that are derived from other people's ideas. I am sorry I have not tracked the sources well or completely. Hopefully it will be sufficient that the ideas are what matter and not who gets the credit. To the extent that there is wisdom and value in this book the glory belongs to God rather than to any of us created beings. Any failures in this book are completely due to my own insufficiencies.

# FORWARD

"Here's to the crazy ones. The misfits. The rebels. The troublemakers. The round pegs in the square holes. The ones who see things differently. They're not fond of rules. And they have no respect for the status quo. You can quote them, disagree with them, glorify or vilify them. About the only thing you can't do is ignore them. Because they change things. They push the human race forward. And while some may see them as the crazy ones, we see genius. Because the people who are crazy enough to think they can change the world, are the ones who do."
Steve Jobs

I believe in the ideas written in this book and I hope the American people embrace them also. Unfortunately, it seems like every issue has become a Third Rail in our politically polarized country. While I am sure that there is something in here that you will disagree with; I hope that you will agree with much of this book and see the wisdom of the solutions. Whether you agree or not let us have a discussion about these and your ideas for solving these problems. Let us come together and find solutions and stop looking to use these continuing issues for political advantage for the next election.

I have been a conservative since I was a teen, though I did not realize that until much later. I began as a national defense hawk and as I matured and experienced the world I added fiscal and social conservative convictions to my values. I became active in the Republican Party during the George W. Bush years because I became concerned about the Party straying from platform and principles. For a long time I thought it was sufficient to elect Republicans to office and they would follow the platform and principles and I could live my life without having to worry much about politics and public policy. That illusion was shattered and I realized that we all need to keep our elected officials both in line and supported. We have to call them out and challenge them when they stray and we need to support them when they toe the line and make sure they know we are behind them when the opposition is attacking them.

We are in a pivotal time in American history when we must decide whether to renew the American spirit and grow the country or settle for a steady decline and an end of American Exceptionalism.

In the first edition, in 2012, I used the nom de plume, Relentless For Liberty, for the book. I believed the ideas are more important than who I am. I was concerned that my name in connection with these ideas could be used to discredit the ideas. Now I am taking a chance and stepping out with these ideas under my own name. It is time to put this in the hands of God. It is my hope that the Republican Party, Tea Parties, the President and Congress, and the American People will embrace these ideas.

I am not married to these specific ideas. These are the best solutions I have found to this point in time. I am continuously seeking more information and better ideas for solving problems. My values have changed over time as I have developed a stronger relationship with Christ. Other than a desire to become more Christ-like I do not anticipate my values changing significantly in any other manner. In terms of specific details about solving public policy issues I am open to any idea that is practical, family and relationship building, economically sound, recognizes real human behavior, and is not dishonoring to God.

I started writing the first edition in 2011 because I was dissatisfied with the ideas being put forth by the Presidential candidates. I began writing from the viewpoint of a candidate putting forth his positions on issues. Some sections of this book still have that viewpoint. Most now simply put forth ideas I believe will solve many of our current problems and help turn us toward a better future. I would love to be the President of the United States to lead our great country down a better path and to make the decisions to implement these solutions. I would not like to be a candidate for the office. I offer my services to the President and any others who wish to incorporate any of these solutions. It is a sign of good leadership to recognize good ideas and not believe they have to have all of the original ideas. Leaders need to identify the best solution available and then sell it and execute it!

I pray that we as a nation and all of the Peoples of the world turn to God for guidance. We are all sinners and are in need of the saving grace that God provided with the sacrifice of Christ on the Cross at Calvary. The world seeking after God and being in relationship with Christ will do more for solving the problems of the world than anything else.

God bless you and the United States of America, today and always!

Mike Rogers, 2016

# 1 PHILOSOPHY AND PRINCIPLES

"Nearly all men can stand adversity, but if you want to test a man's
character, give him power."
Abraham Lincoln

It is important that you know the philosophy and principles behind the
decisions I make in many of the plans described in this book. This chapter is
an overview of some of the values I consider when making decisions. There is
much more mixed in throughout the book where appropriate.

I wish that all candidates for public office would do likewise. This kind of
information is needed by the electorate, especially for the state and national
level offices. There will always be issues that come up during a term in office
that are unexpected. Having a general idea of the philosophy and principles
that they will use to make a decision will help us make better decisions about
who to vote for.

I believe that elected officials are there to represent their constituents. But
they are not there to do what the majority of their constituents want them to
do on every issue. Officials are there to use their best judgment based on their
knowledge, experience, and values. We elect them to study issues and develop
legislation to serve our interests. Sometimes they will have to make decisions
that are contrary to popular opinion when they make them. Knowing at
election time what guides them will ensure having more predictable results
when the tough decisions need to be made.

Many will likely call me a conservative ideologue because they disagree
with my positions and values. If I am I came through the backdoor. I
developed my values first and figured out later that they frequently matched
up with what are called conservative values. I don't like ideas because
someone says they are conservative and dislike ideas people say are liberal. I
study issues and come to my own conclusions about what makes sense and
what is workable in the real world.

There are many labels that come close to describing me. I am a fiscal and social conservative with some libertarian leanings. I believe a strong national defense is essential to secure not only our own peace and liberty but because we are the sole superpower with a relatively benevolent demeanor compared to other past superpowers we help provide peace and stability to much of the rest of the world. Intact families are the building blocks of a strong free society and government policies should always take account of the effect on families and serve to strengthen and not weaken families.

## Fiscal Conservative

As a fiscal conservative I believe the government should not spend more than it receives in revenue. Except for paying for wars or rebuilding from natural disasters and wars and other attacks the government should not run deficits. Even when these exceptions do occur we should pay for them as soon as possible. It is immoral to stick our children and grandchildren with the costs of our spending on ourselves. They will have their own needs and emergencies to pay for.

That is not to say that using debt is wrong. Capital projects that have a long life are reasonable uses of debt in order to spread the costs over the life of the project. For the federal and state governments this should also be rare. These governments have large annual expenditures for capital projects. It will be rare that any single project or even a small group of these projects will exceed the annual appropriations for capital projects. Therefore there should not be a need to use debt to finance them. Other than the exceptions already listed, debt should not be used for current operations. This includes the costs of retirement and other long term compensation of government employees. The cost of labor needs to be paid for when the labor is performed.

The government has to be reduced in size to the essential duties of the government. This will make it less costly and more efficient. Especially when the government cannot pay all of its bills, like now, nonessential and less essential programs need to be ended. Every dollar spent by the government has to be taken from American taxpayers. People who would be able to spend or invest that money as they see fit. That is only fair since they are the people who earned the money.

## Social Conservative

As a social conservative I believe that the state has an obligation to protect life from the moment of conception to a natural death. To do otherwise sets arbitrary limits on who is to be protected. As I wrote before, intact families need to be strengthened and not weakened. Therefore marriage needs to be just between one man and one woman. Most children do best when raised by their natural parents. It is our connections to one another which help to hold society together. Healthy families have strong bonds. Unhealthy families need to be helped to become healthy and not written off.

## Ownership society

We need to return to an ownership society. Not an ownership society like President Bush talked about, the ownership of homes. What I mean is an ownership of responsibility. For too long now there has been an abdication of personal responsibility. For our society to continue to grow and thrive, to still be an exceptional nation, we must take personal responsibility for our lives.

Intact families are the base upon which a stable society depends. For far too long government has been subsidizing the abdication of personal responsibility and made it far too easy for people to opt out of working for their families.

This means that when individuals, families, and businesses get money from the government it needs to be primarily in the form of loans and not grants. Whether it is welfare for individuals or corporations there is no entitlement to this money. The government must take money from those who earn it to give it to others. There are legitimate times when a safety net is needed and is beneficial. We are a compassionate people but our compassion has been abused for many years. When individuals and corporations know that what they borrow will have to be paid back with interest I believe they will only accept what is actually needed.

When much of the money spent by government must be paid back to the government by those who receive it, taxes will be able to be reduced greatly. This allows us to provide a safety net without developing a lifestyle of dependency upon the government as we have now.

Money and other property in the United States belong to the people who earned it and own it. It does not belong to the government. Government should only be allowed to take what is absolutely necessary and no more. Government needs to be limited to restraining evil, preserving order, and promoting justice.

## National Security Requires Economic Strength

Most major issues in the United States have a certain degree of effect on national security. The stability and peace of much of the world is dependent upon the military, diplomatic, and political power and will of the United States. In many ways, that power and will is dependent upon the economic strength of the United States. Excessive debt, pension, and healthcare costs in the United States are increasingly a burdensome structural cost for businesses and the government. This is making America less competitive and therefore reducing our economic power which in turn reduces our ability to maintain our national security.

If this power and will continue to decline others will try to step into our place. The two most likely being China and Russia. Neither of these countries will have liberty anywhere near the top of their priorities if it even makes their list at all. Eventually we will be forced to stand up or back down to them. If our strength is on par with theirs we will take huge losses like in World War II. Our hedge against letting them consider taking us on is our strength and the will to use it where and when necessary.

## Christ is Not a Socialist

I have heard many liberals say that Christ is a Socialist. This is nonsense. Socialism is the use of the government, which by its nature is force, to steal from some to give to others. Christ very clearly said not to steal. Christ is Love or in other words Charity. He calls all of us to love Him and to love others. Loving others is a voluntary action as the fruit of our relationship with Christ. It is not about a philosophy of government coercion. The early Church shared all as the fruit of their relationships with Christ not out of force or guilt or obligation or even the needs of some but out of Love. This can only be done voluntarily. It cannot be done through government or any other type of force.

## Capitalism, Profits, and Free Markets are Good

Capitalism is an economic system characterized by private ownership of property and the means of production. Investments are made by private decisions. Prices, production, and distribution of goods are determined mostly by free market competition. Unfortunately there are too many people in business who want to protect what they have by getting protection from competition or changes in the economy. There are many with too close of a relationship with government. This happens at all levels of government because government has the power to take other people's money. This unhealthy connection between business and political leaders develops into crony capitalism. (Crony capitalism is an oxymoron. Cronyism and true capitalism are opposites.) This is how we get corporate subsidies, bailouts, and selective regulations that harm competitors and protect some businesses. As bad as that is it gets worse. Crony capitalists mistakenly believe that the power is in their hands and that the politicians work for them. That does not last because eventually the politicians and bureaucrats will have the upper hand. Power seeks more power. If this is not stopped and reversed it will eventually develop into socialism with the government in charge of everything and the people slaves to the government. We have been drifting in this direction for decades.

Maintaining free markets and private ownership of property is essential to economic freedom. Economic freedom is essential for political freedom. Free markets provide each of us incentives to work to improve our lot in life, to secure more resources for ourselves and for our families.

Many people, especially liberal politicians like to criticize profits. They act like profits and those who earn them are evil. The very opposite is true. It is profits which grow the economy and help us all to prosper. We should all want US companies to make huge profits. Profits are a sign of success. Profits mean the company paid all of its bills, paid all of its employees, and had money left over for the owners who invested in the company and created the job opportunities. Profits are what pay to increase employment opportunities, they pay for our pension and other retirement assets, provide tax revenue, and grow the economy. Profits should be encouraged and applauded.

## Christ Follower

Most importantly, I am a committed follower of Christ. We are all sinners, we are lost and deserve hell; and the only hope is to place our faith and trust in the Lord Jesus Christ. Eternal life is granted based on what He did, not on what we do. Jesus Christ is the only way to heaven and to the Father. All of us who follow Christ are called to love God with all of our heart, mind, and soul and to love our neighbors as we love ourselves. We are called to be salt and light to the world by sharing the Gospel and caring for each other.

Because we are all made in the image of God I see all people as family, part of the Brotherhood of Man. Some are closer and some are more distant relatives. While it is normal and right to care more and protect family and countrymen over others it is still important to treat other more distant family members with respect and dignity. While non-citizens do not deserve the rights of citizenship they have been endowed by God with the same unalienable rights. These ideas inform my positions on many issues, from immigration, torture, welfare safety net, foreign policy, and many other issues.

There are some people who like to promote different races as superior or inferior and desire to keep a separation of the races. The Bible clearly tells us that we are all descended from Adam and Eve. Therefore the complete mixing of the races is the closest we will get to original man.

My reasons for believing are many. The reaction of the Apostles to Christ's death and resurrection. The lack of evidence and the mathematical improbability of evolution. The incredible fine tuning that exists in the universe that makes it possible for life to exist here on Earth or for the universe to exist at all. I can feel the presence of God in my heart and my life.

Most of the Apostles and many others who knew Christ first-hand were given the choice to renounce Him or be martyred. They chose martyrdom. It is one thing to die for a lie because you believe it to be true. It is far from likely that all these people would willingly die for a lie that they knew was a lie. Not when life and freedom could be achieved by admitting to a lie. They witnessed God incarnate and they willingly became martyrs. They knew He is real and is who He said He is!

I believe that God exists outside of time and created all that we know. There has been no better explanation of the creation of the universe in which we exist. Mathematically even the longest projections of the age of the universe is not long enough to account for evolution from simple molecules to complex proteins to simple single cell organisms to more complex organisms by random variation. That does not even come close to the complexity of humans or even some of the specialized cells in humans. We would literally be seeing evolution taking place in every generation. The majority of genetic changes we do see are usually harmful in the form of cancers or other genetic defects. The remainder is simple variation in already existing genes. Not the creation of new genes. The fossil record also bears this out. We should see fossils with every variation through time but we do not. We only see distinct kinds of creatures in the fossil record. Much as to be expected with a creator.

An example I have heard many times is about Mount Rushmore. Would you believe that it could have been created by random forces of wind, heat, and water? Of course not! You would expect it to have a creator. How much more complex is life—human or otherwise than Mount Rushmore?

I believe the Bible in its original text is the inerrant Word of God. It has been passed down to us materially complete. Passed down more accurately and in far more copies than any other ancient text. If one is to believe in an omniscient, omnipotent God that desires a personal relationship with each of us then it is easy to believe that He could arrange for us to have the Bible to know Him.

Because Adam and Eve ate from the tree of the knowledge of good and evil, we their descendants live in a fallen world where we experience both good and evil. I believe the purpose of life is to learn to love Christ and each other better. This is done by acknowledging Christ as Lord and Savior, confessing our sins to Him, asking for forgiveness, and seeking His help to love better.

If we reject God then the natural consequence is eternal separation from God known as hell. As I understand scripture our souls are immortal. We either go to paradise with God or to hell and be completely separated from God for eternity. An eternity without the influence of God awaits those who go to hell. I believe hell will degenerate into the worst aspects of life here on Earth. Over time people will get worn out trying to hold onto their humanity. There will be hunger and thirst without the means to quench it or death to end it. The characterization of hell as a lake of fire will be due to the only means of controlling others. Because people will feel but not be killed, pain is used to control and the most powerful weapon will be fire.

Many will try to build human governing structures initially. These will not survive because the people who try to protect these societies will wear down over time. As we see in soldiers and police that are under frequent threat, PTSD will become rampant. These protectors will not be limited to a few combat tours or a 20 year career. They will have to sustain themselves throughout eternity. Even the strongest will break. All of Hell will become like the worst parts of failed states. Great violence and rape. Hunger and thirst without food or drink to quench it. Trust in all others will eventually be broken. Over time the minds of all will be broken.

Hell is not God's punishment of unrepentant sinners. Hell is the natural consequence of human beings choosing an eternity of selfishness over love. Of choosing themselves over God!

Those of us who call ourselves followers of Christ cannot bear to see anyone go to hell. It is out of love that we share the Gospel and encourage others to have a relationship with Christ. To do otherwise given our beliefs would indicate our lack of love for another.

It is unfortunate when so-called Christians exhibit superiority or condemnation toward others. These are not the attributes of Christ who we should seek to emulate. How much do you have to hate someone to believe and not share the Gospel and the love we have received from God?

There are whole books written on the evidence to support a Christian worldview. Above is just a sampling of what I believe. In addition to all the head knowledge, I can feel the presence of the Holy Spirit in my life. The good counsel that I am ashamed to say I do not always listen to. Other times I do listen and obey against my own will and judgment and it has led to a better life than I could imagine or deserve.

## Propose Not Impose

Charles Colson has been a great influence in shaping my thoughts about the proper relationship between Christians and the government and society in which we live. He has written many books that go into great detail on these subjects. I urge you to check them out. (http://www.colsoncenter.org/wfp-home) Here is an excerpt from an email by Chuck Colson about this relationship to counter the secular argument that we are trying to impose our Christian beliefs upon others.

What we do is "PROPOSE"—propose a way of life that benefits the common good and promotes human dignity.

Remember, Western liberal democracy (which gives the media the freedom to bite the hand that feeds it) arose from Christian roots.

It was in the monasteries of Christian Europe during the Middle Ages where we begin to find democracy for all—noble and peasant alike. Capitalism, guided by Augustine's writings, took root in the northern Italian states.

In fact, the moral standards that Christianity engendered in Western culture were crucial for the development of democracy: *People must be able to govern themselves and practice self-restraint before they can rule themselves via elected government.* (My emphasis)

...Even beyond modern liberal democracy, think for just a moment about how Christianity made Western culture the most humane culture in history: schools for all, charities, hospitals, the great universities . . . these are all fruits of Christian culture in the West.

The belief in the sanctity of life made Christians defenders of each individual's dignity.

We believe men and women are sovereign creatures made in God's image.

Because we bear His image and were granted free will by God Himself, we enjoy freedom as a right—it's in our nature. (That's also, by the way, why the Church has always defended the right of private property—another hallmark of the West.)

So, the next time a friend or acquaintance blithely comments that Christians seek to "impose" their religion on others, gently remind him or her that we seek no such thing.

We will continue as our forbearers did, PROPOSING that which benefits the common good and promotes human dignity. Western civilization has been shaped by this proposal and every American who enjoys the blessings of freedom—believer and non-believer alike—benefits from it.

We each have a worldview or perspective from which we look at the world. It encompasses our values and beliefs. We each have a right to propose laws and regulations to the community. The laws of the land are made up of the consensus of the people who participate in the process.

Christians have a right and an obligation to participate in the process. As any other citizen we have a right to participate equally with all other citizens. It is only natural that we will propose and work to promote the values we believe are right. We should never apologize for that nor let others convince us that our values need to be kept private. Because of the nature of our system of government we Christians have an obligation to fully participate in the process of self-government. This includes voting, researching candidates, actively supporting the best candidate, actively promoting Christian values, and running for office. Much as we are part of the Body of Christ we are also part of the body of Caesar. As citizens in a democratic republic we are part of the government. We must be ambassadors for Christ in the ways we participate in the body of Caesar.

## When Considering Issues

Here are several things I do when I look at an issue:

I start by thinking about what the ideal end state would be then map out an incremental path to reach that state. In a democracy incremental change is usually the best that can be hoped for because of the need to build a consensus. Although sometimes it is possible to use this process to see past the symptoms of bad laws to make more comprehensive changes. Normally the politically possible is far short of the ideal.

Consider human behavior and natural consequences when designing policies and structuring programs. There will always be people who try to manipulate to gain advantage. Many times there are ways to design things that make this much more difficult. Using natural consequences is especially helpful because they do not rely on police, investigators, or prosecutors to enforce.

When natural consequences are not available, raising the costs of abuse relative to the benefits gained can have a deterrent effect. That is one aspect of understanding the cost/benefit ratio of a program. Understanding the costs that bad actors need to overcome to make abusing a program profitable can aid in the design of more effective programs.

It is not just intentional bad actors who need to be accounted for. A poorly designed program can offer a moral hazard to the people intended to be helped by creating perverse incentives. This is commonly present in welfare and subsidy programs where the benefits discourage personal or corporate ownership of responsibility.

Seek to reduce concentrations of power. Everyone has heard that power corrupts and absolute power corrupts absolutely. (That is both an indictment of concentrations of power and a warning to idealists or populists not to try to concentrate power for the sake of emergency change.) What is not usually stated is that the corrupt will seek out power. Keeping limits on power and making the process to increase the power of positions in government slow will deter this to some extent.

Given human nature, checks and balances on power are essential. It is common for people to try to restructure government to get power into the "right" hands to achieve some change they believe is needed. I have caught myself thinking along those lines at times. It is important to "game" any structure to understand what is possible in the "wrong" hands. This is not only true at a constitutional level but at all levels of government. Checks and balances on power are needed in many other areas, as well, such as contract law, divorce law, bankruptcy law, corporate governance, etc.

Consider whether it is appropriate for an issue to be handled by the government. Many times people try to make government do something that is better done by the private sector or left to individuals. Government should concentrate on what only government can do and do these things well. Intruding into other areas reduces freedom and can dissipate the energy and focus of the government making it less effective in essential areas. Too much government makes oversight difficult. Rentseekers will gravitate to these opportunities to exploit the people. Anything that is capable of being done outside of the government will usually be done more efficiently by the private sector. When the need is gone the private entity will find new needs to fulfill or go away. A private organization has to constantly justify its existence. A government program seldom goes away even when the need goes away.

The effects of change need to be considered. Many times people see a problem and craft a solution based on their own experience. Most do not think about how this change affects other laws or how people will try to take advantage of the change. They have tunnel vision about their particular issue. Anecdotal evidence can point to the need for a change in law or regulation but a much more encompassing assessment needs to be made about the other areas affected before enacting a change. Don't create more problems than are solved.

Another aspect of considering the effects of change is most apparent in laws affecting business or investments. Many decisions are based on current laws and assumptions about the future and need to be made months or years before being implemented. When the laws change it can have serious consequences for companies. When necessary use transition periods to promote stability and full utilization of resources.

Minimize discretion by bureaucrats whenever possible. Try to be specific with prohibitions in law and regulations and as open or general as possible with what is allowable to those being regulated. Too much discretion can lead to solicitation of bribes or coercion by bureaucrats as well as being used as a basis for candidates to solicit campaign contributions. It is also an issue of freedom in that private individuals and companies should have as much flexibility to conduct their business as possible.

Transparency is essential in government. Aside from some aspects of defense, security, and intelligence operations and negotiation strategy there should be transparency in government. Sin loves secrecy! It is natural that people will try to hide illegal activity, work mistakes, laziness, incompetence, poor policies, embarrassment, and other problems. It is important that government activities and information be publically available in easily searchable formats. There must be very strong justification for not being transparent. This will help to head off wrong doing. When attempts are made to hide information it will tip off the public that wrong doing has occurred or that someone intends to do wrong. Reducing the size of government will aid in making government activities transparent. The sheer size of government makes it difficult for individuals, news media, public interest groups, and even Congress to provide adequate oversight.

Making sure the costs of risks are borne by those responsible for incurring the risk. Aligning personal responsibility with rights is required for true liberty. This is most evident in the area of healthcare reform. Many people use medical services that are unnecessary or they fail to lead a healthy lifestyle driving up the cost for everyone. This is also important in many of the financial, bankruptcy, incarceration, and drug war reforms.

A cost/benefit analysis in government is not as straight forward as in the private sector. It is not a matter of choosing between which products to produce or which markets to enter. Frequently, peoples' health or lives are at stake in the decisions by government. There is no way to quantify the value of a human life. Yet we still have to control costs. Priorities have to be set because resources are limited. Part of this balance can be attained by comparing competing programs. That is the easy part.

The more difficult part is determining how much to allow government to burden the rest of society. Determining the amount of GDP to pull from the economy to pay for government. Deciding the right balance between regulations and the cost of the regulations to those regulated and their customers. Too often regulations and taxes impose heavy burdens without providing a significant benefit.

Simplifying processes and reducing administrative costs for government and for those who interact with government. For the average person these are particularly notable in tax reform. Businesses face far more areas where the paperwork and time burdens of complying with regulations is considerable. As in business, these transaction costs seldom add value in their own right. There is a need for documenting these transactions with the government but only the minimum that is necessary should be required. The forms and instructions should be kept as simple as possible. The complexity of the underlying regulations should be minimized.

In most policies it is important that the philosophical underpinnings are sound. In many cases bad policies result from philosophies that do not account for the way people actually behave. How people will react to the policy. That is because many philosophies that people adhere to are based on personal preference or wishful thinking.

Whenever possible empirical data should be used to help design policies. Too often people with agendas do specific studies to meet the policy they have already decided on. Many times data is discounted because it does not fit the philosophical beliefs or other preconceptions of lawmakers. Usually there is more empirical data available after a program has been in place than before. Then it can be used to reform or end a policy. It does not have to be this limited. More should be done to get broader studies that encompass more data from more perspectives when designing legislation.

Politicians like to use anecdotal "evidence" to promote a policy. Frequently these are cherry-picked examples to help them make a point. They are seldom a sound basis for making policy decisions. They help to drive public opinion because people usually relate to such examples better than they can relate to philosophy or statistics. Lawmakers and the public have to guard against making policy strictly from anecdotal evidence. They can use it as the basis to look into making a new policy or reforming an old policy. They can use it to help sell a policy proposal. But the policy still needs to be supportable philosophically and when possible empirically.

Ideally the philosophical, empirical, and anecdotal will align. This is the underpinnings of great public policy!

# 2 GRAND STRATEGY

**"I prefer peace. But if trouble must come, let it come in my time, so that my children can live in peace."**
**Thomas Paine**

## Global Grand Strategy

The United States has not had a Grand Strategy since the end of the Cold War. We are facing many challenges including a crumbling international order, a sluggish economy, many structural impediments to growth, an aging population, and governments that control much of the economy.

Some have proposed isolation, selective engagement, cooperative security, or US primacy. These emphasize military and diplomatic strategy. Our Grand Strategy needs to be more encompassing that just those two areas. For now we will start with these limited areas. We need to incorporate parts of three of these strategies. First, we need to maintain the US primacy as the lone superpower. There are no prospective superpowers who have nearly the respect for freedom and human rights as we do. Second, we need to develop stronger cooperative security arrangements with other democratic republics. Thirdly we need to selectively engage the world to stop aggressive nations and ideologies from enslaving people.

At the core of our Grand Strategy has to be promoting freedom and liberty. We need to fight the major –isms of our day—socialism, authoritarianism, radical Islamism, and cronyism. These are the major ideologies that seek power and to control others.

We need to use our national power—military, diplomatic, political, and economic to promote our values and facilitate change wherever possible in the world. The crosslinks between terrorists, criminal gangs, corrupt governments, and their cronies means that we should use the full resources of the government to thwart them.

We cannot address every problem in the world but we can and should address as many as we can. Prioritizing those with the most effect on the US and our allies and take advantage of other opportunities as they present themselves.

We need to proactively shape the world of the future before others shape it in ways that will be harmful to our children and grandchildren. Do not deceive yourselves into believing that others are not actively trying to shape the world. The mafia government of Russia, radical Islamists, China, and Iran are the most prolific in trying to reshape the world to empower themselves. Their worldviews are not in the best interests of the American people nor of any of the peoples of the world

A major component of our strategy will be fighting in the economic and diplomatic areas and involves the breaking up of concentrations of power that seek to control people, a country, a region, or an industry. Countries like Russia, China, Ukraine, Venezuela, Brazil, Saudi Arabia, Iran, and Egypt have cliques that control large segments of the economy and the government. There is a mixture of government owned or controlled corporations, sovereign wealth funds, and protection syndicates at play. This cronyism is destructive to the freedom of the citizens of these countries as well as to the businesses, citizens, and governments of other countries. The power to manipulate government policy and large segments of the global economy make these cliques unusually powerful. There are few internal checks on this power except from revolution. Externally, the US and our allies need to stand up against these syndicates or they will further undermine our freedoms and our economies. WTO and other trade rules need to be adjusted to push GSEs into the private sector independent of their governments. Fighting this battle will help head off military battles in the future.

The economy and the people of these countries are milked with impunity. In some cases these cliques hide their activities behind the cloak of government, playing factions against each other, playing domestic and foreign audiences against one another, and challenging outsiders if they dare to "interfere in internal national matters." In other cases they hide behind the cloak of capitalism in order to get the West to give them a pass. But large businesses are not synonymous with free market capitalism. These cliques manipulate rather than compete in a free market. They undercut capitalism and free markets with cronyism.

## Reforming the West

We in the West have our own problems we need to clean up. At a lower level of manipulation many Western countries have very controlling, paternalistic governments. They heavily regulate business and labor. In many cases they have nationalized healthcare, energy, transportation and telecommunication systems, and subsidize industries to be globally competitive. For several generations they have been making larger and larger promises to their citizens in areas like shortened work weeks, many types of paid leave, large amounts of paid vacations, under 65 retirement ages, labor regulations, market distorting wage and price controls. These countries are burying themselves in unsustainable levels of debt to pay for these promises and strangling economic growth with regulations. This debt and overregulation is close to breaking these countries and leading to a global economic meltdown.

This in turn will empower radical cliques, demagogues, or populists who may come to power as an alternative. Because the mainstream politicians do not seem to be able to solve the problems, people will turn to radicals out of frustration and fear. The mainstream Western politicians need to develop the courage to solve these problems and pare back the welfare state before they cause the collapse of freedom in their countries. Politicians cannot solve all problems with a government program. Often the best public policy is to stay out of the way of the people.

These welfare states have to reform. Many of the reforms proposed in this book for the US are just as applicable to other nations. They are based on understanding human behavior and economics.

## US Primacy

Some may say that the US is the greatest concentration of power in the world. In a sense that is true. The redeeming factor with the US is the fact that we hold elections regularly to give the people a say in who makes the decisions. This diffuses some of the effects of this concentration of power. Despite excessive regulation, the government still does not control most areas of commerce. Certainly there are many areas where improvement is necessary and some of these are addressed in this book. Some of these are election reforms that level the playing field between incumbents and challengers.

But the ability of the American people to change their government is not what most people think of when they think of the power that is concentrated in the US. It is the might of our economy and of our military, both conventional and nuclear. They believe we have an outsized influence on the world. We certainly do! But the US unilaterally diminishing our power does not do the rest of the world any favors. Except for foreign despots and their cronies. We have seen ample evidence of this under President Obama.

Unlike most major powers in the past, the US has used its power to help other peoples to become free. Our greatest success in this has been with Japan, South Korea, and much of Europe. We have had an influence in many other countries around the world. Our Navy has been a very significant force in maintaining freedom of the seas for all nations. This allows tremendous amounts of global trade to take place.

I am reminded of the speech by Lt. Colonel Chamberlin to the "mutineers" of the 2nd Maine Volunteer Regiment shortly before the Battle of

Gettysburg as portrayed in the movie, Gettysburg. He talked about how the Union Army was something new in history. It was an army that set out to make other men free. It has been so for quite some time. Although there are some with ulterior motives, other than the Indian Wars, the nation as a whole has fought and worked to bring freedom to people around the world since .

The US has repeatedly implored other countries to aid in the fight to make the world free. We would not have such an outsize role if the other free peoples of the world stepped up to the level of effort we have made. But others have coasted and relied on our protection to afford their lifestyles.

## Building Alliances

Our alliances need to have tiered levels of cooperation based on the level of freedom in the country and their proactive support of encouraging freedom in the world. Our trade agreements need to encompass more than just economic values. Favored trade status should be reserved for those who share our values. In order to accomplish this we need our European, Japanese, South Korean, Canadian, Israeli, and Australian allies to join us in a free trade block. Then add other countries to this freedom block as they meet the criteria. Instead of undercutting each other we need to stay unified in setting standards of behavior toward each tier of trading partners. This will keep an even playing field for the businesses of each of our countries. This group constitutes more than half of the world economy

Not one of our countries meets the level of freedom that we should be seeking. As we are helping others reach our level of freedom we need to be moving further along the freedom-slavery continuum towards more freedom.

Strong security requires a strong economy. A strong economy requires abundant trade. Abundant trade requires the rule of law and security. These areas are not exclusive but have a symbiotic relationship. Our security, economic, and trade alliances need to be mutually reinforcing. This will allow the free world to help make more of the world free without force of arms and without undercutting each other.

## Rebuilding Failed States

On the other end of the power spectrum is the failed states. These are safe havens for radicals, terrorists, and criminal gangs. No one is safe when these failed states exist. Whether it is groups like ISIS or al-Qaeda actively seeking our destruction or criminal gangs victimizing others with drugs, human trafficking, or piracy these areas are a threat to international order. In addition to exporting terrorism and crime they export people desperately seeking safety and opportunity. These flows of people are destabilizing to their neighbors and to the EU.

We need to help the locals rebuild these failed states. This will take time and great effort but is needed to ensure our present and future safety. Much like the "broken windows" theory in policing, when there are broken states there will be war, corruption, terrorists, criminal gangs, and other instability drawn to the area.

### Ending Debt and Strengthening Economies

Excessive debt by the US, Japan, and most European countries poses a serious danger to the security of the free world. We and our allies cannot be effective if our governments and economies are burdened by excessive debt. Debt at the national level should only be used for dealing with emergencies. With the current levels of debt we are limited in our ability to adjust to the needs of our countries in times of emergency. The free world governments need to end deficit spending and allow their debt levels to recede until they are gone.

Except for limited purposes, the use of debt by national governments is immoral. It is not the same as an individual taking out a loan. When an individual takes on debt they are personally responsible for it. When a government takes on debt it is a debt owed by all future citizens of the country. Debt is being used for current benefits but the cost is borne by future generations.

Most economists will say that our high levels of debt are sustainable and will not break our economy. Under recent circumstances our debts will not break the economy but when interest rates return to normal levels or the economy takes a turn for the worse as it does at least once every decade then the strain on our finances reaches dangerous levels. It is simply not good enough to barely survive during a recession. We must put a significant cushion in place so that when things turn out worse than expected we can survive it without an economic collapse.

People working a few more hours each week, a few more days each year, and a few more years before retiring can mean the difference between leaving a stable world for our children and grandchildren or allowing the collapse of our democracies under the overwhelming load of debt.

Central bankers have been holding off a collapse with low interest rates and quantitative easing. The next major economic crisis may be too much for the central bankers to manipulate. Their efforts distort markets and keeps the economy from growing properly. The only reason they have to resort to such desperate measures is because the politicians are too cowardly to tell the people the truth about the costs of their government mandated or paid for benefits. This is not a good solution. It is a house of cards built on a fault line. A very unstable way to manage an economy.

### Summary

The free countries of the world need to get our fiscal and moral houses in order. We need to remove the structural impediments to strong families and a strong economy. This will give us the base to take on the global challenges that face us from the forces fighting against freedom.

We cannot solve all the problems in the world. We can and should solve the ones we can. We need to continuously, consistently, and relentlessly work to keep power diffused in the hands of voters. In every country of the world and at every level of government there must be the real ability of voters to make a change at every election. There is no democracy or freedom if voters cannot regularly decide who will represent them in their government. There is no right to power or control for any person or party in government. The veneer of democracy that many countries' leaders try to pass off as democracy must be called out and contested. It will erode our freedom if we allow freedom to be redefined. As Emma Lazarus said, "Until we are all free, we are none of us free."

## National, Local, and Personal Grand Strategy

At the national, local, and personal level we need to focus on properly educating ourselves, our children, and the whole society. There is a great amount of disinformation masquerading as truth. This is detrimental to the health of our civilization. We need to share the Gospel, grow our own relationships with Christ, and disciple others so they know the most essential Truth there is. We need to learn and teach economic history and sound economic principles so that people understand how the economy works and what history has shown does not work and why. We need to understand how our government works and make changes so it is more responsive to the voters.

We need to be more discerning about what we believe. Too often we readily accept what someone we like has said without looking at the evidence. At the same time we too readily reject what someone we dislike has said without looking at the evidence. We become comfortable with certain sources of information and just repeat without doing any critical thinking of our own. As much as many of us complain about the bias of certain media outlets, we also have biases that we need to be aware of. We need to think critically about what people tell us.

People are frequently misled by activists and politicians that want power and will say anything to get it. It is easy for these conmen to trick people when they are not familiar with a subject area. It is difficult when people are knowledgeable about the subject. As citizens of a democratic republic we have an obligation to know the truth and to act with courage and conviction. We need to expect more common sense, integrity, courage, intelligence, honor, and honesty from our politicians and other leaders. That will only happen if we live according to those same traits. We will not respect those traits enough nor develop an expectation of them in others if we do not live them ourselves. We need to expect more from ourselves and our leaders. We are letting our children and all future generations down if we do not. This has to start with each and every one of us!

Like it or not the US is the leader of the free world. Great harm will befall us, our descendants, and much of the world if we cease our leadership or cease being a beacon for freedom. As citizens we have a responsibility to make sure we are keeping our own country free and accountable to the people. From our freedom we can help others to be free. By setting the example and by active promotion of our values. This book presents many ideas for enhancing freedom here and around the world.

# 3 SOCIAL SECURITY REFORM

**"True individual freedom cannot exist without economic security and independence. People who are hungry and out of a job are the stuff of which dictatorships are made."**
**Franklin D. Roosevelt**

When discussing Social Security we first have to make sure we are using a common understanding of the terms. Terms such as lock box, trust fund, and privatization have different connotations to different people.

The Social Security Trust Fund is what exists now that holds the money received from Social Security taxes that is in excess of what has been needed to pay out in Social Security checks. This Trust Fund does not hold money or stocks or marketable bonds. It only holds Treasury bonds that the Trust Fund cannot trade on the open market. The Trust Fund holds these bonds because past Congresses and Presidents have spent the money. Now when we are reaching the years when the baby boomers are retiring and there are fewer workers to support each retiree there is less money coming in from Social Security taxes than we need to pay for all the checks each year. Because of this the Trust Fund is cashing the bonds in with the US Treasury to pay all of the Social Security checks. This requires Congress and the President to cut something else out of the budget, raise taxes, or borrow on the open market to buy back these bonds to make up for this shortage in Social Security taxes. The amount of bonds that the Trust Fund cashes in will keep getting larger each year as more people retire until around 2036 when the Trust Fund will run out of bonds to cash in with the Treasury. (How old will you be in 2036?) Without any changes in the Social Security program the checks will be cut down to 77 percent of what people were getting the month before.

Many politicians have talked about lock boxes for Social Security funds so that Congress could not spend the money and it would be there when people retire. They were either uninformed or lying. To begin with, Congress's power to bind future Congresses is very limited. This is reinforced by the Supreme Court decision that said that Social Security is not a legally binding contract.

(Fleming v. Nestor, 1960) The Congress can change it at any time. Second, the Supreme Court has already held that Social Security taxes are not earmarked and could be considered general revenue of the federal government and Congress can spend it as it sees fit. (Helvering v. Davis, 1937) Frankly, it defies basic macroeconomic reality. If you take money out of the economy and put it in the equivalent of grandma's mattress it will just depress the economy and lose value due to inflation. Finally and most importantly it is simply too late. The money that was supposedly set aside for the baby boomers has already been spent. Now there are not enough workers to raise excess taxes to set aside any for the future.

Privatization involves giving each person their own account in a new restructured Social Security program. This would not apply to those who are currently receiving Social Security or those who are nearing retirement because there would be no time for those people to accumulate the necessary interest earnings. Depending upon the plan that has been pitched it may be a partial or fully privatized system.

Some of the arguments in favor of privatization include providing guaranteed retirement funds for those who contribute and providing a nest egg for people's heirs if the person does not live to retirement. This is especially good for minorities and lower income people who have statistically shorter lives. The most important reason is taking the money out of the hands of the politicians and providing more liberty to each of us.

Some of the arguments against privatization include the belief that the safety net for senior citizens will be gone and that everyone will be subject to possible losses in the stock market that will leave them short of retirement funds. Later in this chapter I will lay out a restructuring of Social Security which has the advantages of privatization and guards against the common concerns.

## Raise the Retirement Age

The current Social Security program is going to run short of money by 2036. But now, long before this point in time the Social Security program is "cashing in" the Treasury bonds that are in the "Trust Fund" in order to pay benefits. Without reform this will require ever greater spending cuts in other areas of the government or major tax increases. Unfortunately, the Democrats only want to increase taxes and the Republicans just want to add means testing and a small increase in the retirement age. The Democrats tax increase proposals will sink our already weak economy. The small changes advocated by most Republicans will only help for a short time.

There are two major factors that drive the costs of the Social Security program. These are retirement age and life expectancy. When Social Security started the retirement age was 65 and the average life expectancy was 68. People worked for a much larger portion of their lives. Now the retirement age is 66 or 67 depending upon when you were born and life expectancy is 79. To make matters worse many retirees begin receiving Social Security at the early retirement age of 62. The costs of Social Security are going up because people are spending more years of their lives on Social Security than in the past.

There are really only three ways to address the costs of Social Security. Raise more taxes to pay for the trillions of promised benefits. Reduce benefits which will negatively affect the neediest among us. Or raise the retirement age to reduce the number of people that benefits need to be paid out to.

For most of the people who receive Social Security it is barely sufficient to cover basic living expenses. Reducing this would largely undercut the purpose of the program. Even with the current level of benefits most retirees without other retirement savings are living in poverty or are one major unplanned expense away from it. This is not a realistic or morally supportable option.

Taxes already take a significant portion of the US economy and it would be economically dangerous to increase taxes further. These would not be temporary taxes; they would have to be permanent. More taxes will slow the growth of the economy. We are already living through the slowest growth economic recovery since World War II. Any increased tax load on the economy could drive the US and the world into a recession.

As economic history shows us there is a limit to the amount of revenue that can be collected as tax rates increase. As tax rates increase the amount of money that can be reinvested is reduced. The incentive to invest is reduced as tax rates increase. The reduced return takes away the benefit of many investment options. This reduces the amount of taxes that can be collected even with higher rates.

The only realistic way to reduce the costs of the Social Security program is to raise the retirement age and early retirement age. People in their late 60s are in far better health now than eighty years ago when Social Security began. It is more practical to have us all work a few more years than to increase the burden on working parents. These working age parents already are struggling under the burden of taxes, raising children, buying homes, starting businesses and for some caring for elderly parents.

The baby boom generation began reaching age 65 in 2011 and over the next 19 years 79 million people will reach age 65. More than four million new retirees per year at an average monthly check of over $1,300 per month. Each one year delay in the retirement age saves $63 billion every year. The following plan will save nearly $1 trillion in just the first ten years. It will save many trillions more over the following decades. While it would have been better to begin this reform years ago, now the earliest it can be passed into law is 2017, with implementation beginning in 2019. President Obama will not sign these reforms into law. Here is what I propose.

| Recommended Retirement Ages-Social Security | | | | |
|---|---|---|---|---|
| Year of Birth | Full Retirement Age | Early Retirement Age | Age in 2017 | Age in 2019 |
| 1937 and earlier | 65 | 62 | 80+ | 82+ |
| 1938 | 65 and 2 months | 62 | 79 | 81 |
| 1939 | 65 and 4 months | 62 | 78 | 80 |
| 1940 | 65 and 6 months | 62 | 77 | 79 |
| 1941 | 65 and 8 months | 62 | 76 | 78 |
| 1942 | 65 and 10 months | 62 | 75 | 77 |
| 1943 | 66 | 62 | 74 | 76 |
| 1944 | 66 | 62 | 73 | 75 |
| 1945 | 66 | 62 | 72 | 74 |
| 1946 | 66 | 62 | 71 | 73 |
| 1947 | 66 | 62 | 70 | 72 |
| 1948 | 66 | 62 | 69 | 71 |
| 1949 | 66 | 62 | 68 | 70 |
| 1950 | 66 | 62 | 67 | 69 |
| 1951 | 66 | 62 | 66 | 68 |
| 1952 | 66 | 62 | 65 | 67 |
| 1953 | 66 | 62 | 64 | 66 |
| 1954 | 66 | 62 | 63 | 65 |
| 1955 | 66 and 2 months | 62 | 62 | 64 |
| 1956 | 66 and 4 months | 62 | 61 | 63 |
| 1957 | 66 and 6 months | 62 | 60 | 62 |
| 1958 | 66 and 8 months | 62 | 59 | 61 |
| 1959 | 66 and 10 months | 62 and 6 months | 58 | 60 |
| 1960 | 67 | 63 | 57 | 59 |
| 1961 | 67 and 4 months | 63 and 6 months | 56 | 58 |
| 1962 | 67 and 8 months | 64 | 55 | 57 |
| 1963 | 68 | 64 and 6 months | 54 | 56 |
| 1964 | 68 and 4 months | 65 | 53 | 55 |
| 1965 | 68 and 8 months | 65 and 6 months | 52 | 54 |
| 1966 | 69 | 66 | 51 | 53 |
| 1967 | 69 and 4 months | 66 and 4 months | 50 | 52 |
| 1968 | 69 and 8 months | 66 and 8 months | 49 | 51 |
| 1969 | 70 | 67 | 48 | 50 |
| 1970 | 70 and 4 months | 67 and 4 months | 47 | 49 |
| 1971 | 70 and 8 months | 67 and 8 months | 46 | 48 |
| 1972 | 71 | 68 | 45 | 47 |
| 1973 | 71 and 4 months | 68 and 4 months | 44 | 46 |
| 1974 | 71 and 8 months | 68 and 8 months | 43 | 45 |
| 1975 | 72 | 69 | 42 | 44 |

Many others have proposed a very gradual increase of the retirement age by a year or two over several decades. This is out of political considerations. The original third rail of American politics. Raising the retirement age is unpopular but it is necessary for the country to put its fiscal house in order. It may be possible to just barely cover Social Security obligations with a small increase. That would still ignore the costs to families that have to pay the taxes. The additional years until retirement will spread out the costs over more work years. Most people are fully capable of working these additional years. The Social Security taxes could be reduced to what is needed for the fewer benefit years. People will be able to keep more of their money for taking care of their families. In the meantime it will help grow the economy.

## Voluntary Delayed Retirement

It is already an option for people to receive a larger retirement benefit when they delay their retirement beyond the full retirement age. An additional incentive to keep people working longer is to allow those who continue working past the early retirement age to be able to do so without paying the Social Security Tax. The employer portion of the tax should either still be paid to the government or should be paid to the employee. Both options have merit. Allowing the employer to keep the employer portion should not be an option. It would disadvantage younger workers.

## Disability

One of the major arguments against raising the retirement age is about the portion of the population that is too disabled to continue working until retirement age. The obvious solution to this is to allow disabled people to begin using their funds earlier under a new disability program.

There should be three tiers to the disability program. The lowest tier, Tier 1, is for those who caused their own disability by recklessness, negligence, or intention. The middle tier, Tier 2, is for those who became disabled through no fault of their own. The top tier, Tier 3, is for those who became disabled due to injuries incurred while performing a heroic activity, whether in an official capacity such as the military, police, and fire fighters or as a regular citizen stepping forward into danger in a time of need. Under all tiers the payments would come from their Social Security XXI account (See Social Security XXI section later in this chapter.) until it is exhausted and then would come from the backup federal disability program.

Under Tier 3, the person would receive benefits equal to 120 percent of the national median wage times the percent of their disability. Under Tier 2, the person would receive benefits equal to 80 percent of the national median wage times the percent of their disability. Under Tier 1, the person would receive benefits equal to 101 percent of the federal poverty rate times the percent of their disability.

By default the disabled person will be eligible for Tier 2. The government will be responsible for proving that a person should only be eligible for Tier 1 benefits. The disabled claimant or their representative is responsible for proving eligibility for Tier 3 benefits. The government has a duty to assist in the procurement of evidence and determining the truth. Fraud, obstruction or bribe seeking should be dealt with harshly as a criminal offense.

If the person has any other disability benefits then the federal disability program amount will be reduced by an amount consistent with the formula used for earned income. This will reduce the burden on taxpayers.

Employers may reduce the compensation of their disabled employees up to the percentage of their disability rating from the federal government if the disability materially affects the performance of the job. The employer must document these limitations and provide a copy to the employee. At no time can an employer pay for less than the percent of work typically performed. For example, someone who is 60 percent disabled but can perform their particular job at 50 percent of average would have to receive at least 50 percent of the compensation of the average employee not the 40 percent that would correspond to their disability rating.

This is meant to provide more work opportunities for those who are disabled and spread the cost across the whole society. It is better than just forcing the whole cost on those employers who hire disabled people who are unable to fully perform the job at the level of an average person without the disability. This should protect employers from discrimination charges while also opening up more employment opportunities for people with disabilities.

This program needs to encourage work to the extent possible for each person. For that reason there needs to be a graduated reduction in disability benefits as they earn. Up to the point where their disability benefit plus earnings are equivalent to a 100 percent disability benefit at their tier there should be no reduction. After which a gradual benefit reduction starting at just ten percent for each new dollar earned and ending with a complete phase out of disability benefits for those in Tier 1 at 90 percent of the median wage, Tier 2 at 120 percent of the median wage, and Tier 3 at the national average wage. This same standard should be used to determine the reduction in federal disability payments due to private or state disability benefits.

## Transferability

It would be highly patriotic and charitable for anyone who can afford it to delay using Social Security and Medicare. An option is a program where someone can assign their eligibility to another person a month at a time for each month they delay. It could go to someone they know or go to a pool to help cover the cost of disabled people who need to retire early. Right now this may help smooth out the bump up caused by the flood of retiring baby boomers.

Unfortunately, under current conditions, Congress would likely waste the money that these people deferred to another less fortunate person. The only way I or anyone else could believe that a delay or deferment program would work is with passage of the Federal Spending Limit Amendment in Chapter 5.

## Social Security XXI

Raising the retirement age will do the bare minimum to make Social Security solvent far out into the future. Unfortunately, as long as Congress has access to the taxes collected, they will spend them. They pretend to balance the budget with the excess money as they did during the Clinton years. What they are actually doing is using excess Social Security taxes to pay for other things now and giving IOUs to the Social Security "trust fund". This slush fund for irresponsible spending will continue to be abused as long as Congress has access to it.

For this reason I propose Social Security XXI, a program of privatized Social Security accounts. This will take the money out of the hands of Congress. It permits those who wish to remain strictly invested in Treasury securities to do so. It provides a safety net for those who do not earn enough during their lifetime. It only needs to provide benefits to retirees for the first 25 years after they reach their full retirement age. After 25 years they revert to a restructured government funded program.

People 55 and over on December 31st of the year when the bill is passed will have the following options. By default they will remain in the current Social Security program and continue paying current Social Security payroll taxes. Or they can choose to have a prorated benefit from the current Social Security program based on previous contributions and begin the Social Security XXI program from this point. People may move toward being fully in the Social Security XXI program at any time after it begins but may not move further away than previously opted.

People 54 or younger on December 31st of the year when the bill is passed will have a prorated benefit from the current Social Security program based on previous contributions and begin the Social Security XXI program from this point. Those with a low net present value benefit under the current Social Security program will be cashed out of the current Social Security program and be required to roll the funds into their Social Security XXI program account.

People should be allowed to make supplemental tax-free contributions for past years worked, up to an amount where the present value will allow a future benefit amount equal to the estimated maximum Social Security benefit for the first 25 years after the person reaches retirement age.

The Social Security payroll taxes will be eliminated for those who do not remain fully in the current Social Security program and the remaining obligations will be paid from general revenues. All wages for those in the Social Security XXI program are mandated to increase by 6.2 percent to make up for the employer portion of Social Security payroll taxes. This would include an increase of the federal minimum wage by 6.2 percent.

## Social Security XXI Accounts

The Social Security XXI accounts are to pay for retirement or disability. While it would be great not to have any restrictions on how we invest our own retirement funds, there is too much risk that taxpayers would be stuck with potentially huge unfunded welfare liabilities when people retire with insufficient retirement funds. This plan attempts to strike a balance between account holder and taxpayer. The investment categories and the restrictions below are an example of a way to balance investment risk and return for the people of the country in their dual roles as Social Security XXI account holder and taxpayer. It permits those who wish to take on less risk to have no restrictions from doing so but also allows those who wish to be more aggressive to be able to do that with part of their funds. Each person will be responsible for the decisions they make about the investments in their account.

## Social Security XXI Account Investment Types
### Type I:
Money market mutual fund

### Type II:
Treasury bonds and other US government bonds
General revenue municipal bonds
FDIC insured accounts
Annuities
Other insured investments

### Type III:
Investment grade bonds or bond mutual funds
Major domestic and international market index mutual funds
    No sales fees allowed
    All expenses must be less than 0.50 percent
Major domestic and international market index ETFs/ETNs

### Type IV:
Other mutual funds
Domestic and international stocks
Other ETFs and ETNs

### Type V:
Below investment grade bonds
Commodities
Derivatives—futures and options
Any investment in a short position

Minimum and maximum limits on types of investments to reduce risk and provide diversification

### Under age 40
Types I, II and III combined: At least 30 percent
Type IV: No minimum amount
Type V: No minimum amount, Maximum of 15 percent

### Age 40 up to 49
Types I and II combined: At least 10 percent
Types II and III combined: At least 40 percent
Type IV: No minimum amount
Type V: No minimum amount, Maximum of 20 percent

### Age 50 up to 59
Types I and II combined: At least 10 percent
Types I, II, and III combined: At least 50 percent
Type IV: No minimum amount
Type V: No minimum amount, Maximum of 15 percent

### Age 60 up to full retirement age
Types I and II combined: At least 10 percent
Types I, II, and III combined: At least 60 percent
Type IV: No minimum amount
Type V: No minimum amount, Maximum of 10 percent

### Over full retirement age
Types I and II combined: At least 10 percent
Types I, II, and III combined: At least 70 percent
Type IV: No minimum amount
Type V: No minimum amount, Maximum of 10 percent

The Type I investments are for expected near-term withdrawals. The Type II investments are generally considered safe or insured investments. The Type III investments are generally good investments with more risk and return than Type II investments. They provide good diversification and over time generally reflect a return consistent with the level of profits of the underlying companies. The restriction in level of fees is because with an index fund there should be very little trading activity or research warranted that would require management fees and no sales fees should be required for a mandatory account. This will maximize the return for Social Security XXI investors and prevent unreasonable gouging with fees.

The Type IV and V investments are for more experienced and

knowledgeable investors and provide for greater returns but at greater risk. When the Type IV and V investments result in a loss for the year, the loss will have to be made up by increased contributions by the worker. If Type I, II, or III investments are part of the same account as the Type IV or V investments they must be segregated in different subaccounts. Losses from Type IV and V investments may not be covered by Type I, II, or III Social Security XXI investment returns. Any total portfolio that does not earn at least the return on investment of a benchmark of the weighted average of all issued 10 year Treasuries during the same running three year time period may be required to reduce the amount of risk in their investments and will be required to make additional contributions to make up the losses to reach the benchmark.

The faster that the Social Security XXI investments accumulate, the sooner that the Social Security XXI account will be fully funded. This will provide for more security for families, result in higher tax receipts from the reduction in income that is set aside after the Social Security XXI account is fully funded, and reduce the likelihood that someone will need to turn to the government for help.

### Contributions Requirements

All workers will be required to contribute ten percent of their gross pay until they reach an amount where the present value will allow a future benefit amount equal to 70 percent of the estimated maximum Social Security benefit for the first 25 years after the person reaches retirement age. When the person has accumulated an amount where the present value will allow a future benefit amount equal to the estimated maximum Social Security benefit for the first 25 years after the person reaches retirement age, all of the employee's future gross wages will be counted as regular wages. Future investment earnings estimates will be based on the lifetime average or the 10 year average whichever is less but not more than 7.0 percent per year after inflation when the calculation of withdrawal limit takes place.

The account holder will be responsible for paying estimated taxes on the excess quarterly and is free to withdraw the excess without penalty. As the balance will vary, the annual tax liability will be based upon the level of excess at the end of the calendar year plus withdrawals of excess during the year. All other funds people wish to set aside for retirement should be done outside of this program.

Ten percent of wages is slightly more money set aside for Social Security XXI as the person and their employer currently pays in Social Security taxes. This is after the wage basis is adjusted by including the 6.2 percent tax currently paid by employers for Social Security and the 1.45 percent tax paid by employers for Medicare and the amount that employers spend on their employees for healthcare insurance.

## Distributions

When people retire at the full retirement age with Social Security XXI accounts they will be able to take distributions up to an amount that will allow them to take the same inflation adjusted distribution for 25 years past retirement age. For the early retirement age this will be for 28 years past the early retirement age. But as a lower limit these amounts will not be below the inflation adjusted amount that someone would receive under the current Social Security program with the same income profile. Every year during this 25 to 28 year period the distribution amount will be recalculated to adjust for changes in the portfolio value.

## Safety Net

For those who run out of funds in their Social Security XXI individual account there is a safety net. They will receive 80 percent of what they would have received under the current Social Security program until 25 years after their full retirement age. For those who are younger than 55 when Social Security XXI begins the safety net benefits will be means tested. Those with outside retirement or pension funds or home equity or other savings and investments will have to use those assets first. Additionally these payments will be a loan and not a grant. The provisions in this section are a part of the new ownership of responsibility by each of us to be diligent on behalf of our own welfare and not just depend on others for retirement. Nobody will be left destitute but they will have to deplete their own resources before drawing on the resources of their fellow citizens.

## Limited Time Period

The privatized Social Security XXI accounts and the supporting safety net provisions are designed for the first 25 years following the full retirement age. This sets a maximum period for which people need to plan for. For those who are still alive after this 25 year time period they will receive a benefit comparable to 85 percent of the current maximum social security benefit, adjusted for inflation. Those who owe money to the government for previously loaned benefits will receive 75 percent until the debt is repaid with the difference. These post-25 benefits will not be subject to repayment.

The time period is limited for practical reasons. It allows people to plan for a specific period of time instead of having to hedge against the need to set aside funds for a possibly much longer life span. Most people will die within the first 25 years following retirement and can maintain a higher standard of living if they only need to plan for the first 25 years. Lower income people will only be subject to the need for safety net benefits for a limited time. The government can plan ahead for the need to provide benefits for a the longest living segment of the population because whether or not the program exists many in this group will need income assistance.

**Borrowing From the Account**

Account owners may borrow up to twenty percent of their contributions from their account. The borrowing is limited to a few key areas.

1. Down payment for a home, up to twenty percent of the cost of a median value home.
2. Make home mortgage payments while out of work.
3. Pay for own or dependents' qualified education.
4. Pay for medical care expenses or medical insurance premiums.
5. Low income people may borrow to buy or repair a car or truck. Must be needed for work and this vehicle must be the only vehicle available to the person.

The account owner will be required to pay interest to their account of the current cost of borrowing for the federal government. This is the cost that taxpayers would pay to borrow to provide a safety net benefit to any person who does not save enough to fund their own retirement. Any federal student loans should require borrowers to pay an interest rate that exceeds the cost of borrowing from their own account by at least two percent. This will encourage people to use their own resources rather than other taxpayers. Borrowing from this account may not be discharged in bankruptcy.

**Community Property and Inheritance Provisions**

Community property is typically a state issue and it would be nice if all married couples stayed together but they don't all stay together. Due to the importance of this program and the ownership nature of the accounts each spouse's employment based contribution should be evenly split between the husband's and wife's accounts immediately. Each should control their own account. If there is a divorce, the ownership will already have been split.

Any funds inherited from another's Social Security XXI account are to be applied to the person's Social Security XXI or Medicare XXI account if the recipient is a physical person until the person's tax free contribution limit is reached. Any funds in excess of this limit will be treated as income and can be received by the recipient as they see fit. Depending upon how the excess is distributed, it may be subject to taxes.

**Enforcement**

The Social Security Administration (SSA) will monitor all accounts for contributions, earnings, and distributions to ensure compliance. The SSA will establish income and account verification procedures. The SSA will establish age-indexed remaining lifetime accumulation tables and tax free contribution limits. The SSA will coordinate with the IRS to collect from those who are short in their accounts.

## Three Legs of Retirement

In the past there were three legs of retirement funding like the three legs of a stool. They were Social Security, pension from an employer, and personal savings. This should be encouraged again but with some changes.

The new first leg is the Social Security XXI program as described earlier.

Defined benefit plans have rightly acquired a bad reputation for dragging down companies and governments under excessive burdens. Much of the problem with these plans has actually been promising too much and then underfunding the plan. The S&P 500 has a long-term average of 6-7 percent inflation-adjusted returns when dividends are reinvested. It is rare that a pension plan will be capable of beating this over the long-term. These plans should not be permitted to claim a greater projected return. The other important factor that requires correction is the need for employers to fund these plans at the time the employee performs the work. When these plans are underfunded they can drag a business or local government into bankruptcy. There is more detail about solving issues with the employer funded pension plans in the Employee Benefit Chapter.

The third leg is personal savings, mostly in the form of defined contribution plans, individual retirement accounts (IRAs), and a home. This will be improved by reforms in the housing market that encourages a return to people paying off their home and not using it as a source of revolving credit. This can be encouraged by significant changes in the tax code that favors saving and investing over spending.

# 4 HEALTHCARE REFORM

**"The first wealth is health."**
**Ralph Waldo Emerson**

## Introduction

Unfortunately the current healthcare system has serious problems. Those with insurance are paying more for services so healthcare providers and insurers can recoup losses from those without insurance and those with government benefits that limit payment for services. In addition, there is only a limited opportunity for healthcare consumers to shop around for insurance and services. The dramatic increases in insurance premiums are placing a severe burden on those employers who can still provide it and on the American people. A great deal of insurance premiums is being wasted on healthy people when these funds could be earning interest for when people really need it. For the average person, approximately fifty percent of the person's lifetime healthcare costs are incurred in the final year of life.

Many have proposed government run alternatives, usually a single payer system. The problem with government run alternatives is that they serve their masters—politicians and bureaucrats. They do not have to compete on economics or service as a private company must. If a private insurance company does not provide good service or does not price its policies at a market viable rate it will not be competitive, customers will go elsewhere and the company will go out of business. On the other hand, a government agency that operates poorly will seek more taxpayer funding to "fix" their problems. The politicians will give it to them in order to tell the people back home that they are providing free or low cost healthcare. In actual practice we will be subsidizing another inefficient government program with our own money in the form of taxes.

Another problem with a single payer system is that the single payer is the only buyer in the system. That buyer will be able to dictate prices and there will always be a bias by that buyer toward short term benefit. This will deprive pharmaceutical, biotechnology, and medical equipment companies of funds needed for R & D which will reduce the pace of progress in the development of new life saving products. The only R & D occurring will be what the government decides should be done which will be based on who has the political clout. This is in contrast to the diverse array of decision makers and innovators that have given us the best healthcare technology and techniques in human history.

The current Medicare, Medicaid, and Obamacare programs are not fiscally sustainable nor are many of the proposed reforms. As long as the people receiving healthcare services are not directly involved in deciding their own care <u>and</u> the financing of their own care there will not be a sustainable solution.

This reform plan will provide Americans with good healthcare coverage while maintaining their independence from government, employer, and union. Healthcare insurance will be completely portable and accumulated funds in the Health Savings Account (HSA) can be used for insurance premiums when someone is between jobs and after retirement. Having insurance will improve healthcare and reduce the possibility of financial hardship due to catastrophic healthcare problems. Healthcare consumers will be able to shop around for services far more conveniently. This comparison shopping will improve market efficiencies and help reduce costs. Employers will not be responsible for healthcare costs and can plan their budgets better. It will give employers more flexibility with regard to hiring more employees vs. using overtime to minimize insurance costs. It will provide more opportunities for flex scheduling and part time work.

## National Security Requires Economic Strength

Most major issues in the United States have a certain degree of effect on national security. The stability and peace of much of the world is dependent upon the military, diplomatic, and political power and will of the United States. That power and will is dependent upon the economic strength of the United States. Healthcare costs in the United States are a burdensome structural cost for businesses and the government. Healthcare is over seventeen percent of GDP and growing. This is making America less competitive and therefore reducing our economic power which in turn reduces our ability to maintain our national security.

## Rationing Care

There has been much talk about various healthcare reform plans resulting in the rationing of care. This is absolutely true but can be misleading if not fully understood. Every reform plan that can be imagined and no plan at all will involve rationing. It is Economics 101; there will always be fewer resources than opportunities to use resources. The important part of the rationing debate is not the existence of rationing but who makes the rationing decisions.

In government run plans such as Medicare, Medicaid, and Obamacare it is politicians, bureaucrats, and lobbyists who make the decisions on what the government will pay for and how much it will pay for it. This is also the case for a severely regulated health insurance industry, medical care sector, and pharmaceutical and medical devices industries. Medicare is already close to bankruptcy and has an estimated $25 trillion in unfunded liabilities for obligations promised to current workers and retirees. For many Americans, their employer, union, or the combination of the two make the decisions about price, type of plan and insurance coverage.

When the government or our employer make the decisions they average everyone together and make these rationing decisions based on averages or the opinions of the decision makers instead of on people's individual needs. With this reform plan, the rationing decisions about what to cover and what is a priority to spend your healthcare dollars on are in your hands. We can each make the decisions for ourselves and our families like we do for most of our major decisions. We can achieve mass customization in healthcare financing, custom-tailored plans to meet our diverse and changing needs at near mass production prices. Enabled by technologies such as computers, the internet, and plan modularization, it will provide market segmentation where every consumer can have exactly what he or she wants. This is more freedom for the individual and the American family.

**Principles of Insurance**

Most people have major misunderstandings about the nature of insurance. Insurance is meant to mitigate the risk of major financial losses to individuals by pooling the costs among a large group of people. Only a portion of the group will have high costs in any particular time period. This allows people to pay a relatively small amount in order to be protected against potentially huge costs if they are unfortunate that year. This has been distorted in several ways.

Primarily when there are mandatory coverages for certain types of care or medicines. Many of these coverages, such as immunizations, cancer screenings, and other preventative care have great health benefits. The problem is that if they are likely expenses for the year the full cost is included in the cost of the insurance. There is no longer a low or medium risk of the expense being incurred for the year. There is a high risk of the expense being incurred. Since the coverage is mandated, people do not shop around for the best deal on these services. This greatly increases the costs. It is better if at least part of the cost is incurred by the patient in order to incentivize the patient to find the best deal.

Other types of coverages used by only a small part of the population will in any given year have a different affect. These coverages truly represent risks. The problem for some of these coverages occurs when first dollar costs are mandated to be paid by the insurance company. Patients need to have responsibility for the first costs of each medical service. This incentivizes them to control the costs. The risk covered by the insurance needs to be limited to when the cost of medical services exceed a certain threshold each year, regardless of the specific medical issue.

This plan provides a structure that protects people from catastrophic financial losses due to medical issues. At the same time it ensures that people will have all of the medical coverages they need. It provides incentives for people to shop around for the best care at the best price. This will bring costs down for everyone.

## To Be Mandatory Or Not To Be Mandatory

There are pros and cons to making insurance in this plan mandatory. How will things be different if this plan is mandatory or not mandatory? A mandatory insurance plan is repugnant to the independent side of America because it is the less free option. However, the problem of free riders drives up the cost of healthcare services and insurance for those who do pay for insurance because healthcare providers charge more to cover the costs that cannot be collected from those who do not have insurance. There is no realistic mechanism that could prevent healthcare providers from shifting costs to those who do pay from those who do not pay, short of allowing healthcare providers deny care to those who do not have insurance. Not only are the American people unlikely to agree to a denial of service policy, many healthcare providers will not deny service to those in need on moral grounds but will still need to recover the costs.

If it is not mandatory there will be a potential unfunded liability when these people need healthcare services in the future. When the uninsured reach retirement age and have not accumulated funds over their lifetime to cover their healthcare expenses in retirement, there will be a push to reinstate a new Medicare program to cover these people. The argument will be made that we cannot turn our backs on these elderly people in need of care. Many people will take their chances and will end up sticking everyone else with the cost when a major expense occurs.

If the program is mandatory it will be less free than a non-mandatory version of this program but will still provide more freedom and independence for American citizens than the current employer based system, Medicare, and any of the nationalized healthcare plans that have been put forward. There is independence of choice concerning which insurance company and healthcare providers people may use. They will not be forced into the plan that their company or union or government bureaucrat has decided is best. People will have the freedom to acquire the best option for themselves and their families and any funds remaining upon the individual's death can be willed to another instead of being absorbed into the government.

We already have a mandated healthcare program—Medicare. This new plan will provide more freedom to Americans than Medicare, provide it at a lower cost, take most of the cost out of the federal and state budgets, and reduce the bureaucracy needed to manage it. It is tempting to make it mandatory. **But in the final analysis, a mandated requirement to purchase something, in this case medical insurance, is un-American and should be unconstitutional whether the Supreme Court says it is or not. This plan incorporates very strong incentives to purchase medical insurance but does not mandate it. Read on for details!**

### Funding the Healthcare Program

**Income-based Contributions**

The Medicare payroll tax is rescinded and the employer portion is added to the employee's base wage. The amount that employers currently spend for healthcare on their employees will be added to the employees' wages. (There are more details later.) Initially the income-based contribution toward the High Deductible Health Plan (HDHP) and Health Savings Account (HSA) is twenty percent of the person's gross income, earned and unearned. This includes all regular wages, overtime wages, holiday pay, vacation pay, bonuses, profit sharing, dividends, realized capital gains, etc. When an employee's HSA accumulates more than their lifetime maximum, the excess will not have to be set aside for healthcare and will be taxed as income.

After the first year of the new program the percentage of the employee's gross wages that is required may be changed. It will be increased by one percent annually until it is twenty-five percent unless it is decreased to as low as twenty percent based upon results from health status testing or adjusted for other reasons (See details further along.). It may be voluntarily increased to as much as thirty percent of gross income. **(To increase clarity in describing the plan, the percentages used are placeholders; while these are likely close to what is needed the actual percentages should be set based on what economic modeling says is needed to sufficiently fund the plans. Then reevaluated periodically.)**

All healthcare expenses that an employer spends on their employees under current plans must be declared to the employees. All employees under a group policy will be treated equally. The total spent under the policy will be divided equally per employee. This will be added to the employees' wages to form the new wage basis from which the HDHP/HSA income set aside is calculated. The assumption here is that total compensation was negotiated and agreed upon between employer and employees and should remain the same. The exception to this is the elimination of the difference in compensation between those who get a single policy, family policy, or no policy from their employer.

This method will balance the benefits costs of the employers of a married couple. Instead of a couple choosing an insurance plan with one employer and not the other and shifting all of the cost to the one employer. For low income people there will be a proportional split between employment sources and the government subsidy instead of all or none from one or the other. All statutory healthcare benefits will be proportional to the total compensation regardless of the wage or the source of wages.

After retirement age is reached, the set aside will continue for earned income. Distributions from retirement plans, including pension, IRA, 401(k), Social Security, etc. may be required to be set aside. If total earned income plus distributions exceed the federal median income level, the portion over that point will be required to be subject to the set aside in the HSA. The set aside from earned income is always required but would be used to offset the amount due because of total income exceeding the federal median income level. The older worker will not be doubly hit for the same income. The reason for this requirement is to mitigate the effect of people making extra contributions to their retirement plans but not the HSA.

### Health status adjustments

There are several indicators and/or tests that can provide a good approximation of someone's health status. These indicators and tests can be used to approximate future healthcare cost risks and establish benchmarks that people can work toward to achieve a better health status. Based on the results of the schedule of tests the percentage of mandatory income set aside can be increased to as much as twenty-five percent. Excellent health will not reduce the percentage of the set aside below twenty percent. It is assumed that those with excellent health will reach their maximum lifetime accumulation in their HSA sooner and will in that manner reduce the amount that is set aside. The purpose of this option is to have people pay for their own behaviors that affect their healthcare costs.

Several factors that may be considered for this are Body Mass Index (BMI), well-baby check-ups, up-to-date on inoculations, results of physicals, cholesterol tests, blood pressure test, triglycerides test, blood glucose test, pap smear, PSA test, mammogram, breast exam, colorectal exam, urinalysis, complete blood count (CBC), STD testing, diabetes testing, Electrocardiogram (EKG), mole exam, hearing test, eye exam, etc. A schedule should be established for how often someone should be tested to continue to qualify for this option. Failure to be tested in a timely manner should result in the maximum increase in the set aside for having a poor result on the test. This will encourage people to get these tests and improve health outcomes through early detection and preventive measures. The costs for these tests should be split 50/50 between the consumer and the insurance company. It will get both parties looking for the best deal on where to have the services done and will likely improve long-term outcomes which should help to bring down risks for both the consumer and the insurance company which will keep down costs for both. The insurance company is more likely to be able to assemble and provide statistical information about outcomes and prices in an efficient and searchable format than the typical consumer.

In order to accommodate this option while protecting everyone's privacy, the raw results of the evaluation will be kept between the patient, provider, insurance company, and federal government auditors. The insurance company will collect the results from all providers and calculate the percentage of set aside for each account and notify the account holder(s) employers, HSA trustee, and the federal government of the result and notify the account holder(s) in detail as testing occurs. The account holder(s) will have to certify to the government at least biennially that the insurance company calculation is accurate to the best of their knowledge. Evaluation more often than biennially is optional for the policyholder(s) to report changes throughout the time period. This is an incentive to not delay making positive changes in their health status.

The purpose of the government auditors will be to compare the filed results with the actual raw results and to confirm that the evaluations have actually occurred. Accounts will be selected randomly and based on inconsistencies between the filed results and billing to the insurance company and/or HSA as reported by the insurance company or HSA trustee, and from whistleblower tips. The auditing agency may require the insurance companies or HSA trustees to look for particular patterns that may indicate fraud and report the accounts to the agency. The raw evaluation results obtained by auditors will be sealed upon completion of the audit if passed. The raw results obtained in audits that are not passed will be maintained until the case and the terms of the settlement are completed and then sealed by the court. There will be no crossover of these medical files with other agencies for US citizens.

## Behavior-based Contributions

There will be contributions by an individual to their own healthcare based on their lifestyle habits. These habits frequently have a profound effect on the individual's health and their cost of healthcare. The behavior-based contributions toward the HSA are below. [NOTE: The research relating healthcare costs to various behaviors is weak. This section should be improved based on better numbers regarding the true healthcare costs of these behaviors.]

### *Abusers of drugs or alcohol.*

People who abuse alcohol and/or drugs tend to have higher healthcare costs and at an earlier age than those who are not substance abusers. This section is intended to put the costs on the substance abuser rather than on taxpayers. Each new offense will start a new time period at the next higher penalty level. The effects will not be cumulative. A person with more than three offenses will have the time period start over if they reoffend. This section requires court adjudication. A criminal conviction for the use/possession of street drugs and/or the abuse of prescription drugs or alcohol or a civil judgment based upon a preponderance of the evidence that use of street drugs and/or the abuse of prescription drugs or alcohol is occurring or has occurred. The civil judgement option allows the government to enforce this provision without seeking a criminal conviction.

1.  First offense will result in an additional one (1) percent of total wages deducted from pay and placed in their HSA for five (5) years with a minimum dollar amount equal to one (1) percent of the national median wage for the five (5) years.

2.  Second offense will result in an additional two (2) percent of total wages deducted from pay and placed in their HSA for five (5) years with a minimum dollar amount equal to two (2) percent of the national median wage for the five (5) years.

3.  Third offense will result in an additional five (5) percent of total wages deducted from pay and placed in their HSA for ten (10) years with a minimum dollar amount equal to five (5) percent of the national median wage for the ten (10) years.

## Mechanism for collection

(For the Tobacco and Alcohol Sections below) The fee is paid to the federal government when the item leaves the production facility. The cost of the fee becomes part of the price of the item. When the consumer purchases the item, they use a card similar to a credit/debit card to have the fee portion of what they paid go to their HSA account. If an individual does not wish to use a card or forgets their card a purchase can still be made and the federal government will retain the fee. Vendors may issue coupons to consumers or use other procedures to credit those who forget their card in order to return to the vendor location to have the fee added to the consumer's HSA. This card should be a deposit only card in order to minimize opportunities for electronic theft. For short duration sales operations, paper records can be generated and used to record collection and then dissemination of the fees. In all cases the consumer is entitled to a receipt. Private contractors should be selected to be clearinghouses for the transactions. It is anticipated that companies that process credit card transactions have the infrastructure that could accommodate such a process for a small percentage fee. Transaction fees should be added to the HSA fee.

### Tobacco use

Tobacco use is a significant source of healthcare expense. Another factor with regard to tobacco use is that smokers usually face serious or terminal illnesses at a younger age than non-users. This means that they need to accumulate more money in their HSA at a faster rate than non-users. Users of tobacco products will pay the following fees. (If marijuana or other drugs are legalized a similar fee should be added to pay for health related costs.

$3 per pack of cigarettes.
$0.50 fee per ounce of smokeless tobacco, pipe tobacco, etc.
$1.50 fee per cigar

### Alcohol use

While occasionally drinking moderate amounts of alcohol may actually help a person to stay healthy, drinking frequently and/or in large quantities is not healthy or safe behavior. A $1 fee per drink (i.e. 12oz beer, 1.5oz shot of liquor, 5oz glass of wine, 12oz wine cooler) will be paid at every purchase.

### High Risk Activities

High risk activities such as skydiving, scuba diving, piloting aircraft, hang gliding, bungee jumping, base jumping, racing, using a tanning bed, etc. should have a fee paid to the participant's HSA account. Studies should be conducted to assess the cost of the risks for these types of activities.

## High Deductible Health Plans

With the deductible and out-of-pocket maximums listed below, the premiums for the plans will be much lower than conventional health insurance plans.

### Single Plan

The individual plan HDHP will have a $3,500-$7,500 annual deductible and a $5,000-$12,500 annual out-of-pocket maximum.

### Family Plan

The family plan HDHP will have a $7,000-$15,000 annual deductible and a $10,000-$25,000 annual out-of-pocket maximum. The annual deductible and out-of-pocket maximum for an individual in the family is limited to that of the single plan at the same relative point in the ranges as the purchased family plan. For example, if the Family Plan has a $10,000 annual deductible and $15,000 annual out-of-pocket maximum then the individuals in the family will have a $5,000 annual deductible and $7,500 out-of-pocket maximum.

## All Plans

People may enroll in an employer sponsored plan or another plan without penalty. The employer will send the income-based contribution directly to the HSA trustee for the employee. The employee will pay for their HDHP with funds from their HSA or by payroll deduction if their employer provides the option. If the employee has accumulated his/her lifetime maximum, then the remainder of the employee's gross income will be counted as taxable income to the extent that it would normally be taxed.

If the household does not receive enough in income-based contributions to their HSA nor have sufficient accumulated assets, they will be eligible to receive a supplement from the federal government. (See the Medicare XXI section.)

A maximum limit should be placed on the amount of HDHP insurance premium that is tax deductible. The limit should be set at a reasonable point so that most individuals and families do not pay taxes on the money used for their premiums. The limit should be indexed for age. Behavior based health care issues that cause higher premiums should not be used as a basis or be considered when setting the tax deductibility limit. A ballpark figure of about $3,000 for individuals in their twenties to about $12,500 for individuals over 75 and about $6,000 for families in their twenties to about $25,000 for couples over 75 sound appropriate. There is no need to make all premiums tax deductible as long as most are tax-deductible and the relative standard is the same for everyone. This will help to minimize problems with illegal kickbacks or 'rebates' and encourage people to shop around.

## Employer Group Policies

Employees may still enroll in employer group HDHP insurance policies which will still offer benefits to employees and employers alike. They have the ability to smooth out differences between individual policies by averaging risk between many households. They provide consistency, convenience, and economy of scale to help reduce costs for employees, employers and insurers. Even though many of the healthiest will probably go with individual policies, because of the pooling by state there will be a balancing effect that will still allow group policies to work without facing exorbitant cost increases. There are likely to be many employees who will participate just to be relieved of the administrative work that an employer typically performs in providing a group policy. Pushing wellness programs and other preventative programs by employers should be helpful in reducing costs for the remaining employees.

No employee will be required to participate in an employer or other group policy. This includes a prohibition from putting such a requirement in a union contract. Although an employee may enroll in an employer or other group plan for one year periods and may be required to remain for the full year. A company is permitted to restrict contributions that exceed the statutory requirements to those who participate in an employer group policy if there is a legitimate economic reason for requiring participation.

When an employee leaves an employer, the employee may stay in the group plan until the end of their contracted year unless there was a medical condition which existed before termination of employment that would have placed a covered policy member in a high risk/high cost category. Then the employee would be eligible for the five years following the year in which the high risk/high cost condition became known. When an employee leaves an employer they can be required to complete their contracted year with the group plan.

Another option for employers is to simply act as an administrative conduit for their employees. In this case the employer finds an insurer or group of insurers and obtains a bulk discount for their employees due to administrative savings. In this case the employees would have the option to get a personalized plan through this conduit.

**Free Association Group Policies**

Similar to Employer Group Policies this will allow any group of people to freely join together to obtain a group policy. Any group can do this whether an extended family, group of small businesses, local credit union members, church congregation, local community or service group, etc. The tax write-off for the administrative costs will be assignable to those who did the work for the group or divided based on who paid for the costs. Write-off of administrative costs should be consistent with rules for employer group policies.

**Basic Policy**

The base coverage plans will include medical, dental, prescription drug, mental health, and optical coverage. People should be able to add long-term care insurance and contribute tax-free funds in addition to the requirements under the standard plan. A minimum level of preventive care and screening will be <u>recommended</u> to help keep costs down through early detection of problems. While many states have mandated coverages that are excessive and unnecessarily drive up costs for many families, there is a minimal level of coverages that will be necessary for this plan to be successful. This base level need not be mandated but set as recommendations with easy to opt out of provisions but with consequences that fall on the individual for their decisions rather than on the rest of society.

Essentially a basic policy should provide customary and ordinary coverages to make comparisons easier and to prevent the sale of policies that cover very little of anything. The base policy minimums will be strong recommendations that policy holders would then have to sign off on to reduce or to make additions. Every base policy for a specific jurisdiction will cover exactly the same thing.

Insurance companies may issue riders for additional coverages not included in the base plan and allow coverage exclusions that may result in a plan with reduced coverages from the base plan. If there are coverages in the base plan that are contrary to the beliefs or needs of the policy holder, they should not have to pay for the coverage nor be individually charged more if the insurance company believes reducing coverage would increase cost. A policyholder should not have to pay for a provision they will not use, but reducing the coverage must be done in writing.

For the base plan it is assumed that the deductible and the out-of-pocket maximum are set at the lowest cost option of the statutory ranges. Pre-existing conditions caused by heroic activities, congenital conditions, and any cause that the patient cannot control such as accidents, genetic defects, AIDS due to infection by no fault of the patient, unknown causes, etc. must be covered under the base plan at the base rate.

The insurance company may place a claim against a third party that is the cause of the condition in order to recover costs in order to pay for the condition and the costs of collection. If the patient, patient's parent, guardian, or heir recovered damages because of a condition, the funds may be required to cover the cost of services due to the condition until exhausted. (Similarly, health care providers may sue to recover costs from the perpetrator for treating an injury or illness caused by someone other than the patient if there is no insurance or inadequate insurance coverage.)

**Macro Insurance Plan Pooling**

The US Congress will set a base coverage plan and each state will be asked to set a base coverage plan. If a state does not have a base coverage plan, the policies of the state's residents will be based on the federal base coverage plan. A company or individual may purchase a policy based on the federal base coverage plan or their state base coverage plan. Each insurance company that is marketing a policy will file it with the state or federal agency that is designated to regulate it. Each insurance company will have only one policy meeting the base coverage plan for a jurisdiction and all policyholders for the company in the jurisdiction will be pooled (1 Federal pool and up to 1 pool per state per insurance company).

All rates must be filed with the federal or state regulating agency and may not be changed more than monthly. A policy in force will be for at least one year and will not be subject to a rate increase more than annually. The base price for a base coverage plan and the base price for any riders are the same for all policyholders. The schedules of rates for the factors below are filed with the regulating agency and follow the same guidelines regarding changes as the base price. Many of the factors can be controlled or eliminated by the individual, permitting a reduction in insurance costs by changing to healthier behaviors. The purpose of this section is to limit the high end of HDHP costs by anchoring it to the base policy cost and market competition will keep the base policy cost as low as is economically practical. Some of the costs for the higher risk consumers will be borne by lower risk consumers but for every one dollar increase in the base policy, there will be up to twenty-five dollars in increases in the cost for the highest risk policy.

Each insurance company can decide for itself the degree to which each factor will affect the policy price up to the maximum rate. The formula or methodology for establishing actual policy prices needs to be filed with the base policy. The combined highest rate price based on these factors can be no more than 25 times the base rate. This will have the insurance companies compete by setting their own price differentials.

The reasons for variation allowed:
1. The amount of deductible the policyholder chooses.
2. The amount of maximum out-of-pocket expenses chosen.
3. Geographic location
4. Age
5. High risk activities
6. BMI
7. Pre-existing conditions due to personal habits or actions such as drug or alcohol abuse, STDs, obesity, Type II diabetes, tobacco use, reckless behavior, etc.
8. Alcohol use.
9. Tobacco use.
10. Court determination of alcohol or drug use/abuse in criminal or civil court.

It should be noted that pre-existing conditions due to heroic actions or to reasons outside the control of the patient are not to be considered for variations from the base policy. It is expected that insurance companies will include these risks in their base policy. This will divide the costs for these conditions among the whole populace.

The base family policy assumes two adults and two children. An insurance company may require up to an additional twenty-five percent of the family policy premium for each additional dependent. Insurance companies may offer discounts for smaller family sizes.

## High risk/high cost policyholder lottery
The lottery is to ensure health insurance coverage for those with high

risks/high costs while dividing the risk on a pro rata basis between the insurers in the jurisdiction. After the lottery most high risk/high cost policyholders will be covered for five years under this category. The exception is the initial transition period.

A new diagnosis may not be used to terminate a policy even at the end of the current contract. After a new diagnosis that does or is expected to incur more than thrice the average annual healthcare cost the policyholder must be allowed to renew their policy for five years after the year of diagnosis. The premium may be adjusted based on allowed criteria.

An increase of healthcare expense may not be used to terminate a policy even at the end of the current contract. After an increase that exceeds thrice the average annual healthcare cost the policyholder must be allowed to renew their policy for five years after the initial year that healthcare costs exceed thrice the average annual healthcare cost. The premium may be adjusted based on allowed criteria.

There are a couple ways for people to be added to the lottery pool. If the average annual healthcare expenses for an individual or a family for the previous five-years is more than thrice the median for the jurisdiction and policy type the insurance company may refer them to the pool. If the individual or family does not have insurance and has a pre-existing condition that will likely result in meeting the risk or cost conditions they can be added to the pool. In addition an individual or family can voluntarily add themselves to the pool. People can reenter the pool if they have already been through the pool and had a policy for at least a year and are not satisfied with their current provider.

**Step One** is an assessment of each individual or family in the high risk/high cost pool. Each individual or family in the pool will have their average costs over the past five years noted and receive a rating based upon probabilistic estimates for costs over the next five years. The organization that makes this assessment should be run by the insurance companies that will be receiving the results of the assessments. The process should be transparent and fair for all participants. There should be an internal appeals process if a participating company believes that an individual or family has not been rated accurately. A second level of appeal would be in the state or federal court system as appropriate.

**Step Two** in the high risk/high cost insurance pool program is a **Reverse Auction**. The individual or family is put in a list that insurance companies may search and make offers of coverage prior to the mandatory lottery. Some insurance companies may have service contracts with hospitals or clinics that are especially good at treating particular illnesses and can offer better plans at better prices and still achieve better profitability than other insurance companies. This will count against the obligation in the mandatory lottery provided that the company had not previously denied coverage to the individual or family in the past five years unless more than ten other insurance companies or more than fifty percent of the insurance companies in the jurisdiction (whichever is less) have denied coverage or offered more expensive policies since the providing company denied coverage. Under the reverse auction program all insurance companies in the jurisdiction will have 30 days to review the household's medical records and the prognosis for future care requirements and costs and to make an offer of coverage. Any offer made to the consumer during this period will be valid until it is time to decide between these offers and the result of the mandatory lottery.

**Step Three** of the high risk/high cost insurance pool program is a **Mandatory Lottery.** Each insurance company will have to report total dollars of health insurance in force. (Based on gross revenue from policies in force.) The high risk/high cost individuals and families will be randomly assigned to insurance companies on a pro rata basis so that each insurance company has a similar proportion of risk compared to health insurance in force. There will be a lottery each month to assign policies for those that have been added to the pool. The previous insurance cannot be cancelled until the new policy takes effect. The assigned policies will be in effect for five years. The policies assigned through the lottery will not count toward insurance in force for future lotteries. The consumer can be in the state and federal lottery and choose the best option. Insurance companies can trade lottery customers with the consent of the consumer. If an insurance company made an offer to a consumer in the reverse auction that the consumer did not accept, the consumer may accept it after reviewing the offer from the company selected for the consumer in the mandatory lottery. The consumer must decide within 30 days if they will accept an offer other than the results of the mandatory lottery or be automatically enrolled with the company selected by the mandatory lottery. When there is an imbalance in the division of this pool after these changes, it is to be corrected with the initial division of the following month's pool.

If a policyholder leaves a company due to death or for any other reason and the high risk/high cost factor(s) remain then the policy is replaced in the lottery in addition to the company's normal allotment for the month. This is to discourage driving high risk/high cost customers away with poor service or difficult to comply with rules.

During the initial year of the new program there will be a very large pool that will need to be allotted. So that many of these policies do not reoccur at the same time they will be divided up by cost rating based upon a reassessment at the end of the initial year. By the midpoint of the second year the insurance company and the policy holder will be notified of the length of the contract. The lowest 25 percent in cost rating will be two year policies, the next 25 percent will be three year policies, the next 25 percent will be four year policies, and the 25 percent most costly will be five year policies. This will provide the most stability for those with the worst health. When any of these policies end the policy holder and insurance company may choose to continue their association by reaching a new agreement in the reverse auction when returned to the high risk/high cost pool.

## Foreign visitors

The federal government will establish minimum healthcare insurance coverage requirements for short-term (Less than 12 months) foreign visitors. Long-term visitors will be required to participate in a plan like a citizen. Through treaty provisions the federal government may set requirements for groups of foreign visitors. (i.e. foreign diplomats) The federal government will be liable for defaults of healthcare bills by foreign visitors. Taxes and fees collected from US citizens and businesses may not be used to pay any bills resulting from this section unless there is a liability directly attributable to the citizen or business. Treaties may be arranged for the US to trade the adjudicated defaults of foreign visitors for those of US citizens from the foreign country. Then collect from US citizens. Another option is a fee added to visas for visitors to the US. Any fees paid when purchasing tobacco, alcohol, or recreational drugs by a non-citizen will be kept by the federal government unless the non-citizen has an HSA set up to receive them.

## Insurance policy maximum limits

Each policy will provide policyholders with at least three options. Options 2 and 3 should cost less than option 1 so the maximum limit should not be part of the 25X limits.

**Option 1:** The insurance policy will not set an annual or lifetime maximum. It will be expected that the insurance company will purchase reinsurance to pay for excessive liabilities. This is the default option in a base policy.

**Option 2:** The insurance policy will set an annual maximum per person but no lifetime maximum per person. The consumer will be responsible for the remainder of their healthcare expenses for the year. The policy may have a variety of different annual maximums that policyholders may choose from.

**Option 3:** The insurance policy will not set an annual or lifetime maximum. For the insurance company, their cost for the policy is limited to an annual maximum payout but any remainder is due in future periods until fully paid. The policy may have a variety of different annual maximums that policyholders may choose from.

## Health Savings Accounts

### Health Savings Account Investment Types

**Type I:**
> Money market mutual fund (For current period expenses).

**Type II:**
> Treasury bonds and other US government bonds
> General revenue municipal bonds
> FDIC insured accounts
> Annuities
> Other insured investments

**Type III:**
> Investment grade bonds and bond mutual funds
> Domestic and international market index mutual funds
>> No sales fees allowed
>> All expenses must be less than 0.50 percent
> Domestic and international market index ETFs/ETNs

**Type IV:**
> Other mutual funds
> Domestic and international stocks
> Other ETFs and ETNs

**Type V:**
> Below investment grade bonds
> Commodities
> Derivatives—futures and options
> Any investment in a short position

Limits on types of investments to moderate risk and provide diversification

**Under age 40**
> Types I, II and III combined: At least 30 percent
> Type IV: No minimum amount
> Type V: No minimum amount, Maximum of 15 percent

**Age 40 up to 49**
> Types I and II combined: At least 10 percent
> Types II and III combined: At least 40 percent
> Type IV: No minimum amount

Type V: No minimum amount, Maximum of 20 percent

### Age 50 up to 59
Types I and II combined: At least 10 percent
Types I, II, and III combined: At least 50 percent
Type IV: No minimum amount
Type V: No minimum amount, Maximum of 15 percent

### Age 60 up to full retirement age
Types I and II combined: At least 10 percent
Types I, II, and III combined: At least 60 percent
Type IV: No minimum amount
Type V: No minimum amount, Maximum of 10 percent

### Over full retirement age
Types I and II combined: At least 10 percent
Types I, II, and III combined: At least 70 percent
Type IV: No minimum amount
Type V: No minimum amount, Maximum of 10 percent

The investment categories above and the restrictions are an example of a way to balance investment risk and return for the people of the country in their dual roles as HSA account holder and taxpayer. It permits those who wish to take on less risk to have no restrictions from doing so but also allows those who wish to be more aggressive to be able to do that with part of their funds.

The Type I investments are for expected near-term expenses. The Type II investments are generally considered safe or insured investments. The Type III investments are generally good investments with more risk and return than Type II investments. They provide good diversification and over time generally reflect a return consistent with the level of profits of the underlying companies. The restriction in level of fees is because with an index fund there should be very little trading activity or research warranted that would require management fees and no sales fees should be required for a mandatory account. This will maximize returns for HSA investors and prevent unreasonable gouging with fees.

The Type IV and V investments are for more experienced and knowledgeable investors and provide for greater returns but at greater risk. When the Type IV and V investments result in a loss for the year, the loss will have to be made up by increased contributions. If Type I, II, or III investments are part of the same account as the Type IV or V investments they must be segregated. Losses from Type IV and V investments may not be covered by Type I, II, or III HSA investment gains. Any total portfolio that does not earn at least the return on investment of a benchmark of the weighted average of all issued 10 year Treasuries during the same running three year time period may be required to reduce the amount of risk in their investments and will be required to make additional contributions to make up the losses to reach the benchmark.

The faster that the HSA investments accumulate, the sooner that the HSA will be fully funded. This will provide for more security for families, result in higher tax receipts from the reduction in income that is set aside after the HSA is fully funded, and reduce the likelihood that someone will need to turn to the low income supplement for help.

When the employee has accumulated their lifetime maximum, all of the employee's gross wages will be counted as taxable wages. The HSA trustee will track the household's demographics and account balance and compare to the lifetime maximum tables. When the account reaches the lifetime maximum the HSA trustee will notify the federal government and the account holder. The account holder will be responsible for paying estimated taxes on the excess quarterly and is free to withdraw the excess without penalty. As the balance will vary, the annual tax liability will be based upon the level of excess at the end of the calendar year plus withdrawals of excess during the year.

## Lifetime Maximums

This plan is intended to continue for a person's lifetime. Therefore there is a need to establish lifetime maximum tax-free accumulation limits. This is necessary so that those who have accumulated sufficient resources to fund their healthcare can have free use of the remainder of their money and to remove the tax-exempt status of this money.

To facilitate the generation of beneficial numbers for establishing limits, the average annual and lifetime healthcare costs need to be estimated each year. Congress will have to establish or identify an agency for this purpose. From these the expected average remaining healthcare cost by age is estimated. An application and approval process should be established so that those with an established healthcare problem or genetic predisposition that is likely to cost the person more than the average healthcare costs to accumulate more than the customary lifetime maximum. In addition, all actual healthcare expenses can be paid with tax free funds even if the funds are earned or otherwise acquired after the expense is incurred.

The HSA account holder can accumulate tax free up to 110 percent of their average remaining healthcare cost in their HSA. The HSA account holder can accumulate tax free up to 110 percent of the average remaining healthcare cost in their HSA for each adult dependent. These maximum limits will be adjusted annually. (The 110 percent in this section is a placeholder. The actual percent should be balanced between the loss in taxes from people accumulating too much tax-free and the cost of providing low income supplement to people who run out of funds in their HSA.) There is no limit to after-tax contributions to the HSA accounts. The funds will be accounted for separately.

For dependent children, the HSA account holder can accumulate the higher of 200 percent of the average annual healthcare costs times the number of years remaining until the child reaches the age of 23 or actual expenses tax-free per year for each child dependent. These maximum limits for the dependents include funds that the dependents received from all sources so child custody agreements will have to take into account who gets to set money aside and how much. Each child dependent who will likely become an adult dependent because of disability will be treated as an adult dependent.


## Opting Out

There are several ways to opt out of the HDHP. Some people will not use healthcare services for religious or other personal reasons. Then there are others who can afford to self-insure. Also there are two conditions based on an informal opting out; failure to designate an HSA and/or HDHP for an employer to send money to and those who are living under the radar.

Those who are formally permitted to opt out will pay taxes on the wages normally set aside for HDHP/HSA as regular income. They will be required to begin participation if application is made for the low income supplement. The maximum set aside will have to be set aside until any low income supplement is repaid. Life insurance to cover low income supplement payments will be required to be carried by most recipients and continue until the low income supplement is repaid. (See low income supplement section.)

Those who do not purchase the full basic plan insurance coverages for their state or the federal plan are not permitted to bankrupt out of uncovered healthcare expenses that were recommended. If they do not purchase any insurance the state plan recommendations will be used as the basis for the bankruptcy bar if the state has a basic plan for this program, otherwise the federal plan recommendations will be the basis. If they opt out of part of their state's plan or the federal plan they will have a bankruptcy bar on the options they choose not to purchase from the plan.

Those who fail to purchase insurance coverage may be required to make up payments from time periods when they did not have coverage in order to resume coverage. People will have two options in this case.

**Option 1:** The person may renew an old policy with a previous insurer and pay the premiums that would have been due during the intervening time. Insurers will be required to allow a previous insured to renew a lapsed policy for five years and will have the option after that point. Insurers may require a medical evaluation along with the renewal application. If a pre-existing condition is found it can be assumed that it has existed for the entire lapsed period unless proven otherwise. Premiums for the lapsed period may take into account the pre-existing condition(s).

**Option 2:** The person may obtain a new policy with an insurer and pay the premiums that would have been due during the lapsed time. Insurers may require a medical evaluation along with the renewal application. If a pre-existing condition is found it can be assumed that it has existed for the entire lapsed period unless proven otherwise. Premiums for the lapsed period may take into account the pre-existing condition(s).

An insurance company is not required to make a new or returning customer make up payments from uncovered time periods. It is expected that the customers without a pre-existing condition will receive competitive quotes from many insurance companies. Everyone will have two years following the start of this program before the provision to make up payments will go into effect.

Those who opt out will still need an HSA card to receive their contributions back from making purchases. If they do not use it, then the money will stay with the federal government. In addition any extra that is required to be set aside due to drug or alcohol abuse will still need to be set aside. They may not use the HSA funds for anything but qualified healthcare expenses and will be able to collect interest on it and will it to another upon their death.

**Will Not Use**

Those who will not use healthcare services for religious or other personal reasons may file notice to opt out of the program. They will be required to set aside twenty-five percent of gross income in the HSA and not use healthcare services for twenty years after filing notice. After the twenty years of no use of healthcare services, the HSA must be maintained but no further funds will have to be deposited except for the contributions linked to high risk activities, and alcohol, drug, and tobacco purchases unless they let it go to the government. This is necessary so that an individual cannot undercut the program by purchasing these items for others at a lower price. These provisions address another concern which is the tendency of people who have generally been healthy, especially young adults to be more likely to want to opt out and then have no funds accumulated when they do need healthcare services. Most people that are just trying to save money will have a healthcare expense within the twenty years and will have resources to turn to. They will be less likely to have to turn to the government for assistance.

**Self-Insurance**

Anyone can opt out of purchasing an HDHP but will not be able to bankrupt out of debts that would have been covered if an HDHP had been purchased. Twenty-five percent of gross income will have to be set aside until the account has assets of 150 percent of the average remaining lifetime healthcare cost for the covered person(s).

### Failure to designate an HSA or HDHP

When an individual fails to designate an HSA and/or HDHP for an employer to send the employee's money to in a timely manner the funds will be sent to the federal government and placed in an individual healthcare reimbursement account invested in Treasury securities. Funds may be withdrawn on a quarterly basis to reimburse qualified healthcare expenses. Funds are taxed as income and withholding will not reduce the amount placed into the individual healthcare reimbursement account. The maximum set aside of gross income will be placed in the account. Funds can be removed from the individual healthcare reimbursement account and rolled over into an HSA account or to purchase an HDHP. Tax-exempt status will be restored to the portion that is rolled over within 180 days from the end of the quarter in which it was earned. This is clearly designed to encourage people to make decisions about their funds.

### Under the radar

This is not actually a formal opting out. The federal government will maintain an account to cover the costs of the homeless and indigent who are living under the radar. Minimum standards will be set for healthcare providers to attempt to identify recipients (Such as picture, fingerprints, and/or DNA sample) to guard against abuse and fraud and to assign costs when possible.

## Medicare XXI

Medicare XXI is the overall name of the whole healthcare financing reform that is described in this chapter. The individual HSA accounts and HDHP insurance and the program that should replace the current Medicare, Medicaid, and SCHIP programs. The Medicare XXI program administers the low income supplement which replaces Medicaid and SCHIP and the retirement program for those who are qualified for the current Medicare. This section describes these two components of Medicare XXI that more closely correlate with the current government programs.

All people who are eligible for the current Medicare program and are 31 years old by December 31st of the year the bill is passed will be eligible for the Medicare XXI retirement benefit. The amount of benefit is conditioned upon the age restrictions below. Those under age 31 and those with less than ten years of Medicare-qualifying work will automatically be cashed out. Funds from the Medicare "trust fund" will be used to cash people out as needed.

In order to encourage healthier behaviors there are some restrictions for the retirement benefit. Beginning ten years after the new program starts the retirement benefit will not pay the portion of the insurance premium for the causes of rate increase that are patient controllable and the taxpayers should not be responsible for the costs. Should the retiree lack the resources to pay the additional premium or fully fund their HSA, they can receive a low income supplement to cover it. The low income supplement will require repayment in the future.

### Age 65 and over

All qualifying workers/retirees who are age 65 and over on December 31$^{st}$ of the year of the passage of the bill will receive the Medicare XXI retirement benefit automatically and receive it for the remainder of their lives. All workers over age 65 will be able to place their set aside of compensation into an HSA.

### Age 31 to 64

All qualifying workers who are age 31 to 64 on December 31$^{st}$ of the year of the passage of the bill will receive a Medicare XXI retirement benefit, by default, that is equal to 2.3 percent of the full benefit times the number of years the person is over 18 and begin to receive it when they reach retirement age and then receive it for the remainder of their lives. (Maximum of 100 percent) Anyone 61.5 years of age and over when the new program starts will qualify for 100 percent retirement benefit. The reason for the bias is because it will be more difficult to grow the assets in the HSA given the shorter time between the start of the program and their retirement age and the higher cost of an HDHP at these ages.

### Younger Than Age 31

All workers who are younger than age 31 on December 31$^{st}$ of the year of the passage of the bill will automatically be cashed out of the retirement program. The cash out will be based on what the Medicare contributions would be worth if they had been invested in 10 year Treasury Notes when the contributions were originally made.

### New Retirement Ages

A new schedule of full retirement ages is recommended. One of the key ways to reduce costs is to increase the retirement age. People are living longer and healthier than when Medicare first started. By delaying retirement just a few years trillions of dollars of liabilities are eliminated from the government budget. That is the least painful way to trim costs. For those who truly cannot work the additional years there is disability and the low income supplement.

Everyone else should plan to work longer or set aside more on their own to retire earlier at their own expense.

| Full Retirement Age-Medicare XXI | | | |
|---|---|---|---|
| Year of Birth | Full Retirement Age | Age in 2017 | Age in 2019 |
| 1955 and earlier | 65 | 62+ | 64 |
| 1956 | 65 | 61 | 63 |
| 1957 | 65 and 6 months | 60 | 62 |
| 1958 | 66 | 59 | 61 |
| 1959 | 66 and 6 months | 58 | 60 |
| 1960 | 67 | 57 | 59 |
| 1961 | 67 and 4 months | 56 | 58 |
| 1962 | 67 and 8 months | 55 | 57 |
| 1963 | 68 | 54 | 56 |
| 1964 | 68 and 4 months | 53 | 55 |
| 1965 | 68 and 8 months | 52 | 54 |
| 1966 | 69 | 51 | 53 |
| 1967 | 69 and 4 months | 50 | 52 |
| 1968 | 69 and 8 months | 49 | 51 |
| 1969 | 70 | 48 | 50 |
| 1970 | 70 and 4 months | 47 | 49 |
| 1971 | 70 and 8 months | 46 | 48 |
| 1972 | 71 | 45 | 47 |
| 1973 | 71 and 4 months | 44 | 46 |
| 1974 | 71 and 8 months | 43 | 45 |
| 1975 | 72 | 42 | 44 |

**Low Income Supplement**

A sliding schedule is used to supply a low income supplement. This supplement will pay 100 percent of HDHP and HSA supplement for those without income or assets and decrease as income increases. In addition, the high cost/high risk people may qualify for the supplement based upon their actual costs in relation to their income. The sliding schedule needs to account for the projected insurance and out-of-pocket costs. This supplement will replace Medicaid, SCHIP, and any other means-tested targeted government healthcare programs.

Those with funds in an HSA and/or other assets will receive a prorated amount. The amount of assets will be divided by the average life expectancy plus ten years minus current age.

$$\frac{\text{Amount in HSA + other counted assets}}{\text{Avg. life expectancy} + 10 - \text{current age}}$$

If the person is already past the average life expectancy, the amount in the HSA and assets will be divided by ten until age 100, thereafter it will be divided by five. The resultant amount will be deducted from the income based benefit. This will be repeated each year the low-income supplement is needed.

There are some assets that should be excluded from consideration. This should be done in order to make it possible and easier for a household to recover and more quickly become financially self-sufficient again.

**Home**:  primary residence, equity up to 100 percent of the national median home value. The national median home value used is the average of the past four years. This will slow the change of the limit. The government will place a lien against the property.

**Retirement accounts**:  IRAs, 401ks, etc. up to a reasonable threshold based on age, expected life expectancy, and projected future earnings. Projected future earnings should be considered conservatively if there are any existing health conditions which may reasonably limit future income.

**Automobiles**:  equity up to $15,000 (2016 dollars) per working age adult in the household with a current valid driver's license. This limit should be indexed to the inflation rate.

The government should limit the amount of distributions from retirement accounts, reverse mortgages, and other assets that provide the funds for living and healthcare expenses after retirement age. At a minimum the distribution should be enough so the household does not live in poverty. Double the federal poverty level is reasonable. At a maximum the government should limit the restriction of assets to providing 25 years of retirement income at double the federal poverty level. Any amount in excess of this should not be restricted. This is to limit the burden on taxpayers and creditors that could be left holding the person's debts.

Those receiving more than forty percent of their healthcare funds from the low-income supplement will only be eligible for a base plan unless less is desired or more is necessary due to pre-existing conditions, family history, or other substantial reason. Any state base plan coverage that exceeds the federal base plan coverage the state will be responsible for covering that portion of the low income supplement that exceeds the federal base plan coverage.

The default supplement for the HSA is 110 percent of the national average used two year's prior for comparable size and age of household or the household's out-of-pocket maximum, whichever is less. Those who need more than the default may apply for up to their annual out-of-pocket maximum. Application for the additional supplement will also trigger an alert that an audit may be necessary.

One-third of the unused standard low-income supplement provided for a person's HSA and any interest earned will be able to be retained in the person's HSA. This portion will not have to be repaid at any time in the future. The other two-thirds will be returned to the government. This is to incentivize recipients to be careful about their spending. By default, owned dollars are spent before low income supplement dollars.

## Low Income Supplement Repayment

There will be a mandatory repayment of previously used supplement. Prior to death the repayment formula will be related to the beneficiary's income after adjusting for the standard deductions and personal exemptions for the household. After the deductions and exemptions, ten percent of the remaining income will be garnished. It is also reasonable to require most of the household's income that exceeds twice the average income for the same size household to be garnished until the debt is repaid.

When the household income reaches 120 percent of the federal median income, life insurance will be required to be maintained until the previously used supplement is paid off. It may be most cost effective for the government to contract for a group policy for all people who owe the government money. This may help bring down the cost for higher risk people.

At death, any unused HSA funds will be used to repay any supplement used during the person's life. The remaining funds will be considered part of a person's estate and may be willed to another person. It will be tax-free if it goes into the beneficiaries' HSA or Social Security XXI account. Taxed as regular income if accumulated tax-free and is not rolled into another tax-deferred account. It will be required that it goes to the beneficiary's HSA first, then Social Security XXI account second if they have not reached their lifetime maximums.

## Retirement Benefit

The full retirement benefit is calculated similar to the low income supplement benefit. The used benefit does not need to be repaid. The person may keep and own one-third of the unused full annual HSA benefit at the end of each year. The unused benefit will not reduce benefits in future years but will need to remain in the HSA.

## Converting Employer Retiree Health Benefits

The legacy health plan will have several options. It may make payments as the first payer for the beneficiaries. It may use the average benefit from final years before implementation of Medicare XXI and index it for inflation and provide an annual lump sum for each beneficiary's HSA. It may collect healthcare cost information under Medicare XXI for beneficiary pool and calculate what it would have paid out under current rules. Then use the average to provide a lump sum benefit to the beneficiaries. It may cash out of the benefit by providing a lump sum to each beneficiary for the NPV of the benefit. These options may need to be adjusted or weighted for some reasons such as age, pre-existing conditions, family size, or other reasons. A hybrid of these options could work also. Congress will need to decide what options will be available and then the contracted parties to the plan will need to decide which option they prefer.

## Paying for Medicare XXI

The money that is already spent on Medicaid and SCHIP will be diverted to this program. The money currently spent on Medicare from the payroll tax will be replaced by general revenues and used for the program. The Earned Income Tax Credit (EITC) will be gradually reduced and eliminated over three years and these funds will be diverted to the program. The low income supplement healthcare benefit is more valuable to low income working families than the EITC.

Preferably the remainder of the costs will come from reductions in lower priority spending and tax expenditures. As more baby boomers retire the costs of the retirement program are expected to increase so spending will need to be reduced in other areas of the budget to get over that hump until the number of people eligible for the full retirement benefit decreases again. It is possible that debt financing will be required to smooth out the hump due to the baby boomer retirement surge. When cashing people out of the old Medicare program it should be done with Treasury bonds of varying duration to spread the cost over the person's working lifetime. More debt in the transition period can be justified only by the elimination of much larger liabilities that the restructuring will accomplish.

Most of those who receive the low income supplement will pay that back directly when their income increases later in life or through the mandatory life insurance requirement. Over the long-term the costs of this program should be greatly reduced and lower than any other alternatives that have been pitched.

## Charitable Contributions

There are many situations where people are in need of help in paying for healthcare expenses. It is in the best interests of the state, community, and individuals involved in making this easy. Everyone knows someone who has suffered from a catastrophic illness like cancer, stroke, or heart attack. This is one more way we can help out family or friends in need. It will also greatly help reduce the cost to taxpayers. Every dollar of reduced taxes means three or more dollars of targeted help for those in need. This will reduce the amount of low income supplement needed in the future.

Contributors may contribute tax-free funds to another citizen's or legal foreign worker's HSA regardless of relationship provided it does not exceed the recipient's actual expenses plus remaining lifetime maximum limits. A receipt is necessary for tax records and anonymous donations are allowed which would not be tax deductible. Anonymous donations that result in excess contributions may be donated to another HSA or taxed as income.

This mechanism could also be used to shift money from one person to another easily. Parents can fund an HSA for their children even if the children are not mature enough for the parents to give them cash. When there is a large party or family reunion and a single individual purchases the alcohol. The person can be reimbursed in cash and distribute set aside money from their HSA to the other peoples' HSAs.

## Implementation Strategy

To aid in the transition to Medicare XXI, immediately pass a law during the new administration that requires any employer that provides medical insurance to employees to provide a High Deductible Healthcare Plan and Health Savings Account option. They will not have to have two plans but if they do provide insurance there will have to be a HDHP and HSA option. The money that the employer saves on the HDHP premium compared to the traditional plan must be paid out to employees in their HSA. The employer does not need to arrange for HSA accounts for employees. The employees may obtain their own HSA account to improve portability.

While it is desirable to pass and implement Medicare XXI as soon as possible it may take some time to accomplish. The greatest issue most people have with HDHPs is the fear of having to pay a high deductible. Most years people do not have high healthcare expenses. Over time people will realize that they can save the money in low expense years to more than make up for high expense years. This experience will aid in building support over the long term that can help pass Medicare XXI in the future if it cannot be accomplished in the short term.

As a reinforcement to this strategy, traditional Medicare and Medicaid should have HDHP and HSA options designed like the Medicare XXI plan.

## Other Healthcare Reform Ideas

### Truth in Healthcare Provision

These provisions are to aid consumers in comparison shopping for healthcare services. Anything that can be reasonably standardized with regard to formatting of common documents/forms, presentation of information, payment processing, etc. for simplifying comparisons should be done. There is certain information that nearly all healthcare providers and insurance companies collect or need. These should be standardized to the extent possible to improve clarity and speed up the transfer of information between users. Standardized definitions for terms, procedures, and coverages should be set by the federal regulating agency in consultation with a broad range of stakeholders.

All healthcare providers must maintain a website with prices for materials and services and provide patients with an itemized estimate ahead of time unless it is an acute emergency. Also, if a provider has a financial interest in other providers such as a pharmacy, clinic, or imaging center that interest must be disclosed. This will be necessary for consumers to more efficiently shop around for healthcare services. With consumers more free to adjust their spending based on price, this should force healthcare providers to become more efficient and push down costs by free market forces instead of unrealistic and inefficient government price fixing.

There should be a searchable online database of healthcare providers with a past or pending malpractice claim with a description of the incident from the claimant and/or defendant and the court's findings if it is adjudicated. If it is still pending, certain limitations should be in place to protect litigants' rights. Any complaints to the various licensing organizations for healthcare providers should be in this database, also. The patient's identity should be in the master database that can be accessed by court order but not in the publicly available database.

Each healthcare provider will report care quality information to an easily searchable online government database. The information that is documented will be determined by panels that the federal government will establish with a mixture of healthcare professionals, insurance professionals, and knowledgeable citizens. A different panel or perhaps sub-committees may be necessary for different segments of the healthcare industry. (Doctors, hospitals, pharmacists, medical specialties, etc.)

## Free Market Reforms

In many states and local markets there are very few insurance companies from which consumers can chose. This is not conducive to the competition that is needed for this plan to work. With 1300 health insurance companies in the country there should be hundreds of plans to choose from in every jurisdiction. Some new requirements are needed to foster more competition.

1. No insurance company may restrict a provider from servicing a patient with another insurance company or no insurance. There can be no different level of reimbursement from an insurer to providers based on whether or not they see patients with other insurance.

2. No insurance company may blacklist a licensed provider that a patient wishes to use unless the provider has been convicted of fraudulent billing. If the provider does not abide by the new industry recordkeeping and documentation standardization then the reimbursement may be reduced by the estimated actual added cost to the insurance company to process the claim. The provider may not directly bill the patient for the added transaction cost.

3. No insurance company may contractually lock up more than twenty percent of the healthcare providers work hours of any specialty in a defined political division. This will include all towns, villages, cities, counties, and states.

4. No provider may deny service to a patient based upon the insurance plan that they have, provided that the company abides by the new industry recordkeeping and documentation standardization and the patient agrees to the price for the service.

5. Providers may not charge more than their posted price provided the insurance is with a company that abides by the new industry recordkeeping and documentation standardization.

6. An insurance company does not need to have a physical presence in a state to market a policy in the state. Companies can market through the internet and/or independent agents.

7. The federal government will establish regulations concerning the reserve and capital requirements and the quality of investments for the insurance companies. There needs to be one national standard for insurance companies. The federal standards will apply to all insurance companies with a national plan or with plans in more than one state. Any insurance company present in only one state will be subject to the state regulator in these matters. An insurance company operating in multiple states may opt to be under the regulatory jurisdiction of the individual states instead of the federal regulator if they do not have a nationwide plan. If the state chooses they can opt out of regulating these matters and just require the companies to be subject to the federal regulator and standards.

## Portable Healthcare Information

While having a centralized database for all of a patient's records would be ideal for having a complete record, the cost may be prohibitive trying to digitally link everything and everyone and there are clear and substantial concerns about patient privacy. Here are several near-term ideas for consolidating and transferring a patient's records:

1. Healthcare records, whether they are text, images, x-rays, CT scans, etc., should be designed to be digitally transferable between patients,

healthcare providers, and insurers on common computer platforms and operating systems.

2. Healthcare providers should be able to place a read-only copy of a patient's records on a USB flash drive.

3. A patient could be allowed to go online and download a copy of their healthcare records. Each healthcare provider could provide an online account for each patient that could be accessed by the patient and by future healthcare providers that the patient allows to access it. The patient would then have to maintain a list of account names and passwords and carry them on their person for emergencies.

4. Insurance companies, major healthcare organizations, or database management companies could allow people to establish cloud accounts that all of the person's healthcare providers can send a copy of the person's records to for archiving and retrieval by future healthcare providers. The patient would then have to carry an account access card with the URL and their password on their person for emergencies. With a secondary restricted permission password the patient could allow their healthcare providers access to all of their medical records, allow providers to post but not delete documents, and to add information and provide updated copies of documents but no deletions to information on documents in the account.

## R&D Cost Shifting Resolution

Americans frequently pay far more for the same medicines and medical equipment than people in other countries. Other countries with nationalized healthcare can negotiate much lower rates because they are the only buyer for the country and can choose to not purchase a particular drug or from a particular company if they do not meet their price target. Sometimes companies are threatened with replacement by similar generic drugs. Another factor is the inability of underdeveloped countries to pay full price because of the wage scale in the country. The current practice has US patients picking up the bulk of the R&D costs of new medicines and devices.

There have been calls for US citizens to be able to purchase medicine from overseas at a lower price. This will offer an immediate cost benefit for healthcare consumers. Unfortunately, this could bankrupt pharmaceutical companies or force them to severely cut back on R&D. Either way it will hurt the progress in finding cures for other diseases or conditions. In addition, there is a potential loss in chain of custody for medications from FDA regulated enterprises to unregulated enterprises.

There are a couple of facets to the solution. First, negotiate trade rules that set stronger restrictions and penalties on the use of generic alternatives before a patent expires. Also, extend the length of time until a patent expires for medicines. After a new compound is created, frequently as much as half of the twenty year patent period is used up by development and clinical trials before it is released commercially. Extensions of up to ten years should be granted to cover reasonable development time and trials. This should help to lower the cost of name-brand drugs by increasing the time available to recoup R&D costs before losing market share to generics. Renegotiate WTO rules to provide this protection worldwide.

There should be some authority that has discretion to set the time period of the extension based upon reasonable development and testing needs. This authority should also determine if the company had a reason to delay releasing an alternative or substitute for a current product and conduct an investigation into whether the new product was intentionally delayed and by how much. To discourage this manipulation the time that a product was intentionally and unreasonably delayed should be reduced from the extension. Additionally the 1984 Hatch-Waxman law could be updated to not only allow generics makers the ability to sue to bust the patents that are not strong innovations from previous drugs but also to contest the length of time of the patent extension.

With increased time to sell new medicines, industry and government will be better positioned to provide medicines to the truly poor around the world at or below cost.

## Physician Training

There are restrictions on the number of medical school slots and residencies for doctors. These restrictions limit the supply of doctors and increase the cost of healthcare. The argument of the American Medical Association and others is that these restrictions increase the quality of doctors. There is no evidence to support this. It merely serves to keep more doctors from being trained and bringing down what they can charge. As in every other sector of the economy, when wages rise more people are encouraged to provide services. Thereby bringing wages down. If wages go down too much fewer people will enter the profession. A rough equilibrium is established by market forces.

Any such laws and regulations need to be removed. It is reasonable to require a set level of professional qualifications for licensure. It is not reasonable to establish limits on the number of people who can be trained. Removing these limits will bring down the cost of medical school and of medical care. Market competition will force this to happen. This savings will ultimately result in less expensive medical care for all of us. It will provide more trained doctors for rural and inner city hospitals and clinics without the need for an expensive government program.

## Indian Health Service

Currently the US has treaty obligations that require us to provide healthcare services to more than 2.5 million Native Americans. The service is a chronic provider of substandard care that is ripe with cronyism and incompetence. Instead of having dedicated government hospitals and clinics the people being served should receive money in an HSA to purchase an HDHP and to pay for part of the deductible and out-of-pocket maximum. An inefficient and corrupt government agency is replaced. The people can use any healthcare provider of their choice. They will not be trapped into using a substandard government provider.

There are some who will complain that these are the only hospitals and clinics serving some of these communities. That will change. The existence of people with health insurance will bring in medical providers. These providers will have to provide good care or the people will vote with their feet and go elsewhere. Now they are just trapped into using a substandard government provider. They are poorly served and taxpayers are poorly served.

# 5 FEDERAL SPENDING LIMIT AMENDMENT

**"The American people want a balanced budget. They want Congress to stop this barbaric practice of perpetual deficit spending. It really, if you think about it, is a form of taxation without representation. We fought a war over that issue and we won that war."**
**Mike Lee**

Over time the federal government has been consuming increasing amounts of the national economy. This excessive burden upon the people of the country is a theft of our liberty. The proposed Federal Spending Limit Amendment to the US Constitution is needed to restrain the government and force the politicians to set priorities and not just keep telling everyone "Yes".

The President should use the plans in this book to propose a budget that limited taxes and spending to eighteen percent of GDP. Compromise and agree to limits of twenty percent of GDP if the Congress passes this or a similar constitutional amendment and sends it to the states. The President should tell Congress the order that he will sign the appropriations bills and the limits he will accept. Any other sequence or exceeding the limit should require the Congress to override his veto. If necessary shut down those parts of government for which there is no timely agreement reached.

Until the Congress passes this amendment, the President should not sign a debt limit increase bill. If the debt ceiling is hit shut down parts of the government starting with the lowest priorities unless there are statutory restrictions to that sequence. Social Security and Medicare would still be paid by incoming FICA taxes up to the amount of current tax revenues. Then their "trust fund" Treasury bonds could be traded for the receipts from Treasury bonds sold on the open market.

This should not be a problem for any Republican President because we should all be in favor of cutting spending and making a strong stand for fiscal discipline. A Democrat President wants excessive spending and will play games like threatening to cut high priority spending like Social Security or the military to scare the Congress and the People into not having a budgetary standoff. For Republicans, being able to set priorities and cut lower priority items from the budget is a win-win situation.

## Section 1.

The Power of the Congress to authorize spending and to lay and collect Taxes, Duties, Imposts, and Excises shall be limited to twenty percent of the Economic Output of the United States; with the following conditions and exceptions.

Twenty years after passage, the limit shall be nineteen percent of the Economic Output of the United States. Thirty years after passage, the limit shall be eighteen percent of the Economic Output of the United States. Forty years after passage, the limit shall be seventeen percent of the Economic Output of the United States.

## Section 2. Conditions

Defense outlays are limited to seven percent of the Economic Output of the largest national economy of the world.

Twenty years after passage non-defense outlays are limited to twelve percent of the Economic Output of the United States. Thirty years after passage non-defense outlays are limited to eleven percent of the Economic Output of the United States. Forty years after passage non-defense outlays are limited to ten percent of the Economic Output of the United States.

## Section 3. Exceptions

Defense outlays may exceed the Economic Output limit during periods when a majority of both Houses of Congress declares that the United States is at war or involved in fighting an internal rebellion or when Congress declares and defines the existence of a clear and present danger to the nation. These outlays must be directly related to defense expenses.

Non-defense outlays may exceed the Economic Output limit for expenses directly related to reconstruction and recovery from natural disasters, war, internal rebellion, and other attacks. This exception requires two-thirds of both houses of Congress to approve.

Non-defense outlays may exceed the Economic Output limit by a maximum of two percent of the Economic Output of the United States for expenses directly related to stabilizing the federal budget during an economic crisis. This exception requires two-thirds of both houses of Congress to approve.

Total receipts and/or outlays may exceed the overall Economic Output limit as needed to meet one or more of the other exceptions.

## Section 4. Implementation

Non-defense outlays exceptions will be in discrete identified appropriations.

All defense outlays will be in discrete appropriations separate from non-defense appropriations.

Congress shall make Laws which shall be necessary and proper for the refunding of excess tax collections.

Exceptions must be voted for each fiscal year and may not be continued without meeting the requirements of this amendment.

Congress shall reach compliance with the initial outlays limits of the amendment by the end of the third full fiscal year following the passage of this amendment.

Congress shall reach compliance with the initial receipts (tax) limits of the amendment by the end of the sixth full fiscal year following the passage of this amendment.

At least six months prior to each fiscal year, the President shall transmit to the Congress a proposed budget for the United States Government for that fiscal year in which total outlays and total receipts meet the conditions of this article.


## Explanation of Each Section

You will notice that there is no requirement for a balanced budget. A balanced budget does not prevent excessive taxation and spending. It just requires that the government does not have a deficit.

Incurring a deficit over the short term during a recession, depression, or war should be available so that the government can spread the costs over a longer time period and limit the drag on the economy during these times. Long term debt is intergenerational theft but short term debt to help maintain stability in the budget and mitigate the effects of natural disasters, war, terrorist attacks, recession, or depression is an important tool that the Congress should have.

Economic conditions change from the time that a budget and appropriations are set until the fiscal year and the tax receipts occur. There will frequently be fluctuations that could cause regular crises and provide uncertainty in the economy that could be a drag on the economy. Frequent emergency adjustments to comply with the constitutional constraint add unnecessary complexity and uncertainty into the economy. The limitation on the total economic output that the government may take and use should be a sufficient limitation.

You will also notice that there is no requirement for a super majority for increasing taxes. This is an unreasonable micromanagement of the Congress. With an overall limit on how much of the economy that the Congress can take, the decisions under that cap should be left to the discretion of the Congress each year. They are elected to decide what the spending priorities are and the types of taxes imposed. If we disagree with their spending priorities then we need to vote them out not tie their hands with the Constitution.

## Section 1.

**The Power of the Congress to authorize spending and to lay and collect Taxes, Duties, Imposts, and Excises shall be limited to twenty percent of the Economic Output of the United States; with the following conditions and exceptions.**

This section begins similar to Article I, Section 8 of the US Constitution. Added to it is a new limit to the power of the Congress to raise revenue. Congress will be limited to twenty percent of economic output each year. In addition, there would be a new type of limitation—a limit on the ability to authorize spending. Both limits are necessary to prevent excessive debt financing to get around the taxation limit. Debts that future generations will have to pay!

This is superior to a balanced budget amendment. With a balanced budget amendment there is no limit on how much the government can tax and spend. The limitation only requires that the government has to raise as much taxes as it spends each year. As we have seen repeatedly when Democrats have held both houses of Congress and the Presidency since the 1970s, they cannot restrain their spending and strongly desire to redistribute the wealth (private property) of the people of this country to their supporters. The allure of saying yes to overspending has also frequently affected Republicans, though to a lesser degree than Democrats. With this they will all be limited.

**Twenty years after passage, the limit shall be nineteen percent of the Economic Output of the United States. Thirty years after passage, the limit shall be eighteen percent of the Economic Output of the United States. Forty years after passage, the limit shall be seventeen percent of the Economic Output of the United States.**

Currently and for the next several decades the baby boom generation will be retiring and using Social Security and Medicare which will prevent us from bringing down the spending right away. Over time as the Social Security XXI and Medicare XXI programs are implemented the tax and spending demand on the federal government will decline. It is important that politicians not be allowed to keep spending at these levels. The set asides required of workers in the new programs will limit the tax base and with most entitlement spending off the books of the federal government there is no need to keep spending at current levels. The American people are not working for the government.

Another option that is worth considering is delaying the reduction in taxes to five to ten years later than the reductions in spending in order to reduce the federal debt.

## Section 2. Conditions

**Defense outlays are limited to seven percent of the Economic Output of the largest national economy of the world.**

Six percent of economic output was the approximate level during the Cold War when we maintained a much larger military than today. Here it is set to seven percent to adjust for the possibility that some time in the future we may be challenged by a nation or group of nations with greater economic output than the US. This is also why the limit is related to the largest national economy. It is unlikely that we would ever have to exceed that level without a declared war but this is a hedge against that possibility. Our recent levels of defense spending at the height of the wars in Iraq and Afghanistan have been around four to five percent of economic output. Separating out defense spending will take away the temptation to gut the military in order to avoid making the tough decisions which need to be made with Social Security, Medicare, Medicaid, and other government programs. There is a temptation to not put a limit on this for security reasons but over time more of the budget would get classified as defense in order to get around the non-defense caps.

Congress will need to formally define what is covered by the meaning of defense in this Article and possibly include it in this Article. There is the potential that additional areas will be placed under this in the future to meet cap requirements such as Homeland Security, the intelligence agencies, foreign aid in areas where the military is fighting, etc. This should be decided before passage of the amendment and adjustments to the percentage made, appropriate for any additions over what was considered defense in the past.

**Twenty years after passage non-defense outlays are limited to twelve percent of the Economic Output of the United States. Thirty years after passage non-defense outlays are limited to eleven percent of the**

**Economic Output of the United States. Forty years after passage non-defense outlays are limited to ten percent of the Economic Output of the United States.**

Again as in Section 1, currently and for the next several decades the baby boom generation will be retiring and using Social Security and Medicare which will prevent us from bringing down the spending right away. Over time as the Social Security XXI and Medicare XXI programs are implemented then the tax and spending demand on the federal government will decline. It is important that politicians not be allowed to keep spending at these levels. The set asides required of workers in the new programs will limit the tax base.

## Section 3. Exceptions

**Defense outlays may exceed the Economic Output limit during periods when a majority of both Houses of Congress declares that the United States is at war or involved in fighting an internal rebellion or when Congress declares and defines the existence of a clear and present danger to the nation. These outlays must be directly related to defense expenses.**

The Congress does not easily make a declaration of war because of the significant impact that has on the country, the world, and our relationships in the world. An internal rebellion on the scale of the Civil War would require greatly exceeding normal limits. Also if we have another Cold War, this time with a nation or nations with more economic output than the US, Congress needs the power to declare a clear and present danger and exceed normal limits. In national security situations there should not be any hindrances to making necessary spending and taxing decisions. For that reason this provision does not require two-thirds of both houses of Congress to approve; just a majority vote of both houses of Congress.

**Non-defense outlays may exceed the Economic Output limit for expenses directly related to reconstruction and recovery from natural disasters, war, internal rebellion, and other attacks. This exception requires two-thirds of both houses of Congress to approve.**

These expenditures are usually not foreseeable at the time budgets are approved and are needed at short notice. The two-thirds requirement for both houses of Congress to approve these outlays is so that Congress does not try to shift routine amounts of disaster relief to this from the regular budget. There is always a certain amount of relief needed for hurricanes, floods, tornadoes, etc. every year. This base amount should still be in the regular budget. This provision is only for the years when these needs peak. It is hoped that at least one-third plus one member of a House of Congress will be fiscally conservative enough to prevent abuse of this provision.

**Non-defense outlays may exceed the Economic Output limit by a maximum of two percent of the Economic Output of the United States for expenses directly related to stabilizing the federal budget during an economic crisis. This exception requires two-thirds of both houses of Congress to approve.**

This is not meant to be an appeasement to Keynesian economics but a recognition of what happens to economic output during a recession. Recession or depression by definition is a decrease in the economic output of the country. This will usually mean a drop in incomes and taxes. In order to maintain stability in the federal workforce and federal programs this provides the Congress with a temporary way to maintain the status quo. It is likely that Congress will frequently if not always push right up to the limits of the provisions in this amendment. If all of the provisions of this amendment are approved and non-defense spending is progressively limited from fourteen percent to as low as ten percent then this is even more likely. It will be up to future Congresses to determine if this exception is the right policy or if cutting spending or a mix of both is most appropriate at the time.

**Total taxes and/or outlays may exceed the overall Economic Output limit as needed to meet one or more of the other exceptions.**

This is self-explanatory. Except when defense spending is well below its limits the other exceptions are likely to require an exception to the overall limit.

## Section 4. Implementation

**Non-defense outlays exceptions will be in discrete identified appropriations.**

**All defense outlays will be in discrete appropriations separate from non-defense appropriations.**

These two provisions are intended to provide transparency to the spending made under the exceptions to prevent the abuse or evasion of the limits. Obviously there may be some defense appropriations that cannot be transparent but hopefully any abuse will be exposed by the loyal opposition.

**Congress shall make Laws which shall be necessary and proper for the refunding of excess tax collections.**

It is a rare situation that a Congress will know exactly how much money will be taken in by the tax policies in effect. Budgets are set based on estimates. This provision requires that any excess tax collections must be returned. It will be up to Congress to decide who will get the refunds. As a **refund,** it must be returned to those who actually paid taxes. As Congress is likely to spend every cent they can within the limits of this amendment this provision will likely be used by Congress to hedge against shortfalls in revenue by setting tax rates higher than necessary. At least they are required to return the excess and not just spend it. Hopefully Congress will establish the refunding policy at the same time as the tax policy is established. That will provide some predictability for taxpayers and guard against playing different constituencies against each other for political payoffs.

**Exceptions must be voted for each fiscal year and may not be continued without meeting the requirements of this amendment.**

The Congress has a bad habit of using Continuing Resolutions instead of passing appropriations bills in a timely fashion. While this provision is not intended to prevent the use of Continuing Resolutions, it is requiring that the basis and requirements for the exception still be adhered to. For defense exceptions there must still be a declared war, internal rebellion, or declared clear and present danger. For non-defense exceptions the approval of two-thirds of the Congress is required each fiscal year.

**Congress shall reach compliance with the initial outlays limits of the amendment by the end of the third full fiscal year following the passage of this amendment.**

**Congress shall reach compliance with the initial receipts (tax) limits of**

**the amendment by the end of the sixth full fiscal year following the passage of this amendment.**

These two provisions allow Congress to gradually reach compliance so it is more orderly. The limitation on spending will take effect first so that any excess taxes can be used for debt reduction if the Congress wishes.

**At least six months prior to each fiscal year, the President shall transmit to the Congress a proposed budget for the United States Government for that fiscal year in which total outlays and total receipts meet the conditions of this amendment.**

This is necessary so that the President cannot just propose an unrealistic budget and put the entire onus for making tough decisions on the Congress. The President is required to show how he would meet the conditions of this article and show his priorities.

If all of the fiscal reforms in this book are implemented and the major entitlements are out of the federal budget we can achieve a total federal budget of less than ten percent of the national economic output within forty or fifty years. This amendment does not attempt to reach that far. It is better to be conservative now and let others rein things in further at that time.

# 6 TAX POLICY

**"You cannot build character and courage by taking away man's initiative and independence."**
**Abraham Lincoln**

Tax policy needs to be linked to government spending. Therefore, as any other changes are made, it is preferable that federal expenditures should be limited to a percent of GDP with the Federal Spending Limit Amendment. Future Social Security and Medicare obligations should be accounted for in this. Initially, any excess tax receipts should be used to cash people out of the old Social Security and Medicare programs into the Social Security XXI and Medicare XXI programs.

There should be a shift in the sources of taxes collected by the federal government. The Social Security and Medicare taxes should be eliminated with the move to the Social Security XXI and Medicare XXI programs. There should be a new national Value Added Tax (VAT), a reduced and simplified Corporate Income Tax and a simplified Personal Income Tax. The shift to another tax structure needs to be gradual to allow everyone to make adjustments in light of the changes. The final rates should be set without sunset clauses. Certainty and consistency are important for better allocation of resources in a market economy.

We should use the VAT to replace the FICA taxes while transitioning to the Social Security XXI and Medicare XXI programs and reduce the individual and corporate income taxes. Most individuals and families who make less than $100,000/year would be able to file a one page form. This will eliminate the complexity for tens of millions of taxpayers. Most will only need to total their income then subtract standard deduction, personal exemption, healthcare expenses, retirement contributions, and charitable contributions. Then figure out their tax, if any, from a tax table. This will reduce the administrative burden on individuals and businesses, and greatly reduce the volume and complexity of returns that the IRS would have to process.

The whole tax code needs to be overhauled and made smaller and simpler. (For a detailed look at tax complexity and the compliance burden read, The Economic Burden Caused by Tax Code Complexity by Arthur B. Laffer, Ph.D. which can be found at http://www.laffercenter.com/the-economic-burden-caused-by-tax-code-complexity/.) The cost of complying with the tax laws should be greatly reduced from the $400+ billion per year that it currently costs us to comply with the tax laws and for the government to collect the income taxes. By keeping the tax code simple and easy to comply with the government can collect more money at a lower cost to the American people. This is better for economic growth.

## Personal Taxes

### Personal Income Taxes

The personal income tax rates should not have to be increased nor should they be increased. The rates should be brought down gradually as the subsidies, credits, and other distortions are eliminated and as the VAT is implemented. A flatter, simpler tax is the goal and rates should be brought as low as possible while meeting the Federal Spending Limit Amendment conditions and the other specific changes included in this book. With the change from payroll taxes to general revenues for payment of Social Security and Medicare we will need higher income tax rates for the wealthier among us for a generation or two until the privatized system takes over the costs of those programs. Hopefully through economic growth and reduced spending we can get even lower than these but I think it will be likely that we can get down to at least the following rates for a married couple (The dollar amounts would be one-half of these for individuals.) for income remaining after the other changes:

**20 percent of income under $250,000**
**30 percent for $250,001+**

### Standard Deductions and Personal Exemptions

These should be gradually increased as the VAT is implemented and increased to reduce personal income taxes and compensate for the reduction and elimination of targeted deductions. Within five years a standard deduction for single filers of $8,000 ($16,000 for couples) and personal exemptions of $7,500 in 2016 dollars would be reached. The current targeted deductions and credits, as well as the itemized deduction option would be eliminated as these are raised. This would include sensitive items like home interest deductions, earned income credit, state and local tax exclusion, and the various child and education credits.

This will allow all people to benefit equally from the tax rates because they won't have to conform to specific actions set by politicians. A reduction to just a single flat tax rate in the future would be much easier to achieve given that so many people in the lower income ranges will not be subject to income taxes. A family of four with twenty percent set aside for Medicare XXI and ten percent set aside for Social Security XXI will not pay income taxes until their income approaches $66,000. A single person will not pay income taxes until their income is over $22,000. A single parent with one child will not pay income taxes until their income approaches $33,000. Even more income can be excluded from taxation by charitable contributions and contributions to 401k and IRA plans.

## Charitable Contributions

The charitable contributions deduction is one of the few deductions that should be continued. The huge benefits to society that results from these contributions greatly eclipse the reduction in tax revenues. For each dollar of charitable contributions, the federal government only loses out on less than 40 cents in taxes, depending upon the person's tax rate often much less. Even less with the proposed tax reforms. Additionally, each person can direct where the contributions go which is the best type of oversight in spending. This makes it much more likely that it will be well spent, especially in comparison to decisions by Congress.

There are three limits that would make sense to reduce abuse of this deduction. The first is to reduce the tax savings by 50 percent if the contributor or family member of the contributor retains control over the charity receiving the contribution. This should only apply to annual contributions exceeding $10,000. This will allow church pastors/elders and leaders of charities to make contributions to their organizations but still prevent others from sheltering large amounts of money that they can control to make purchases or investments or take losses to assist their profit making operations.

The second limit would be a denial of the deduction for an amount equal to the compensation received by relatives of the contributor. Along with this is a prohibition on trading contributions with others to provide employment for relatives. Again this would only apply to annual contributions greater than $10,000.

The third limit relates to the level of administrative expenses of the charity relative to their overall income. This would not apply to religious organizations. Contributions to charities with administrative costs greater than 40 percent of income will be ineligible for tax deductibility. For the charity itself the income used to pay the administrative expenses greater than 25 percent will be taxed. Income used to compensate an employee of a charity in an amount that is greater than 125 percent of the wages authorized for the President of the United States will be taxed. Both categories will be taxed at the highest personal income tax rate.

## Home Interest Deduction

The home interest deduction helps to make the housing industry more unstable by encouraging people to use their home as collateral for a revolving charge account with home equity loans. There is plenty of room in the new personal exemption and standard deduction to greatly mitigate the loss of this deduction for homes up to the median home price. It will help return homes to a place of long term investment and something people want to pay off as soon as possible.

Eliminating the deduction will level the playing field between homeowners and renters who have been subsidizing homeowners under the current deduction. Shifting away from this to a standard deduction will allow renters to save more quickly in order to have the money for a down payment and closing costs to buy a home.

The home interest deduction should never have been permitted to extend beyond what was needed for an average middle class home. Once basic housing needs are met the government has no compelling interest in subsidizing the industry. There is certainly no need to subsidize expensive housing as the current law allows.

Under the Social Security XXI program home buyers can borrow up to twenty percent of their account to help with the down payment on a primary residence. This will help offset the effects of this change on the housing industry.

## Earned Income Tax Credit

The Earned Income Tax Credit (EITC) is a backdoor welfare payment that frequently returns more taxes to low income workers than the workers paid in taxes. This is a redistribution of wealth that is hidden from the welfare appropriations in Congress to make it look like welfare programs are smaller than they are. The reality is that most people who qualify for the EITC need welfare or need to cohabitate with another to survive even with the EITC. It only encourages a limited amount of work. Once the sweet spot of the EITC is hit it discourages many from further work because it is financially counterproductive unless they can make significantly more money than the benefit payment. It does not make sense to do part here and part in the welfare programs. It costs much more to administer the welfare programs when they are divided up into many little chunks in several agencies. This is addressed more fully in the government reform chapter.

Larger standard deductions and personal exemptions make the basic level of income needed by a family free of income taxes. That is already a great incentive for people to work and earn more. The EITC discourages people from working beyond the minimal amount to get the maximum EITC benefit. Other taxpayers then have to work more to pay these people to not work. The EITC should be phased out over three years to give people the time to adjust with more work or apply for direct welfare benefits.

### School and Education Credits

The goal of these is laudable but don't belong in the tax code. There is plenty of room under the standard deductions and personal exemptions for individuals and families to save the money for their or their child's education. Additionally the government provides substantial help in the form of student loans. Under the Social Security XXI program parents and students will be eligible to borrow against their accounts to fund higher education.

### Limit on Tax Exempt Employee Benefits

There should be a maximum amount of tax-exempt employment compensation. This will discourage the sheltering of income in non-cash benefits. Excessive benefits frequently do not add significant value for the employee, they only enrich benefits administrators. A limit of $10,000 in benefits sheltered from income taxes and twice this for couples should be established if Social Security XXI and Medicare XXI are not implemented.

The entire value of benefits should be subject to FICA taxes or the set asides for Social Security XXI and Medicare XXI. The Social Security XXI and Medicare XXI set asides are exempt from income taxes. This will encourage more efficiency in benefits allocation and provide more incentive to switch to High Deductible Health Plans and Health Savings Accounts.

### Estate Tax and Gift Tax

These two taxes should be permanently eliminated. Nobody should have to pay taxes on money given as an inheritance or as a gift nor should heirs have to pay taxes on what they inherit. Property, whether it is money, a business, or real estate belongs to a person not the government. It is not on loan from the government. The purpose of government is to serve people; people are not here to serve the government.

If there are capital gains due on the investments of the deceased person they should have to be paid. If the length of time that the deceased held the investment cannot be determined it should be backdated as far as evidence allows or the purchase date should be set to the day prior to death whichever period is longer. The heir should then be able to use the deceased person's purchase date to determine the capital gains due when the investment is sold. This provides for the investment to be taxed once instead of twice.

### State and Local Tax Exclusion

This is an especially disgusting exclusion. It should be eliminated with the elimination of the itemized deduction. It shifts the tax burden from those states and communities with high taxes to those who have been more responsible and kept their taxes lower. This is a gift from high tax politicians in Washington to their counterparts in high tax state capitals.

## Marriage Penalties

There are several places in the tax code where the benefits for a married couple are not at least twice that for individuals. This should **never** occur. It is another sign that many in Congress think the American people work for the government instead of themselves and their families. Just because there is money present does not mean it is right to tax it. These instances are penalizing people for doing the right thing and being married. Marriage is a key building block of civil society and provides tremendous benefits to couples, their children, and the communities they live in. Instead of penalizing marriage the tax code and the rest of government policy should be geared toward promoting marriage.

## Corporate and Investment Taxes

There have been many who promote an elimination of taxes on dividends and capital gains to try to eliminate the double taxation on corporate income that occurs at the corporate level and the personal level. This is the wrong place to correct this over taxation. The appropriate place is on the corporate side by reducing the tax on distributed corporate income. By doing it on the corporate side it helps all shareholders equally, regardless of income. Many shareholders in tax exempt retirement accounts would not benefit from elimination of taxes on dividends and capital gains. They will be able to grow their retirement accounts much faster with the tax reduction on the corporate side. This will make them less dependent on the government.

## Interest and Dividends

Interest and dividends should be taxed as ordinary income. They are received as payment for the "work" that their capital has done. The work of capital should not be favored over the work of labor but be treated equally.

## Very Short-term Capital Gain

Very short-term capital gains should be taxed at 125 percent of ordinary income. They are from gains in the value of investments held for less than 31 days. (Author's definition) Because the investment is held such a short time, there are far fewer risks than exist with longer term investments. These are more appropriately called bets than investments and are frequently used to milk the profits from true investors. These very short-term holding periods should not be prohibited because they do add liquidity to the markets and are used for legitimate hedging of investments in order to limit losses. Gains from hedging are typically offset at least in part by losses on regular investments.

## Short-term Capital Gains

Short-term capital gains should be taxed as ordinary income. They are from gains in the value of investments held for more than a 30 days but less than one year. (Author's definition. Standard definition is gains from investments held up to one year.) Because the investment is held such a short time, there are far fewer risks than exist with long-term investments.

## Long-term Capital Gains

Long-term capital gains are from gains in the value of investments held for more than one year. Because the investment is held for lengthy time periods, there are more risks than exist with short-term investments.

Another consideration with capital gains is the fact that most job growth is in small businesses, especially in new small businesses. Providing a better long-term capital gains tax rate for investments in new small businesses would provide incentives to invest in new small businesses and help entrepreneurs to get started and help investors offset some of the additional risk inherent in such investments. Perhaps this would also encourage community banks to become local business development centers. They can grow their business by helping to find equity investors as well as providing the debt financing. They can aid a pool of investors in performing due diligence on the projects.

**Standard Rates:**
**Half the regular income tax rate with a minimum of ten percent. Optional alternative: taxed as regular income after adjusted for inflation.**

**Rates on Investments in Businesses with Fewer Than 100 Employees and Less Than 5 Years Old When the Investment Begins:**
**Fifty percent of the tax that would be assessed under the standard rate.**

## Corporate Income Tax

In reality corporations are just tax collectors for the government. The corporation's customers are the ones who pay the taxes by paying more for what the corporation sells. With that understanding completely eliminating the corporate income tax sounds like it would be great but it is not practical. The concern with no corporate income tax is that income will be parked in corporations instead of being used for its best economic purpose. On the other hand it is important for the rate to be globally competitive to reduce the cost of doing business here. The current high rate drives corporations overseas. Our high corporate tax costs millions of jobs for American workers. It reduces workers' pensions, other retirement accounts, and wages. As an added incentive for corporations to not hold onto cash unnecessarily, a lower rate for distributed income will allow shareholders to put their dividends to best economic use.

**Corporate Income Tax Rate for Undistributed Income:  20 percent**
**Corporate Income Tax Rate for Distributed Income:  10 percent**

**Repatriated Income**
Repatriated income is money that corporations earned overseas and bring back to the United States. It is usually taxed where it is earned so it would be burdensome to tax it again at regular corporate rates. On the other hand we don't want corporations with operations overseas to have an unfair advantage over corporations with operations here. These corporations benefit from the stability that the US brings to the world. One other factor in this issue is that overseas profits will be left overseas if the tax here is too high. If we try to force payment on overseas profits the parent corporation could be incorporated overseas. The second best option that fits reality is to set a rate that does not undercut companies here but still provides an incentive to repatriate the income and invest it or distribute it here. In combination with the recommended reduction in the corporate tax rate the recommendation here should help repatriate more corporate income and drive more investment in the US.

**Corporate Income Tax Rates for Undistributed Repatriated Income:**
**The US corporate rate minus the taxes paid overseas or half of the US corporate rate; whichever is less.**

**Corporate Income Tax Rates for Distributed Repatriated Income:**
**Half the rate of undistributed repatriated income**

The best option is to go to a territorial income tax system combined with a VAT. This still provides tax revenue to help pay for the stability that the US brings to the world. The VAT removes much of the bias toward sending US manufacturing overseas and then importing the products back into the US. Foreign and domestic products and services will be taxed equally by the VAT. Much of the production of US corporations' overseas operations is for sale outside of the US. Regardless of the tax structure much of that will continue simply because they want to keep supply chains short to be more responsive to local markets. Similar to foreign corporations putting some of their facilities in the US. This helps them to keep their costs lower and be more efficient. Making the corporations stronger and more profitable.

## Carried Interest and Stock Options

There has been much talk about taxing carried interest as regular income. At the moment when this **compensation for work or performance** is vested to the person or company then it should be treated as regular income. Any interest earned after the moment of vesting should be a capital gain. The same treatment should be made for similar forms of compensation such as stock options. Any agreement should specify when vesting occurs.

## Interest Deduction Reform

There has been a bias in favor of debt financing over equity financing in the tax code for a long time in the form of the interest expense deduction. Debt financing can help a company grow while minimizing the dilution of ownership from issuing new stock. Too much debt financing can be destabilizing to a company. If the company hits hard times or if the economy takes a downturn then it can push the company into insolvency.

To reduce this financing distortion there needs to be a reduction in the value of the deduction for the company. On the other hand, deduction of interest is a legitimate business expense. The key is to pass the value of the deduction to the shareholders but limit its value to the corporation.

A way to do this is to require that the value of the interest expense deduction be distributed to shareholders. This will be a minor issue for a well-capitalized corporation but could be a significant restraint on a highly leveraged corporation. It will help to promote the moderation of risk over the long-term.

Because this would be a major change in how the tax code treats corporate financing it should be implemented gradually. This will allow highly leveraged corporations the time they need to shift over to more equity financing. Stability is not enhanced by forcing this on corporations quickly. Debt that is in place at the time of passage should retain the current deduction until the maturity date. If the maturity date is greater than 20 years then the debt will retain the current deduction for 20 years then convert to the new policy.

## Capital Expensing

Businesses should have the option to use depreciation/depletion or fully expense capital purchases. We are in a global economy where conditions change more quickly than in the past. This will provide businesses with more flexibility.

Forcing a business to depreciate property instead of expensing it reduces the value of the deduction. The time value of money dictates that carrying over the deduction for capital purchases for years after the cost is incurred forces a business to pay taxes on money spent to make improvements. This reduces a business's ability to make improvements.

## Value Added Tax (VAT)

Payroll taxes and part of the current personal and corporate income tax should be replaced by a VAT to help make US products and services more competitive. The payroll taxes and income taxes increase the costs of all products and services produced here. Employers have to pay enough to their employees to provide an adequate after tax compensation. Businesses have to have sufficient after-tax income to obtain financing from banks or investors. By shifting more taxes to the point of consumption from the point of earning or point of manufacture, people pay taxes on what they spend rather than on what they earn. There is more opportunity and incentive for workers to save and more incentive to earn. Reducing it will make American products and services less expensive and more competitive because these taxes will be paid equally on things "Made in the USA" and things imported. Because every economic factor is considered when placing a factory here or overseas, this will be a factor in helping to keep companies from moving overseas resulting in more jobs for Americans. The VAT is reimbursed on exports which will make American exports less expensive.

In the European Union countries the VAT varies from 17 to 27 percent. The VAT for other major trading partners include; China at 17 percent, Mexico at 16 percent, and Canada at 12-13 percent depending upon the province. For this example we will use the UK rate of 20 percent to keep the math simple. When a US product that sells in the US for $10,000 is exported to the UK the 20 percent VAT is added so that the product costs $12,000 in the UK. Now let's reverse this and have a product that sells for $10,000 in the UK, including the VAT, imported to the US. Upon leaving the UK the VAT is reimbursed so the product only costs $8,333 in the US. With the income tax and payroll taxes US exports are taxed twice versus imports that are not taxed. By reducing or eliminating payroll taxes and income taxes and replacing with a VAT US products are more competitive globally.

Now let's consider how it will effect products sold in the US. The cost of US made products will not change significantly. The cost of payroll taxes and the income taxes will simply be replaced by the VAT. The competing imports on the other hand will be ten percent more expensive with a ten percent VAT.

The VAT is a more efficient means to collect taxes than the income tax. Only businesses would have to deal with tax filings. Some believe there is a potential moral hazard with shifting to the VAT in that the level of taxes is less evident to the average person. It makes people more susceptible to accepting more taxes because they only see it in small amounts. This is mitigated if we can pass the Federal Spending Limit Amendment. To make the VAT visible it should be required that sales receipts list the amount of tax paid.

**The VAT should be applied to all products and services purchased—imported and produced in the US.** Implementation and operation of this tax should be kept simple. When there are exemptions there will be greatly increased accounting costs for both businesses and the government. The best way to offset any increased burden on low income people or retirees is to increase the standard deduction or personal exemption on the income tax and increase welfare and social security benefits. These other means do not increase transaction costs which are a waste of money. It will be less expensive and simpler for businesses to calculate and pay the tax if there are no exemptions. The other problem with VAT exemptions is that once there is one exemption then lobbyists will keep pushing to add their favorite exemption. We will have pressure on the politicians and the same distortions that are a problem with the income tax. So there should be no exemptions for anything or anyone.

### Collection of the VAT
1. Every person and business will pay the VAT when purchasing goods or services.
2. Taxes on imported items will be paid when they enter the country. To avoid carousel fraud, imported items should have the tax paid before goods are released by the transportation company. In addition, every business as part of their business insurance will have to carry coverage that will pay the tax if bankruptcy or some other problem arose to prevent normal payment.
3. The taxes paid on exported items will be reimbursed when they leave the country.
4. Taxes paid by state and local governments will be reimbursed by the federal government.

It should be implemented gradually such as two percent the first year and increasing by two percent every year thereafter until it reaches ten percent. This will allow an implementation that businesses, individuals and trading partners can become familiar with and plan for. In addition, it will allow for a gradual reduction in income taxes without resulting in a deficit or excessive taxation. The total increase should allow more than 70 percent of people to be able to file a single page income tax form. The exact total percent of VAT should be estimated and the whole total with each increment listed should all be in one piece of legislation so that everyone can predict the tax consequences of their decisions well ahead of time. Predictability is essential for making long term decisions.

Many consider a VAT to be a regressive tax. Perhaps it is. But it is not healthy for a republic to eliminate all taxes for any group of citizens. With the proposed changes in the income tax code most low and middle income people will not pay income taxes. They will have to pay the VAT, but can reduce their taxes by reducing their spending.

In terms of trade it is better to remove the structural imbalances that hurt US businesses rather than engage in a trade war with tariffs. Changing over to the VAT is a key part of this structural change. Another factor is opening up oil, gas, and coal for unrestricted export to reduce our trade deficit. Changing our tax code, regulatory regime, and healthcare financing are other key factors. Limiting the existence and power of government sponsored enterprises (GSE) around the world is the most significant external factor in improving US trade.

### User Fees and Taxes

There are many areas of the federal budget where user fees or targeted taxes specifically apply to areas of the budget. These should only exist if needed and should generally pay for the full costs of the budget area for which there is a direct connection.

### Federal Gasoline Tax

The federal gasoline tax should be set at a sufficient level to pay for US and Interstate highways. No more and no less! It should not be used for state and local roads except for intersections with federal highways. Walking or biking trails, dog parks and anything else that are for locals should be paid for by state and local taxes.

### Air Transportation Taxes and Fees

The cost of airports, TSA and other security activities at airports, FAA personnel and equipment should be paid for by taxes and fees on the users of the airports. These costs belong being paid for by the users. Normally there should not be a need to include this as part of regular appropriations.

### National Parks, Forests, and Other Public Lands

The expenses for these public properties should be paid for with user fees, royalty payments, admission fees, etc. They can have discounted rates for low income people but overall they should be restructured to be self-supporting.

## Internet Sales Tax

There have been a variety of efforts to tax online sales. It is unfair that online retailers do not have to collect sales taxes when local retailers do have to collect it. It is also impractical to have online retailers collect and pay sales taxes to every tax jurisdiction in the country. The solution is to set a single online sales tax that all online vendors collect on out-of-state sales. Set it at the median state sales tax from the 50 states, rounded to the nearest tenth of a percent. It will be updated on January 1st each year.

The retailer will send a single payment each pay period to the federal government which will distribute it to the states. The retailer will upload a spreadsheet with a list of how much tax they collected from each state when they pay the tax. Online retailers will still collect and pay sales taxes from instate purchases according to state laws.

## Property Taxes

Property taxes are currently a state issue. States and local governments should keep property taxes at modest levels and rely predominately on income taxes and sales taxes. Preferably relying on sales taxes. The property taxes act like a fixed cost on the people and businesses of the state and are included in the cost of business. Shifting more to sales taxes will spread those tax costs to imported products and lessen the burden on what is produced in the state and in the country. Property taxes should not be completely eliminated. There needs to be a modest level of property taxes to deter the storage of wealth in property and slowing down the velocity of money in the economy. This should improve the business climate in the state and help the country.

# 7 ENERGY POLICY

**"Historically, the United States has had a wonderful energy policy. We're blessed with a diversity of resources. We have oil. We have gas. We have coal. We have nuclear. And renewables. And as a result, one of our biggest competitive advantages has been affordable energy. You need a strong economy and you need affordable energy to fuel that economy."**
**John S. Watson**

Energy policy has become critical to national security. Until recently most of the remaining gas and oil reserves were believed to be located overseas. Much of these overseas reserves are located in countries that leave the US and our allies subject to influence or coercion. The US must develop realistic alternatives to supply our energy needs in the coming decades. In addition, we must develop realistic conservation measures that reduce consumption, are beneficial to the environment, and are economically responsible and sustainable. Market forces should be used as much as possible to influence future directions.

The federal government should have two major roles; influence changes before a crisis develops and help fund promising research that does not have sufficient private funding. This should not involve wealth redistribution with grants, tax credits, or subsidies as many government programs involve. This should be done with loans with recourse on the principals if it is a failure. Not necessarily for the full loan amount but enough to ensure that they seriously believe in the viability of their proposal. Additionally taxpayers should be part owners of any patents developed by government funded R&D. It needs to be limited to R&D and some demonstration projects. Beyond that market forces are a better way of implementing full-scale production. If it is commercially viable then private investors can finance the project. If not it will simply be a waste of taxpayer funds for the government to subsidize the project.

As a Christian I believe that we have a responsibility to be good stewards of our time, talents, and treasure. The natural environment is one of our treasures and we need to be good stewards of it so that it is in as good or better condition than the way we received it. Our environmental policies should strive to prevent damage, allow for the harvest and use of natural resources, and clean up past damage in a fiscally responsible and family friendly manner.

## Domestic Coal, Oil, and Natural Gas Drilling and Extraction

Nearly all U.S. land and water area should be available for coal, oil, and natural gas exploitation. States should be able to restrict drilling and mining within their borders and off their shores but there are consequences for a NIMBY policy. The reduced economic growth and taxes from these restrictions will result in more of their money leaving the state.

Due to advances in natural gas extraction from fracking there has been a great reduction in the cost of natural gas in the US as the supply has increased. That has not been the case for the rest of the world. The cost for much of the rest of the world is 3-6 times what it costs in the US. Under current law, exports to countries without a free trade agreement (FTA) with the US require approval by the Department of Energy (DOE). The Obama DOE has been very slow in approving permits.

There has also been resistance by the US manufacturing and chemical industries to US exports because they want a competitive advantage in being able to buy natural gas much more cheaply than their competitors. On the other hand the low price in the US has depressed new exploration and drilling because companies cannot make a profit. By permitting an open market we can generate thousands of new jobs and billions of revenue and taxes from exports. It can significantly reduce our trade deficit. Even though prices for US consumers will go up they are still likely to stay lower than they were just a few years ago. Higher prices will just encourage more drilling which will increase the supply and keep prices down.

One of the ways that fossil fuel exports are limited is from excessive environmental impact assessments when companies seek to develop port facilities and other transportation infrastructure to bring these products to the international market. These assessments as with all assessments done by the government need to be done as quickly and fairly as possible. It is not the responsibility of bureaucrats to undermine the law, they are there to efficiently and effectively make an objective assessment. Environmental groups increasingly have been pushing federal, state, and local governments to not only evaluate the local environmental impact but to consider the global impact of more fossil fuel use in order to try to stop projects. Companies have been able to meet the required environmental standards so the green groups attempt to make impossible standards. There is no place in government policy for such foolishness.

Expanding fossil fuel supplies in the world will keep energy costs down. It will improve economic growth in most of the world. The US can secure a greater global market share. This will change the geopolitical power of countries like Russia, Iran, and Venezuela who are highly dependent on energy sector revenue.

## Deep Tunnel Geothermal Systems (DTGS)

Current efforts in new large scale Geothermal Systems are called Enhanced Geothermal Systems (EGS). Research and development on EGS involves fracking high temperature rock formations to develop heat reservoirs. Unfortunately with the current projects they expect to deplete the heat reservoir after a couple of decades at each location.

Going beyond current scientific thought I believe R&D should be considered for a deeper system with a network of closed circuit water tunnels at a depth of 2-15 km (1.3-9 miles). I call this Deep Tunnel Geothermal Systems. (The deepest hole ever drilled was about 15 km deep.) The geothermal gradient in the earth's crust averages about 25° C (75° F/mile) per kilometer of depth. Directional drilling can be used to produce a network of water paths at different depths and different angles. At these depths the water will be heated to steam and develop high pressure for turning turbines. Switching between different water paths using smart well technology should allow the Earth to continue reheating water indefinitely. These tunnels would run between several power plants that are 10+ km apart.

In the early stages drilling will be to the minimum depth with sufficient heat and deeper water paths will be drilled periodically after the electric power plant is online. Over time a large and deep heat reservoir will be tapped by many flow regulated tunnels. This will allow the income earned in each phase of the project to help finance future phases at ever deeper depths.

There is enough heat energy within 10 km of the surface of the earth to supply the electricity needs of the world for many centuries. It is a clean, abundant, sustainable source of energy that is produced domestically. The skills needed to build and operate these systems are the same as are already in the drilling, mining, and electricity industries. Instead of disrupting the workers in these industries, we would strengthen them.

Eventually, after many different water paths have been constructed in the 2-15 km zone and the procedures and processes are mature this will also likely become a very cheap source of electricity. Provided there is enough geologic stability and the costly drilling is completed the power plant may still be producing electricity for decades after these input costs have been paid for.

In conjunction with these power plants there should be an alternative energy source such as coal, natural gas or nuclear. This is for two reasons. The first reason is to extend the length of time that heat can be harvested from the location by allowing heat from around the heat reservoir to reheat the reservoir. The second reason is in case seismic activity or another cause damages the wells and prevents operation. If the geologic conditions at current power plants permit there may not be a need to build new plants for some areas. The geothermal produced steam could be integrated into the existing plant processes.

There are many locations in the world with sufficient heat in the 2-5 km depth range. Most of the planet should have sufficient heat by the 10 km depth. The energy potential warrants further R&D and possibly demonstration projects to prove the commercial viability of this energy source. It is amazing how much money has been wasted on wind and solar projects that will never be more than niche sources of electricity. Very little has been spent on geothermal which holds great promise in supplying base-load electricity and is more environmentally friendly than wind or solar.

This may not be financially viable until fossil fuel supplies decline considerably. At some point in the future geothermal will form a considerable part of the world energy production mix. There are countries that may find it beneficial to explore this to achieve energy independence sooner than then for energy security and independence. The country that comes to mind as the most likely to begin exploring this further is China. They have the desire for energy independence, a great need to improve their air quality, and the financial resources to fund the R&D and construction.

Geopolitically, this could be a great equalizer for nations. If a cost effective method of harvesting the local geothermal energy can be developed every energy consuming nation can also be their own primary energy producer. It will not eliminate resource competition or wars but it could reduce a significant source of these conflicts.

The initial need is to determine the theoretical potential of this type of system and what would be needed to construct it. There are numerous design variations that can be tested.

## Conversion of Coal and Natural Gas to Synthetic Fuels

The ability to convert coal and natural gas to a variety of fuels has been around since the 1920s and was used for mass production by Nazi Germany during World War II. It generally has not been cost competitive with oil.

Recently researchers around the world have announced that they have developed catalysts and processes that are much faster, more efficient, and cheaper than previous processes. They indicate that their process will convert coal to oil at about $30-$50 per barrel. Encouragement is needed to continue improvements and to demonstrate it on a larger scale. This process will produce a feed stock that is compatible with regular oil refining processes and can be refined to make gasoline, diesel, and aviation fuels compatible with the engines already in general use. Researchers said that the same process can be used with natural gas and since natural gas is already closer to oil than coal it would be less costly. This would provide us with the means to use our huge coal and natural gas deposits for motor fuels instead of importing oil in the future. The current glut in oil makes this an option for the future but not likely to be a substantial part of the current supply.

## Home Energy Efficiency Improvement Program

A considerable percentage of energy use is in the home. Some common areas that could use improvement in many homes are insulation, sealing, tankless hot water heaters, new windows, shrubs and trees for shading, geothermal heatpumps, solar and wind systems. Tax credits or grants are a wealth transfer that should be eliminated. The federal program that provides a 30 percent tax credit for improving home energy use should be replaced with a loan program. (The parallel state tax credits should be eliminated as well.) The program should provide low and middle income homeowners low interest loans for energy efficiency improvements. These loans should cover the cost to the federal government and administrative costs. The lien should stay with the home if there is a sale. Full recourse to the borrower should be required if there is an uninsured loss to the covered improvement or in cases of fraud by or to the borrower concerning the covered improvement. It is more appropriate that the homeowner is responsible for improvements to their own home and not the taxpayers. This will also help to improve the chances that the energy savings exceed the cost of the improvements.

## CAFE Standards, Gas Taxes, and Gas Prices

CAFE standards should be eliminated. It puts an unfair burden on US car manufacturers. It costs manufacturing jobs by forcing companies to allocate resources inefficiently. This is another tax on red states much like the federal tax deduction for state taxes. There tends to be more need for large vehicles in rural and suburban areas, and small and medium cities than in major cities. When there is a need for a larger vehicle it is usually more efficient and uses less gasoline than trying to do the same job with a small more fuel efficient car. Also people should have a right to a safer vehicle as larger vehicles typically are.

A more efficient means to influence people to buy more fuel efficient vehicles would be to increase the gas tax or create a carbon tax. That puts the burden on those who use more gas rather than on all vehicle buyers. Car makers could then manufacture what sells rather than what is needed to meet government mandates. The end user would then be responsible for the costs instead of all who buy US made vehicles.

A two cent per gallon annual increase in the gas tax for 25 years would put modest, gradual pressure to increase gas mileage or decrease driving. It should be contingent upon passage of the Federal Spending Limit Amendment so that this tax does not increase total taxes but only replaces other taxes. This would be less burdensome, less costly to administer or comply with, and offer more freedom than the CAFE Standards.

People can then weigh the pros and cons of what is most suitable for their own lives when buying a new vehicle. By increasing the tax gradually but surely all stakeholders would be able to make knowledgeable decisions. Auto makers will know that R&D into better gas mileage will likely be beneficial to future sales. People and businesses will not be immediately burdened by increased gas costs so that current vehicles can be fully used before being replaced but will know that gas prices will steadily rise.

With the growth of energy use in China, India, and elsewhere gas prices will be steadily increasing over time. There will be times when prices fluctuate higher or lower but the trend will be toward greater consumption as time goes by. Even with new oil deposit discoveries and conversion from coal or natural gas the cost of extraction and production will be higher than they are for current deposits. This alone will likely drive oil prices higher and provide a natural consequence to low gas mileage and is the most appropriate market force to increase mileage of vehicles.

Transportation costs are a drag on the economy so the government should usually minimize the costs it imposes upon transportation to only what is needed to maintain the infrastructure. The structure of this gradual gas tax increase will allow users to offset the tax cost with reduced gas consumption. Replacing one structural cost with another. Minimizing the overall effect.

## Carbon Tax

There has been some discussion over the past couple of decades about the implementation of a carbon tax to reduce $CO_2$ emissions. This is far better that cap-and-trade which is just a scam to milk the economy by financial insiders. There are two requirements necessary to make a carbon tax a palatable option. The first is the passage of the Federal Spending Limit Amendment. This will require that the carbon tax replace other taxes and not be an economy stifling additional tax. The second is that it be implemented contingent upon an international carbon tax agreement. Such an agreement would require all WTO members to impose a common carbon tax rate indexed to the per capita GDP. As nations become more prosperous businesses will either pay higher taxes or get their energy suppliers to become more efficient and reduce $CO_2$ emissions. This will minimize the cost differential between businesses in different countries. For this to work there has to be a parallel divestment of Government Sponsored Enterprises (GSEs). Not only are GSEs dangerous for free market competition in the world economy but in this program they could largely shield these businesses from the true impact of a carbon tax. (More about limiting GSEs in the Trade section of the Foreign Policy Chapter.)

## Pipelines and Refineries

There has been a great increase in the amount of oil and natural gas found in Canada and northern parts of the US. Additionally, much of the coal that may be converted to synthetic fuels is in northern and middle states. It seems more logical that new refineries should be located closer to these supplies and not send these feed stocks to the Gulf Coast to be refined and then sent north again. Having our refining capacity spread around the country will also reduce problems from regional disasters such as hurricanes or from vulnerabilities in future wars. This lack of dispersion was caused by the location of past oil deposits and more recently by a NIMBY attitude in many states about having a refinery. The energy industry has concerns about investing in new refinery capacity when the green movement has had such power in government lately. Reasonable environmental regulations along with market forces should determine the general location and capacity of refineries and pipelines. Continuity of supply should be a factor for both markets and the government for economic and national security reasons.

## Greenhouse Gases

There are strong doubts about the evidence and conclusions by the climate change community. There is no clear evidence that there is continuing global warming. We seem to have hit a plateau for the past decade. They do not have definitive evidence to conclude that past temperature change was caused by man and not from natural causes.

With that said, as God's stewards of the world he has given us we have a responsibility to be on alert for problems and be proactive in solving them. Study should continue. At the very least we are altering the composition of the atmosphere and the oceans with more $CO_2$. We should try to change this back to more natural levels but it needs to be done economically. Until then we risk more real damage to people than the hypothetical damage predicted by the climate change crowd.

Toward this end we should encourage those who are passionate about this issue to look for ways to use the $CO_2$ and methane that is produced. Having a market for it would greatly mitigate the cost of sequestration and eliminate the opposition. Much as George Washington Carver did in finding uses for peanuts and soybeans to develop a market for these crops. His research encouraged crop rotation to restore nitrogen to the soil depleted by repeated cotton crops. This should be the model for reducing greenhouse gases. Find valuable uses for $CO_2$ and other greenhouse gases.

## Energy Summary

The United States has the means to be energy independent within a generation. By gradually shifting over electricity production to the deep tunnel geothermal systems we can greatly reduce the need to use coal and natural gas in electricity production. The coal and natural gas at the same time can be shifted over to conversion to synthetic fuels which when united with domestic oil production could supply our transportation fuels for several hundred years yet.

We can become oil and gas exporters to Europe and Asia. In addition to being great for our economy, this would allow the world to become less dependent upon the Middle East, Russia, Venezuela, and other unstable, undemocratic countries and result in a new era in international politics and economics. These countries will have to deal with the world on different terms. Additionally, the technology for converting coal and natural gas and for developing EGS and DTGS could help head off the geopolitical conflicts with China or others that would result from global energy shortages. This is a far more likely and dangerous situation than any potential climate change problem.

Should oil prices drop below the coal and natural gas conversion cost it would be expected that the companies involved would be hedging on the commodities markets to even out the fluctuations. Additionally it is expected that most of these coal and gas conversion refineries will be owned by integrated energy companies that use traditional oil and could take advantage of the lower cost in the other part of their business. There should not be any government subsidy or market manipulation to set a market floor. Lower prices will result in more consumption which will bring prices back up. Economic growth in the developing world should keep the oil prices from dropping below the conversion price for significant periods of time.

This policy should also create many good paying jobs throughout the country. I expect eventually a geothermal plant outside every large or medium city. I hope that many of the new coal and natural gas conversion plants and refineries would be placed in the coal and natural gas producing states or between there and the pipeline they will feed. As well as being good economically, it is also better for the environment and national defense than the current structure.

With all of the lies in the climate change research community it is difficult to know if global warming is even occurring. If it is occurring it is more likely to be part of a natural cycle than being caused by man. But whether it is or not the EGS and DTGS initiatives along with changing over the electricity production in the United States from coal and natural gas should appeal to environmentalists.

More research needs to be done to ascertain precisely where the research is and the time frame for maturing these technologies. But this is a basis for constructing a viable energy policy for the United States. Even if some of this is not possible immediately all of these ideas are likely to play a role in the future. In the short term promoting energy independence should also help bring energy costs down now. Fears in the market will be reduced and oil producing countries will try to keep the price down enough to discourage rapid introduction of new technologies.

Mostly the federal and state governments need to get out of the way of innovators and energy producers. The government needs to stop trying to pick winners and losers and let the free market grow. They have tremendous economic incentive with the growing energy needs in the world.

# 8 GOVERNMENT REFORM

**"Experience hath shewn, that even under the best forms of government those entrusted with power have, in time, and by slow operations, perverted it into tyranny."**
**Thomas Jefferson**

My first thoughts on government reform are about repeal of some of the bad legislation that has been passed over the past decade. Obamacare is the worst of the lot. It is already driving up insurance costs and will soon drastically drive up costs to taxpayers, cause millions of Americans to lose their medical insurance, and force rationing of healthcare services on the American people by bureaucrats in Washington. Following this is the need to repeal the Dodd-Frank financial reform bill. It seeks to micromanage financial services by unaccountable bureaucrats while not ending too big to fail bailouts. Then there is Sarbanes-Oxley. It drives up compliance costs and drives companies private or overseas without significantly improving corporate governance or financial reporting. The repeal of these three examples of bad legislation will save billions of dollars and be significant factors in reviving the economy.

The next order of business is to end subsidies and bailouts. The only exception is for areas that are directly related to national security needs. There are some things that only become profitable during wartime. It is better to subsidize specific needs during peacetime to ensure that these things are available when needed. This should typically be limited to paying for excess production capacity that will only be needed during wartime.

The government has a very poor record of usually picking losers when it subsidizes or bails out companies. In some cases it creates losers by not requiring some companies to compete in a free market. Well managed companies providing what people want or need do not need to be bailed out or subsidized. Even more importantly the federal government does not belong trying to pick winners and losers. Every time that government takes money from people they prevent people from making their own decisions about what to invest in or spend their money on.

This money does not belong to the government it belongs to all of us taxpayers who earned the money. This should include not bailing out the states and territories. There are several states that have made promises, especially to public employees, which will be impossible for them to keep. The taxpayers in states that have been fiscally responsible should not have to bailout these other states. President Obama and the Democrats have already provided some bailout money in the stimulus plans. The states should be forced to get their own finances in order.

In addition we need to consolidate several Cabinet departments and get rid of many duplicative and unnecessary agencies and programs. The welfare system needs major reform and consolidation into one program. Limits to government employee compensation need to be established. Major regulatory reforms need to be implemented. Reforms of the unemployment compensation program and the national flood insurance program are needed.

## Consolidating Cabinet Departments

There are a huge number of government programs that are duplicative, obsolete, wasteful, outside of the proper role of the federal government and unnecessary. While reducing these programs and the agencies that run them it will be possible to consolidate departments. This is only a sampling of ideas. A detailed examination of each program and department needs to be done to decide the fate of each. It should be possible to eliminate or consolidate a considerable number and reduce the federal civilian employment. The next Administration should require a comprehensive review to be conducted in the first six months in office. Then work with Congress to pass reform legislation before the end of the first year in office.

### Merge Departments of the Interior and Agriculture

Merge both of these departments into a new Department of the Interior. The food stamp program should be moved to Health and Human Services with all of the other welfare programs to be administered as a single unified program. Interior and Agriculture both administer large tracts of federal land. A merger will unify the administration of these lands under one department.

Agricultural subsidies need to be phased out. They primarily go to large commercial operations that should survive in the free market.

The federal government needs to begin selling off land. For example, land that has been leased long term to the same rancher, lumber company, or paper company should be considered for sale to them. There does not need to be a rapid selloff. Parcels should be sold as a competitive market becomes available in order to maximize value for taxpayers. The federal lands that are retained should be managed to be self-supporting. They should not need to draw upon tax revenues.

## Merge Departments of Commerce, Labor, and Education

The essential remnants of these departments should be merged into a new Department of Commerce. While the education of our students needs to be about more than just preparing them for employment, the federal government's limited areas of responsibility concern primarily financing college and preparing people for work.

## Eliminate Department of Housing and Urban Development

Eliminate this department after moving the housing assistance program to Health and Human Services with all the other welfare programs to be administered as a single unified program. The free market is a better motivator of efficient housing markets and urban development. It is better if the government does not distort the marketplace and stops trying to pick winners and losers. Local governments should minimize zoning regulations to make low income housing more affordable.

## Eliminate Department of Energy

The Department of Energy was started in the 1970s to help end our dependency on imported energy. They have utterly failed at this mission. The free market can handle developing our energy resources. They have done far more than the department has accomplished without costing billions of dollars of taxes. Instead the private sector has generated billions in tax revenue. The agencies and programs within the department that are necessary should be divided among the other Departments such as Defense, Commerce, and Interior.

## Continuity of Government

In recent years we have seen the national capital shut down for snowstorms and hurricanes and attacked by terrorists. The federal government needs to remain operating during these emergencies. In the future the capital will be shut down again by weather emergencies or may be shut down due to terrorist or other attacks.

The bulk of the federal government employees should be spread around the country so that continuity can be maintained. While it is necessary for the top leadership of most departments and agencies to reside in the DC area much of the mid-level and rank and file workers have no compelling reason why they have to be there. With the internet and cloud data storage, government workers can collaborate from around the country.

## Welfare Reform

The federal government has over 175 means-tested welfare programs that should be consolidated into one unified program. There are programs that provide assistance to needy families, housing assistance, food assistance, energy assistance, medical assistance, childcare assistance, WIC, and the earned income tax credit. Over $700 billion is spent each year on these programs by the federal government and they are expected to double in the next ten years. The states spend an additional $250 billion on these programs. An additional problem is that they are divided between different departments and agencies making coordination very difficult. Recipients of aid have to apply multiple times with multiple case workers in different agencies for assistance. There is much waste in time and bureaucratic duplication under the current setup.

The duplication should be eliminated and a single unified program set up in place of these programs. It will improve administration and reduce the structural costs of the programs. Rather than paying a caseworker in each of these programs to review the same income information it would save time and money. Some of these savings can be realized in the budget and some can be used to provide counseling and case management to aid recipients in becoming self-sufficient.

The appropriations should not separate the funds into separate categories such as cash, medical, housing, heating, childcare, and food assistance. The program should use the total funding as needed for each category. The cash assistance should be the first part phased out for recipients as they have earnings. The last part phased out is the low income medical supplement. The heating assistance should be automated to adjust for recipients based on heating degree days for the local community. Only those with health issues sensitive to the heat should receiving energy assistance for air conditioning. This should be automated as well based on cooling degree days.

When someone begins a welfare case that will constitute the base point in time. At the point when the recipient has received 24 months of full benefits there will be no cost of living increases. This is an incentive to encourage recipients to only take the aid that is truly needed.

There will be a point system that corresponds to the benefit schedule. The beneficiary will receive one point for accepting 100 percent of the monthly benefit allowed for the size and composition of the household. After the accumulation of 24 points the recipient will no longer receive cost of living increases. Each month that a recipient accepts a partial benefit they will only accumulate a partial point comparable to the percent of the benefit.

The welfare benefits shall be a loan and not a grant. As long as their points stay under 24 no interest will accumulate. When their points are 24 or greater they will have an interest rate equal to the cost of borrowing for the

US government plus one percent. When their income grows they will have to make payments to pay the loan back. (See Low Income Supplement section in the Healthcare Reform chapter for example. They may voluntarily begin repayment earlier.) When they repay enough to get below 24 points interest will stop accumulating.

The points will determine when cost of living increases end. When recipients pay back part of past benefits to bring their points below 24 and then receive benefits in the future the cost of living increases will resume until the recipient reaches 24 points again. This is an additional incentive for people to actively repay past benefits when they can afford it. This will restore a stronger safety net for their future.

Every adult that receives assistance should be required to put a plan together with their case worker at the start of the case to become self-sufficient. If significant progress is being made toward becoming self-sufficient then they will be eligible for cost-of-living extensions. There are a maximum of three in order to allow someone to complete a bachelor's degree.

All recipients should have an online account and all expenditures will be verified by automated controls and case worker verification. Most of these will be preapproved regular payments like rent, insurance, and utilities. Exceptions can be made for communities or individuals without easy access to a computer. This should be rare because most public libraries have free computer use and there can be terminals in the lobbies of government buildings with access restricted to government websites. Additionally, it would be advisable for local school districts to have their facilities open to the general public, including their computer labs, on weekends and evenings.

Everyone will have a basic level of food, shelter, clothing, transportation, insurance, and medical care. The recipients will not have cash available for non-necessities such as cigarettes, alcohol, cable or satellite television, presents for others, etc. Only a small cash allowance will be available for clothing, vehicle expenses, toiletries, and cleaning supplies. These provisions are incentives for people to work for any extras and only stay on assistance for as long as necessary. This is a true safety net which is preferable to establishing a way of dependency for people.

The Medicare XXI low income supplement will be the last part of the program people will be phased out of because of the significant financial consequences of not having medical insurance when it is needed.

With a nationwide program the recipients will be able to move anywhere in the country and transfer their benefits. There will be a benefit based on the national average minimum need. The program benefits will be adjusted for cost-of-living differences by county throughout the US. Any recipients living in jurisdictions with a minimum wage greater than the federal minimum wage will only be eligible for a maximum of the national average minimum need.

This is to discourage states and local communities from raising the minimum wage and causing more people to be receiving welfare.

States may partner with the program to provide a supplement for their residents from state funds. High cost states generally have higher incomes. This permits the same tax rates as less expensive states while generating larger tax revenues for use in cost-of-living supplements. The way the program is structured, financially it will be better for states to keep their minimum wages at the federal level. Recipients have their benefits reduced gradually and less than the amount of their earnings. States can save money by keeping the minimum wage down so there are more jobs available. The combination of federal benefits and a job should greatly reduce the need for a state supplement.

## Minimum Wage Laws

Generally minimum wage laws reduce the number of entry level jobs available. They limit the opportunities for the workers they are supposed to help. In an ideal world there would be no need for a minimum wage. Wages would rise or fall as the supply and demand of labor changed. We do not live in an ideal world. We do not live in a world with static conditions.

In the real world the minimum wage should be at the bare minimum for an individual to pay for their minimum needs. It is not meant to support a family. People need to improve their skills and combine the incomes of two parents to support a family.

The current minimum wage is $7.25 per hour. The average and median inflation adjusted minimum wage from 1938 to 2012 was $7.09 in 2012 dollars. Adjusting the $7.09 for inflation it would be $7.37 in 2016.

Politically, the minimum wage will not go away. The $7.09 in 2012 dollars should be set as the reference point. The minimum wage should be set to automatically adjust with the inflation rate up to a point. If there is a recession or depression with high unemployment and a high inflation rate an automatic adjustment may slow a recovery by keeping too many people out of the workforce. The inflation adjustment should be limited to five percent per year and suspended when the unemployment rate is greater than eight percent. In following years the inflation adjustment can be caught up as the unemployment and/or inflation rates drop.

From 1914 to 2015 the average annual inflation rate was 3.3 percent and median inflation rate was 2.8 percent. In that time, there have been 25 years with an inflation rate above five percent with the last time in 1990. There have been 55 years with an inflation rate below three percent.

Unfortunately the Democrats and their union allies use the minimum wage for political purposes and to generate union dues and advantages. At a basic level they make it look like they are fighting for the common man in order to provide a living wage. The reality is that many union contracts explicitly peg their wage agreement to the level of the minimum wage. When the minimum wage increases the union wage automatically increases by the same amount or the same percentage. Another factor in play is that when union wages increase then union dues increase. This provides more money for union activities including supporting the very same Democrat politicians who increased the minimum wage. But the most cynical use of a minimum wage increase is in the states and cities that exempt unionized workers from the minimum wage law. This pushes employers into hiring unionized workers in order to get lower wage employees. Against the best interests of employees who receive less than the minimum wage the unions benefit by receiving dues from more union workers. Enriching the union leadership at the expense of workers. Shamefully cynical manipulation.

## Salaried Minimum

There has been debate about the minimum level of wages salaried workers should receive so employers are not required to pay overtime. These are wages paid to executives, managers, supervisors, and professionals. There are some employers who try to use this status as a way to avoid paying overtime. The minimum should be sufficient to reward the responsibility of leadership and/or professional skill. While those earning the salaried minimum may be new in these positions, they are likely the more experienced and valuable employees in these businesses. They should not have to take a reduced wage in order to receive a promotion.

Every minimum is going to be an arbitrary setting. Two thoughts on the matter are that it should be about twice the hourly minimum wage and the other is that it should be about the median wage for adults. At this time, both of these are close to the same.

Another, perhaps better option for executive, managerial, and supervisory positions is to relate the minimum to the typical wages paid to those being supervised or managed. A minimum equal to 125 percent of the average wage for 50 hours of work per week for the workers being supervised. This last option will offer flexibility for different industries while keeping employers from abusing the salaried status. Supervising employees who all earn the federal minimum wage would result in a salaried minimum of $25,919.

Most employee positions have a wage scale. The salaried minimum should be calculated based on the midpoint of the wage scale multiplied by the number of employees in that employee classification. If there are multiple employee classifications supervised then each group should be averaged together to set the salaried minimum. This will discourage the salaried employees from increasing their employees' wages in order to increase their own.

## Social Services Reform

Too often the social workers who work for social services agencies spend a significant amount of time doing paperwork. Most got into the field to help people. We need to leverage technology to facilitate more help for clients and to reduce the time needed for social workers to document their work.

Perhaps an audio/video recording system to record interviews with clients where the case worker can append written notes to the recording. An automatic voice transcription of the interview would help. This will provide a more complete record and make it more easily searchable. Some of this is beyond current technology. This would be a more valuable project for society than more games. IT professionals should be encouraged to grow this technology.

Another technical improvement is the ability to set up audio/video surveillance systems in the common areas of homes of families where abuse or neglect has occurred. During live surveillance specialists will monitor to intervene when necessary with the police or simply with coaching to improve marital communication or parenting. Audio systems will alert for loud noises or key words to draw the attention of specialists. Particular events can be noted and recordings sent to caseworkers for follow-up meetings with the family.

These systems need to be very user friendly. The purpose is to minimize the time needed to do documentation and maximize social worker time to help rebuild families.

### Separating Dual Mandate

In many states social workers have a dual responsibility. One is to protect children from abuse and neglect. The other is to try to put a family back together. This can cause social workers to make a decision about which of the mandates they prefer for each family and only pursue the one course of action. While many try to meet the requirements of both mandates everyone has a bias. The process needs to be restructured to provide both strong protection for children and strong help to rebuild families.

To allow the state to meet both mandates there should be two separate agencies. One is responsible for investigating abuse and neglect and making referrals to the other agency, prosecutor, and/or corporation counsel as appropriate. The other agency works with families to facilitate counseling, parenting classes, supervision of visits, case management, home visits, etc. This other agency will be required to report abuse and neglect to the investigating agency and open its files to them. Their mandates and their personnel will be separate. Both tracks can be pursued in parallel. Those social workers who prefer a particular focus can work for that particular agency.

**Information Folders**

Social workers and police frequently go to homes with families in trouble but are unable to do anything because certain thresholds have not been crossed. County social service agencies should compile folders of flyers for parenting classes, counseling services, domestic violence shelters, etc. The folders can be assembled by volunteers. Police and social workers can keep a box of these folders in their vehicles to hand out to people they think could benefit from the information.

The folder should also include a letter from the head of the agency explaining how they work, criteria for removing children from a family, what types of help are available, other issues of concern about the agency in the community, etc. Many people are afraid of seeking help out of concern that a social worker will take their kids. Everyone has heard stories in the media about kids being taken after an accusation of spanking. By the time most people get to the point where they think they need help they are afraid of how past actions will affect them. They need to know that when they voluntarily seek help they will be given the benefit of the doubt and be helped and not have their family torn apart.


## Regulatory Reform

Regulations add huge costs to businesses, families, and individuals. It is important that there is a vital interest achieved by the regulation. Regulations against fraud, theft, misrepresentation, or unsafe actions toward another are vital and necessary. Too often politicians and government bureaucrats impose regulations as a way to control or limit behavior they do not agree with. In just the first 6 years of the Obama administration an additional 184 major rules were imposed costing $80 billion per year. There are thousands of lesser rules that impose costly burdens on individuals and businesses. These new regulations have been added to the hundreds of billions of dollars in existing regulations. According to the Competitive Enterprise Institute federal government regulations cost Americans $1.9 trillion per year.

**Red Tape Obstruction**

One component of this problem is the excessive and many times arbitrary delays in making decisions or deciding that they need more information that politicians and bureaucrats use for political purposes or to try to kill something they don't like. An excellent example of this is the delays imposed on the Keystone XL pipeline project. Even after all of the regulatory hurdles had been met, President Obama still pushed off making a decision until after the 2012 and 2014 elections for political reasons.

This is a $7 billion dollar construction project that would send 700,000 barrels of oil per day from Canada to a Texas oil refinery. It would create thousands of jobs, result in more than $5 billion per year in tax revenues for the states that it crosses, and allow us to buy oil from a friend instead of an enemy. Pipelines are the most efficient and environmentally friendly method to ship large volumes of oil. There are already more than 50,000 miles of pipelines in the US. Modern pipelines have pressure and flow sensors that can detect leaks when they occur. When this happens pumps can be quickly shut down to minimize the leak. Oil companies do not want to lose their product. It means they have less oil to sell. With regular environmental inspections there is no chance they will escape cleanup costs.

Instead the President and his environmentalist friends will force the oil to be shipped by truck and rail which will cost more and consume more energy. The environmental impact will be much greater because the oil is transported by less safe modes. There have already been several train derailments carrying the oil that have caused fires and environmental damage exceeding the likely impact of a pipeline. The sheer volume of oil transported by rail has raised the cost of rail transport because of more demand than capacity. Rail companies are reluctant to increase capacity significantly because of the expectation that the pipeline will eventually be approved and cause a drop in rail transport demand.

## Regulatory Waivers

A favorite tactic of some politicians and bureaucrats is to put in regulations and then have a way for people or businesses to apply for waivers. This is particularly common in the worst bills and regulations that are imposed. They claim this is to provide needed flexibility so that those who are "inadvertently harmed" by the regulations can seek relief. On the surface this seems like a reasonable option. Unfortunately, this appears all too frequently to just be a way for politicians or bureaucrats to have power over people or businesses. Bureaucrats can coerce companies to change their behavior in ways unrelated to legal requirements in order to receive a needed waiver. Politicians use their power to help get waivers to get campaign contributions or to help political allies and hurt political enemies. It is a way of granting favors. This is dangerous in a representative democracy.

This tends to help large businesses over small businesses because only the large businesses have the resources to lobby or seek waivers. This favors the Democrats over Republicans. The Democrat philosophy of the government controlling business is easier to do with fewer large businesses than with millions of small businesses. Having more of the population as workers for large businesses aids their attempts to play workers against business. Millions of small businesses with their owners who see the effects of what the Democrats are doing to business in America hurts them at the ballot box.

## Prevailing Wage Laws

Another facet of the regulatory problem is expensive requirements that drive up the costs of construction projects that receive government funds. The Davis-Bacon Act requires that federal contractors pay at least the "prevailing wage" as set by the US Department of Labor. Many states have similar prevailing wage laws for government contractors at the state and local funding levels.

This has typically been interpreted as the union wage. The reality is that the method to determine the prevailing wage is flawed and corrupted. It is complex documentation and relies on voluntary reporting. The only ones who tend to report are unions and employers with unionized employees. This keeps them from being underbid by nonunion shops. Audits have also shown that these reporters frequently inflated wages.

The law should be redefined as requiring the average non-management wage to be at least the average of the state's and county's median wage where the project is being built. This would not likely affect the skilled workers, only the unskilled who now receive far more than they could otherwise earn. This would also encourage the unskilled to evolve into skilled workers as in other types of jobs. This would save tens of billions of dollars every year that would allow us to repair more of our infrastructure each year.

By taking the average of the state and county median wages there will be a balance that holds up wages in low income districts and keeps them from being statutorily inflated in high income districts. This plan will also eliminate the need for extensive surveying and paperwork by businesses and government bureaucrats to determine what the prevailing wage should be each year.

## Interpretation of Legislation Problems

This is a two-fold problem. Part of the problem is vague legislation by Congress that puts too much of the responsibility for interpreting the meaning on the bureaucrats that have to write the detailed regulations. The other part of the problem is bureaucrats stretching the authority that has been given to them to impose burdens or restrict actions that were never intended in the legislation and in some cases were explicitly voted down in Congress.

One example of this is the National Labor Relations Board ruling that Boeing violated fair labor practices by opening a new factory in South Carolina. The law allows a company to make economic decisions. It does not say that closed shop states are to be preferred over right-to-work states. No new company will open a factory in a closed shop state if they are prevented from then opening one in a right to work state. Even worse will be companies sending factories overseas that would have been placed in other states but will not now because of the fear that they will be shut down.

Another is the attempt by the Environmental Protection Agency to regulate carbon dioxide under the Clean Air Act. This has been explicitly denounced by Rep. John Dingell (D-Michigan) one of the original authors of the Clean Air Act who said "This is not what was intended by the Congress,…and by those who wrote that legislation…"

## Reigning in Regulations

Congress has let down the American people by not maintaining effective oversight on the executive agencies and their regulations. Too often they want to avoid the tough votes and punt the details and the consequences to the regulators and the rest of the country suffers for it. The way to reign in the destructive regulations is to force Congress to sign off on them before they go into effect and to set sunset clauses on the regulations to force them to renew their approval periodically.

Another idea is an option in Congressional procedures that allows 25 percent of the members of a house to sign a petition to force an up or down vote by both Houses of Congress on the elimination of any existing regulation. This would prevent leadership from blocking efforts to reform regulations and force legislators to take a side on specific regulations.

Congress also has to set better minimum standards on evaluating the economic cost of regulations. Any bill that proposes new regulations that needs additional considerations in evaluating the economic cost should have them included in the bill. Part of the reason for Congress to sign off on new regulations is to have a say after the estimated costs are established. This lets Congress decide if the benefits are worth the costs. If they vote against the new regulations the appropriate Congressional committees should take up the regulations and attempt to make them suitable for approval by the Congress. Until Congress actually approves them they should not take effect.

That will be a cumbersome practice. It would be better if the Congress and the Executive Branch work together to establish the details and have CBO and OMB score the regulations before the bill is initially passed. This will help Congress to be more accountable and careful when they are passing laws. It will also quell some of the uncertainty that the markets have to deal with wondering how new regulations will affect them. Many times it is difficult to know if legislation is good or bad until the detailed regulations are written later. This option puts the details up front and clear instead of having to wait to find out what is in the bill.

Another needed reform is reasonable grandfathering rules. When a regulation requires costly changes to capital assets a reasonable amount of time must be allowed for the transition. The normal life of equipment should be allowed to run before equipment should have to be replaced. Retrofits should be allowed to be delayed until customary overhauls or rebuilds. Any affected company should be able to schedule the change with the regulator within a reasonable time period. Repeated changes to regulations that force companies to meet costly changes before the normal life of the equipment is over adds unnecessary economic burdens and costs jobs. Also by waiting it may be possible to consolidate multiple retrofits into one period of downtime instead of multiple periods. Since some equipment needs to be ordered years in advance this needs to be taken into consideration when implementing new regulations.

## Unemployment Compensation

Typically unemployment compensation was limited to 26 weeks but during the recent recession President Obama and the Democrats added extensions leading to up to 99 weeks of unemployment available to out of work Americans. On the one hand, the higher that the unemployment rate goes up the longer it takes for people to find a new job because there is more competition for the available jobs. On the other hand, increasing the number of weeks that someone can collect unemployment checks tends to delay the time until they will take a job. As long as money is coming in people tend to be more selective about what job they will take until that money is nearly gone.

This proposal attempts to find a middle ground in the program. First, we will maintain the original 26 week program. Second, states can opt in to participate in the second tier of the program. The federal government will supply half of the funding for the second tier and the states the other half. This tier will be paid from general revenues and not from unemployment taxes on employers. Under the second tier, one additional week of eligibility will be available for each one-tenth of a percent the state unemployment rate exceeds seven percent.

The second tier is a loan program rather than a grant program. Our workers will not be abandoned to poverty but will also not be disrespected by making them dependent upon the government. Under both tiers they will become eligible for a total dollar amount based on their weekly benefit amount times the number of weeks they are eligible for in the tier. If they use a partial weekly benefit amount because they are working part-time their total benefit will only be reduced by the amount they use. Their total number of weeks will therefore be extended but the total benefit amount will not. This will encourage people to take work as soon as possible.

If by the time someone reaches the end of their second tier eligibility set when they started the second tier and the unemployment rate has increased they can become eligible for additional weeks. If the unemployment rate drops their eligibility can be reduced as long as the person has at least eight weeks of eligibility remaining. Less than that notice could blindside someone and create undue hardship on the family.

## National Flood Insurance

The government should not be involved in the insurance business. This program needs to be phased out. First it should be split into two categories. One is the area that the Army Corp of Engineers recommends to be used as a flood control area. The other is the remainder of the areas that the federal government insures.

In order to facilitate the generation of flood risk maps there needs to be a dedicated continuous operation. Given the satellite and GIS technology available, the entire country should be able to be classified at least every twenty years with likely areas every ten years. This would involve more than just the regular rivers and shorelines to include detecting areas susceptible to flash flooding. Ideally this would be an interactive GIS system that would allow states and cities to edit with local changes between satellite scans. This system could be designed to work as a simulator to permit governments at all levels to try out options before construction to see how it would affect flooding. Users could set temperature and precipitation levels to see how the terrain handles various scenarios.

Property owners in the flood control areas would be allowed to choose between government insurance and private insurance. Within three years, the government insurance should have to be actuarially sound. In these areas the government program will continue to insure the structures on the properties until the structure incurs a fifty percent or greater loss. Under the government insurance the property owner will be given a couple of options.

1.  The owner can give up rights to the property at the time that the government has to pay for damages. Homeowners can set a variety of deductibles so that the point when the government pays will vary. After the government takes over the property it will be used as a buffer against future floods and be used with minimal structures. Possibly park space that when combined with adjacent property the state or local community will take over and manage.
2.  The owner gives up the right to rebuilding on the land but retains ownership of the land for camping, docking a boat, etc. The government could still recontour the land for flood control purposes.

Under the private insurance the property owner will be given a couple of options. They can rebuild and reinsure privately. After the property is severely damaged they can sell the land to the government or they can sell their rights to build on the land to the government. These last two options are essentially equal to the options available under the government insurance. If the Corp of Engineers needs the property or needs to recontour the property they will still have the option of negotiating with the property owner or using eminent domain. The property owner will retain the right to sell on the open market as well. No new construction will be eligible for government flood insurance.

In the non-flood control areas the federal flood insurance should be phased out within ten years. It should be actuarially sound within three years. This will give property owners time to find a new insurer and for more insurers to enter the market now that they are not going to be undercut by the government insurance.

Any rural areas that are designated for flooding to save cities should be assisted to minimize the cost of this flooding. Any new or rebuilt roads or buildings should be raised above the flood level so that only fields and forests are covered by water. Assistance to property owners in these zones should be available to meet elevation and other zone standards. Compensation for lost crops or the inability to plant crops and for the care of livestock should be made to people in the flood zone. Property owners need to be adequately and timely compensated for reconditioning cropland and other damage. The Corp of Engineers should try to minimize the areas that are needed to be used for flooding.

## Public Employee Union Collective Bargaining Privileges and Setting a Compensation Relationship to the Private Sector

There has been a great deal of rhetoric and emotion over the efforts by some state governments to reduce the collective bargaining privileges of state and local government employees. They should be called privileges instead of rights as the unions call them. As privileges public workers can serve the public as the public needs but as rights the public unions become the tyrants and enslavers of the people. When the government sees itself as the most important part of society it becomes a tyrant. This is true whether it is a king, a dictator, an elected representative, or a union. As a society we can allow public employees the privilege of providing input into their jobs because that is just good common sense. What we cannot do is let them control the job as a right because the job belongs to the people, all of us taxpayers. The servant cannot be greater than the master.

The effort to reign in public employee collective bargaining is largely due to the high level of compensation for public employees relative to the private sector. After state and local governments have cut everywhere else in their budgets there is nowhere else to go. Personnel costs are a substantial portion of most state and local governments. In school districts it is frequently as high as 80 percent of the total budget. Much of this excessive compensation is due to collective bargaining and politics.

Public sector unions can generate a lot of money and votes for candidates, especially local candidates. Local elections tend to have a very low voter turnout which greatly increases the effect of the union power. It becomes difficult and in some districts impossible to get elected without local public employee union support. This takes the power from the general taxpaying public. The result is that the public employee unions sit across the bargaining table with the people they elected and tend to get as much as they want. When they do find elected officials that say no to them they just delay reaching an agreement until after the next election.

The situation in Wisconsin in 2010 drew a great deal of attention. Unions were delaying agreements by 18 months or more from the expiration of the previous agreement. They were so stubborn about their positions of increased wages and benefits that their Democrat allies in power before Governor Walker could not reach an agreement with the unions. They did not agree to any concessions until they thought they might lose collective bargaining privileges. There is a section later that has recommended wage and benefit guidelines that would curtail many of the abuses of public employee collective bargaining. That section is also instructional about the current abuses that rob taxpayers.

When unions started they were important in the fight against abuses by employers. They were on the side of liberty. Most of the protections for workers that originally spawned unions have been part of state and federal laws for decades and apply to all workers. For government workers these are enhanced in many jurisdictions by civil service protections that prevent abuses like filling positions with political cronies or firing without cause. These protections are more than most private sector workers enjoy. No one is trying to get rid of these worker protections but union abuses do need to be dealt with.

Today, unions are frequently fighting against liberty for their members and for society as a whole. They fight to require that workers must belong to a union and pay union dues even if they do not wish to be members. They fight to set up rules to force more people into unions against their will. They inhibit free market reforms in health insurance and trade and tax policy. They push companies into bankruptcy or overseas. These convictions are held most strongly by union leaders but the rank and file is still responsible for these abuses. I understand that most people are involved in their lives and families and do not take the time to fully understand what their union is doing. It is easy to become complacent in overseeing those you believe are looking out for you. (I did the same thing with the Republican leaders.) Union leaders have been manipulating their members for their own political power and wealth. I know many union members who are conservative on most issues but still vote Democrat because they are union members. They are involved in life and do not pay attention to much of the political issues that their union supports. Unions lie and manipulate to keep their members in the dark.

There are basically four options to maintain protection of taxpayers against subversion by public employee unions. One is to restrict what they can bargain for and limit the automatic collection of union dues in order to cut the funding at election time. The second is to continue with collective bargaining on everything but set statutory limits in state law but these limits are likely going to be up for sale by politicians. The third is similar to the second but the limits are part of the state constitution which is much more difficult to change than state law. It will also be much more difficult to put in the constitution and the unions will fight tooth and nail to prevent it. The fourth is to cut loose all lower level governmental units from access to any state or federal funding and make them sink or swim on the local tax base. Then only the local residents are affected by the overspending. This is unlikely to last long because of political pressure.

Here is a plan that still permits collective bargaining for public employees but sets an average compensation limit in relation to the private sector. This could be applied to public employees at the federal, state, and local levels with laws at the state and federal level. This would be best in the state and federal constitutions because it would likely be watered down or removed periodically if it is just in the statutes.

**The average Full Time Equivalency (FTE) employee compensation for the civilian public employee pool shall not be less than the average FTE employee compensation for the pool of all private sector full-time employed persons who reside in the employer's jurisdiction nor will the civilian public employee pool average FTE employee compensation be greater than seven percent over the average FTE employee compensation for the pool of all private sector full-time employed persons who reside in the employer's jurisdiction. Any jurisdiction that is out of compliance with this provision has five fiscal years after passage to be in compliance.**

The seven percent above is a placeholder. It is likely to be in the ballpark of an appropriate differential from the private sector given the higher average level of education needed for most government positions. There are many dueling studies that say either that public workers are overpaid or underpaid. This plan will collect the complete information and set the relationship of public sector to private sector compensation at a level the general public agrees is appropriate.

### Establishing the process

In Box 14 of W-2s of all employees the employer could place three pieces of information. The first is the total value of compensation for the employee. The second is the letters PUB for public employees and PVT for private sector employees. The third is the FTE value or hours worked for the employee at the job.

Compensation should include wages, pension contributions, insurance premiums, free or reduced rate meals, vacation, sick day pay, employee's share of costs for unemployment and workman's compensation insurance, bonuses, merit and effectiveness pay and any other quantifiable compensation received from the employer. The employer should have to convey an itemized list of the types and amounts of compensation to each employee at the same time as the W-2 is distributed. The W-2 will also show whether or not each worker is contributing to Social Security or Medicare and that can be used to get more accurate averages.

On income tax forms two lines will be included for reporting this information. One will be for reporting public employee compensation and the other for private employee compensation and the hours worked for each. Separate lines are needed for those who have income from both in the same year.

The IRS and state departments of revenue will collect the information at the time tax forms are filed. This data will then be conveyed to the appropriate agency for calculation of the private sector averages for the federal government or state and each municipal employer in the state. States without an income tax can have employers report the information directly, have employees send in a copy of their W-2s, obtain the information from the federal government, or require municipalities to collect it.

Because the year being budgeted is not the same year for which the last complete set of compensation data was collected an estimate will need to be used to set the future maximum average. The appropriate agency will make a recommendation of what these estimated future maximum averages should be. The government employer will set aside five percent of planned compensation for the completion of the tax collection reporting and from that make a final payment that complies with the constitutional limit.

Any employer that is exceeding the maximum average at the time this goes into effect should as a minimum freeze wages at their current level. A reasonable time should be set for the union and employer to begin negotiations after enactment of this provision and reach an agreement to implement a plan to reach compliance with these limits by the start of the third fiscal year following passage.

In order to make good compensation comparisons the outliers among the working population should be excluded. This should cut out those who work more than 2600 hours per year and those who work too few hours to be considered full-time from the comparison. This lower threshold should vary based on the average number of hours worked by the employees of a public employer. Salaried employees should be assumed to work fifty hours per week unless otherwise documented.

## Recommended wage, benefit, and contract guidelines

This is a list of guidelines based on items that are frequently included in collective bargaining agreements for which taxpayers get stuck with the bill and should not have to.

Right to work should be the law of the land. No free person should be required to be in a union or pay union dues in order to have a particular job. Especially a job with one's own government! The government should not require anyone to be in a union and should not collect union dues for a union.

Any defined benefit plan should use the average of the actual inflation adjusted return from the plan and the inflation adjusted return of the S&P 500 for the past 50 years as the estimate of future returns. Plan allocations should be enough to keep the plan fully funded each year. Frequently bargaining agreements ask for extravagant pension and retiree medical coverage and the costs are not fully paid in the year when the work was performed. Unrealistic rates of investment returns are estimated in order to give a benefit that is unfunded so that the current budget looks good but in later years taxpayers are stuck with having to make up this funding. That is what is happening now after many decades of not assessing the true costs of benefits. The union leaders know these are unrealistic estimates but still push for them so that they can get more of the current year's money in other forms of compensation. This is a fraud perpetrated on the public that has to stop. The true costs need to be estimated and accounted for in the year when the work is performed. We can't keep passing these costs on to our children and grandchildren. The federal government should tie all federal money for states to reforms in this area. The states have an estimated $2-3 trillion in unfunded employee benefit liabilities. If this does not end soon there will be a strong push for bailouts when these plans bankrupt in the next few decades.

The quantifiable costs of rules which are not related to safety in collective bargaining agreements should have to be covered under the compensation limits.

The expense of union bulletin boards and literature should be borne by the union.

The use of government phones, computers, email, mail, intra-institutional mail, vehicles, facilities or other material for union activities is forbidden unless permitted for the same use by the general public. The legislature should establish penalties for violation of this provision consistent with the use of similar materials by legislators for political purposes.

No employer should provide wages or benefits for union members to conduct union activities or attend union meetings and conferences. The union may purchase time off for union officials to miss normal work hours to conduct union activities or attend union meetings and conferences. No union official should be scheduled for mandatory overtime during union activities or attending union meetings and conferences that the employer was notified of at least 14 days in advance.

No collective bargaining agreement should require union-employer meetings during normal work hours for the employee representative(s). The collective bargaining agreement should not state that the employee will be paid and accrue any benefits from the employer during employer/union meetings. The union may compensate its representatives from its own funds. Alternatively, the employer should not require the union employee(s) to miss regularly scheduled work to meet with the employer without providing compensation equal to that which would have been earned had the time not been used for the meeting and reasonable travel time.

Bargaining unit employees, including union officers and representatives, should not conduct any union activity or business on the employer's time except as specifically authorized by the employer on a case by case basis for meeting with the employer. It should be understood by the union that the primary function of employees is the performance of their job-related duties. Union activities should be done outside of the job.

The union and the employer should split the cost of printing a copy of the agreement for each employee and each supervisor of union employees. The Employer should post and maintain a copy of the agreement online and notify employees where to find the agreement online.

Seniority should not be considered for public employees, skill and ability should have priority.

Shift stacking should be prohibited. This is the practice of taking a sick day for their regular shift and then coming in to work the next shift. Collecting regular pay for the paid sick day and receiving overtime for the other shift. This drives up costs without providing a benefit to taxpayers.

Double dipping should be prohibited. Retirement benefits should be reduced by the amount of current earnings.

Outsourcing of non-core operations should not be a subject of collective bargaining.

Uses of public facilities outside of bargaining unit uses should not be a subject of collective bargaining. For example, schools are a natural place for community activities in the evening. Public use of the sports facilities, libraries, computer labs, meeting rooms, evening childcare, etc. These should not be subject to teacher's union collective bargaining restrictions.

All overtime should be approved by the employer. Mandatory overtime should be distributed as evenly as is reasonable amongst qualified employees. Voluntary overtime should be distributed as evenly as is reasonable amongst qualified employees who volunteer. Priority should go to those qualified employees who volunteer for the overtime. Mandatory overtime rules should be the subject of collective bargaining as long as they don't interfere with an even distribution of the overtime.

Retirement age should be no earlier than the federal retirement age. Going forward retirement benefits that begin before the federal retirement age for the former employee should be reduced so that the value of an early retirement and one at the federal retirement age will be equal at age 85.

The net present value of the lifetime increase in costs for severance packages and early retirement benefits and other end of employment benefits should be included and paid for in current year budgets and fit under total compensation caps. This should effectively end the costly payments for early retirements. Under current rules early retirements tend to save money in the short run but tend to be very costly in the long run. Another way that politicians have pushed costs down the road.

The specific provider for insurance should not be a subject of collective bargaining. The employer and employees should establish a committee to regularly discuss issues related to the insurance plans in order to make recommendations for improvement in the benefit.

Employees who are placed on leave with pay due to being charged with a crime should be limited to receiving the wages and benefits to one year. If convicted and the conviction is the cause of the termination of employment then the wages and benefits costs paid out while on leave should have to be repaid to the employer.

Only base wages should be considered for calculating retirement benefits. Under many collective bargaining agreements retirement benefits are based on the person's highest wage year(s). That is more reasonable if just base wages are counted. It is unreasonable when employees are allowed to work a lot of overtime in the final years before retirement in order to drive up their retirement package. Excessive amounts that taxpayers have to pay for decades with no added benefit to society. A more fair option for taxpayers would be to use the inflation adjusted average of all of their years with the employer as the wage basis.

Cafeteria plans offer the greatest flexibility in benefits for employees. This allows employees to favor the benefits that help them the best. All public employee benefits should be done through a cafeteria plan. A specific dollar amount or percentage of wages for the benefit plan should be set. This will be especially helpful for less than full-time employees. In some cases part-time employees do not receive any benefits. Far more often with public employees the part-time employees get full-time benefits. Neither situation is fair. With a cafeteria plan it is easier to provide a prorated benefit package for part-timers.

Public employee collective bargaining agreements should not be longer than the term of office of the elected officials responsible for approving a contract. No automatic renewals should be permitted. When the terms of office of the elected officials concerned are staggered the length of term for a collective bargaining agreement should be such that the contract does not expire in the final year of the same batch of officials. Unions should have to hold a recertification vote from 30 to 90 days prior to the beginning of scheduled negotiations with the employer. If a union is decertified it should take effect when the existing contract expires. A reasonable period like twelve months should have to elapse after a decertification vote for there to be a new vote for certification.

Establishing these types of guidelines for specific items should resonate better with the general public. Most people are unsure exactly what collective bargaining rights/privileges are and become concerned when they hear that rights are being taken away. Providing clear details will be easier to understand. This is much like specific conservative referendums that pass even when a conservative candidate loses a district. When union members have to start paying for many of these things out of their union dues there will be a reckoning with their own leadership and likely many union members that refuse to pay the dues. These issues and expenses will then be internal to the union where they belong.

### Roundabouts and LEDs

An easy way for governments to save money is by reducing the number of traffic signals and replacing them with roundabouts. There is a tremendous reduction in initial and maintenance costs that are saved by not having the traffic signals in place. There is also a reduction in accidents and a reduction in the severity of accidents compared to traditional intersections. This will reduce insurance costs for drivers. Not having to sit at red lights will save on gas and wear and tear on your vehicle's engine.

This does not mean a wholesale reconstruction of all of our intersections. They should be modified as the roads come due in the normal construction schedule or if a cost/benefit analysis shows that it should be moved up in time on the schedule. In the meantime, zoning laws should be adjusted to make sure there is room for roundabouts in the future.

In a related area, LEDs can now be used for traffic lights and street lighting. LEDs need much less electricity than other types of lights and can reduce the electric bills for local governments. Again, this should be done thru normal attrition. In northern climes an additional heater element is needed which will use a little more electricity during winter months because LEDs do not generate the heat that traditional lights generate. Snow and ice accumulation does not melt as on older lights.

# 9 FINANCIAL REFORMS

**"Money is a terrible master but an excellent servant."**
**P.T. Barnum**

## Too Big To Fail

The very concept of some companies being too big to fail and therefore need to be bailed out by the government is un-American, anti-capitalist, and an insult to American taxpayers and everyone else competing in the free market. The common excuse is that some companies are so big or have an effect on so many other companies or the economy that the government must step in to prevent an economic catastrophe. There are reasonable actions that the federal government can take to head off a cascading economic collapse both before a company has a crisis and when it has a crisis.

These large institutions need to be transparent about their holdings and obligations. The companies that are designated as posing a systemic risk should be required to maintain wind down plans as though they faced a potential bankruptcy. Their regulators should review these plans with them annually or when a major change occurs in the corporation that would materially affect the plan. This should be designed as much as possible to be consistent with good management and internal controls practices.

In some cases it may be helpful for them to put firewalls between different parts of the business. For example, in the big banks, walling off the areas insured by the government and the proprietary trading operations would be good for them to maintain those operations but shelter the taxpayers from risk. Brokerage operations should be firewalled from proprietary trading operations to avoid conflicts of interest.

Under bankruptcy law there should be a new section dealing specifically with companies that are designated as posing a systemic risk. It should provide for much faster resolution. The Federal Reserve should maintain a pool of people identified as capable to step in to help the judge oversee the continued operation and subsequent resolution of the situation. Additionally,

119

all significant stakeholders should be able to immediately present resolution plans instead of having to wait for management to present one. Bankruptcy rules need to be transparent and the seniority of obligations of the companies in bankruptcy need to be clear and inviolate. To be otherwise is to invite political interference as occurred with the financial and auto industry bailouts.

## Progressive Contingent Capital (CoCos)

The First Tier is an idea originated by Mark Flannery of the University of Florida and described by Charles W. Calomiris in the Wall Street Journal on May 29, 2014. It involves a requirement that the big banks maintain a 10 percent book equity-to-asset ratio. Additionally, the bank is required to issue 10 percent of its debt as contingent capital. Debt that converts to equity if the equity-to-asset ratio drops below 10 percent on average for a period of 120 days. Setting the debt to convert at a 5 percent premium to face value will encourage bank managers to maintain sufficient capital to prevent conversion. It will be more expensive for current shareholders if 10 percent of their debt converts than if the bank issues more stock in smaller amounts without a premium as needed to maintain the equity-to-asset ratio. This is the first and hopefully only Tier that is needed by big banks to stay solvent.

The remainder of the Tiers in this recommendation is a progression of debt conversion as needed to prevent insolvency either in a formal bankruptcy court order or in an emergency order by the Federal Reserve. The remainder of the formal long-term debt will be assigned to Tiers 2 through 10 when it is issued. Tier 11 is for obligations remaining from trading operations. Tier 12 is for short-term debt, accounts payable, and amounts owed to employees. Tier 13 is for amounts owed to the federal, state and local governments.

The lowest number Tier is converted first and progress sequentially to Tier 13. Tiers 2 through 13 will convert at the full face value of the debt obligation. As each Tier is converted it dilutes the ownership of the original shareholders and shareholders resulting from previously converted Tiers.

Ideally the formal creditors and shareholders will provide the necessary oversight to keep these corporations from ever reaching the point where these debts need to be converted. If they do not prevent it before conversion they are likely to sack the existing management and work to prevent the further dilution of value. This method should provide more oversight of management and operations. To protect themselves management is more likely to put practices in place that will make conversions rare. This is a much better method than allowing the politically connected to be bailed out by taxpayers.

When the formal long term debt is issued it will be done so in tranches specifying the Tier it is part of or the whole issue will be assigned to a Tier. The debt in each Tier will be valued differently. The lower the Tier number the higher the interest rate will be or it will sell at a discount. If lower numbered Tiers have higher nominal rates then the effect of converting a Tier is enhanced by removing the higher interest rate debt before lower interest rate debt.

Although this was originally designed for the large financial institutions it can be applied to most large corporations. Rather than fighting over which companies should be designated as posing a systemic risk this could be applied to any corporation with a market cap or assets under management over $20 billion. (This amount is a placeholder. I am uncertain that anybody can come up with a solid basis for where this threshold should be. In the end it will likely be an arbitrary point decided by Congress.) Let companies self-select by choosing to be under or over the threshold. An instant change is not practical. All new debt will be placed in a Tier. All legacy long term debt will be placed in Tier 10. Obligations that meet the Tier 11-13 criteria will automatically be placed in those Tiers. This same pattern should be used for all companies as they enter this group.

Managers will have to meet higher standards and have a shorter leash from shareholders and creditors. This is better than current bankruptcy procedures or government regulators. It is a quick and sure way to remove failing management and replace it with new managers. Smaller corporations should be able to adopt this model voluntarily. It may aid some in securing financing.

## Improving Accountability in Bond Rating

One of the factors that led to the recent economic downturn was the inflated ratings for bonds. This was in part due to the fact that bond issuers pay the bond ratings agency to rate their bonds. Companies will ratings shop for the best bond rating in order to get the best price for their bonds. (The top three rating agencies made $3.6 billion in fees in 2009.) There is an inherent conflict of interest in this relationship.

Unfortunately, there is no perfect answer to this conflict of interest because someone has to evaluate the bonds and someone has to pay for the evaluation. The only entities that could realistically be expected to pay for the evaluation are the issuers who wish to sell the bonds. This means there needs to be sufficient checks and balances on the process and participants to achieve a fair and accurate rating. The solution to this problem is to make the ratings agencies' interests align with the bondholders' interests even though they are paid by the issuer of the bonds. This can be done with two simple changes.

First, require that ratings agencies are largely paid for their services in the bonds that they are rating and require that they keep the bonds to maturity, until called by the issuer, or until liquidated pursuant to the rating agency going through bankruptcy. These bonds may not be called until all other bonds from the issue have been called. Essentially the rating agency will be the first in and last out. If the rating agency is inaccurate in their evaluation then their compensation is degraded along with the return of the bondholders. The need for rating agencies to be price competitive will be balanced with the need to receive sufficient bonds to be profitable.

For example, the rating agency rates the bonds. Then the bond issuer will auction the bonds after the rating. The average price that the bonds are sold at will determine how many bonds are needed to pay the fees for doing the bond rating. If the rater overrates the issue, they will likely be undercompensated. If they underrate the issue they may be overcompensated but the issuer may use a different rater the next time around. Overall, this payment scheme should make the ratings agencies more conservative in their ratings, thereby protecting bondholders from taking on more risk than they intend. If a rating agency consistently underrates bond issues the market will notice and adjust accordingly which is another natural check on the process.

Another option is to require a variable level of compensation to be paid in bonds based upon the rating of the bonds. Higher bond ratings would result in a greater percentage of the compensation being paid in bonds. Lower bond ratings would result in a higher percentage of compensation in cash and less in bonds. While there may be pressure to downgrade for this reason there will be a balancing pressure from bond issuers taking their business to other raters in the future if they believe there is a compensation bias. For the rating agency, an accurate rating should result in the same net present value whether paid in cash or bonds.

If there are multiple tranches in the issue, then the rating agency will receive their compensation from each tranche. The bonds used for compensating the rating agency will be from each tranche in the same proportion as the tranche makes up of the total issue.

The entire securities portfolio for the ratings agencies must be public, updated regularly with all trading documented and the historical records must be easily searchable. This is to allow others to evaluate whether a rating agency is hedging against losses from the bonds they received for rating an issue. A reasonable minimum time should be set for ratings agencies to be barred from directly hedging against losses from the bonds they receive for rating an issue.

Second, require that a significant portion of executive compensation at ratings agencies be deferred to correspond with interest and maturity payments of the bonds rated during their tenure. Their compensation should vary with the performance of the bonds over time. The ratings agencies should also have a policy of deferred compensation for all employees that have a significant contribution to the ratings process and decisions. This will help keep their interests aligned with the agency and with bondholders.

## Implementation

The shift to this payment method will have to be gradual in order to keep the rating agency from suffering from a cash flow problem while waiting for bonds to mature. Below is a suggested ten year transition.

| Bond Rating | Year | 1 | 2 | 3 | 4 | 5 | 6 | 7 | 8 | 9 | 10 |
|---|---|---|---|---|---|---|---|---|---|---|---|
| Prime | Percent Change | 6% | 6% | 7% | 7% | 8% | 8% | 9% | 9% | 10% | 10% |
| | Cumulative Change | 6% | 12% | 19% | 26% | 34% | 42% | 51% | 60% | 70% | 80% |
| High Grade | Percent Change | 5% | 5% | 6% | 6% | 7% | 7% | 8% | 8% | 9% | 9% |
| | Cumulative Change | 5% | 10% | 16% | 22% | 29% | 36% | 44% | 52% | 61% | 70% |
| Upper Medium Grade | Percent Change | 3% | 3% | 4% | 4% | 5% | 5% | 6% | 6% | 7% | 7% |
| | Cumulative Change | 3% | 6% | 10% | 14% | 19% | 24% | 30% | 36% | 43% | 50% |
| Lower Medium Grade | Percent Change | 1% | 1% | 2% | 2% | 3% | 3% | 4% | 4% | 5% | 5% |
| | Cumulative Change | 1% | 2% | 4% | 6% | 9% | 12% | 16% | 20% | 25% | 30% |
| Non-Investment Grade Speculative | Percent Change | 1% | 1% | 1% | 1% | 1% | 1% | 1% | 1% | 1% | 1% |
| | Cumulative Change | 1% | 2% | 3% | 4% | 5% | 6% | 7% | 8% | 9% | 10% |
| Highly Speculative or Lower Rating | Percent Change | 0% | 0% | 0% | 0% | 0% | 0% | 0% | 0% | 0% | 0% |
| | Cumulative Change | 0% | 0% | 0% | 0% | 0% | 0% | 0% | 0% | 0% | 0% |

There is a strong case for setting a maximum time limit that a rating agency would need to retain the bonds used for payment. It is extremely difficult to predict economic conditions and the effects of new technology, corporate governance, and government regulations beyond a certain threshold. The Congressional Budget Office uses ten years as the limit that it will score legislation because of the increasing level of uncertainty. For bonds with maturities beyond ten years potential bond purchasers can look to ratings of more recent issues from the same company and past performance from the issue in question. As long as it is recognized in the bond investment industry that rating agencies are looking at primarily the first ten years then investors can account for that in making their decisions. Obviously, material information that is known at the time of the rating about the period beyond this time period should be noted and considered.

A similar process could also be set up for when other securities are rated for a fee or for the payment of outside auditors and consultants. This would likely be more effective and less costly than Sarbanes-Oxley.

## Fannie and Freddie Must Go

Fannie Mae (Federal National Mortgage Association) and Freddie Mac (Federal Home Loan Mortgage Corporation) have been the largest companies insuring mortgages and buying and packaging the mortgages for sale of mortgage backed securities on the secondary market. Their status as Government Sponsored Enterprises (GSE) created an environment where their power and connections with the government undercut their competition. Their cost of borrowing was reduced by an implicit backing by the federal government. They provided high level positions to politically connected people. Many senior people obtained below market rate loans with companies that did business with Fannie Mae. Campaign contributions were used to gain support in Congress with members from both parties which allowed them to neutralize their regulators with Congressional interference. They have repeatedly been found to have misreported their financial information to hide embarrassing results. This is a perfect example of cronyism where private investors reap the profits and taxpayers get stuck with the losses.

When the financial crisis hit Fannie and Freddie they needed to be bailed out by the federal government moving from an implicit backing to an explicit backing. Even if they fully recover from the huge losses from bad mortgages they will still suffer from the same problems as before. Taxpayers will be on the hook for their future corruption and losses.

The only solution is to phase out Fannie and Freddie and have the private sector take over the mortgage insurance and securitization businesses. Many companies will be able to compete with each other on a level playing field. They will not be able to accumulate the same kind of influence with Congress. This transition should be done over a period of about ten years.

It should involve a gradual reduction in the maximum loan that they can buy and guarantee. Within five years the maximum loan should be limited to the median single family home value for each state. During the final five years the maximum loan should be further reduced by ten percent each year. Then end new business after ten years.

They should begin divesting their portfolios of mortgages. At the end of ten years all that should remain are two small companies that will collect the guarantee fees that remain from their previous business, act as market maker for their previously issued securities, and managing the remaining underperforming mortgages that they cannot get rid of at a reasonable price.

Congress should help the process along by reducing the affordable housing mandate for low and moderate income borrowers for all entities to 15 percent of their portfolio. This will allow the selective writing of mortgages for those that are a better risk in this income range but also limit the risk to the overall economy and taxpayers. (The requirement imposed by the federal government had reached at least 55 percent by 2007 which greatly increased the risk to the economy. This led to greatly more risk taking by lenders and borrowers alike.) Competitive free market banks will find a way to assess borrowers better in order to find the better risk people from among low income borrowers

## Mortgage Standards and Documentation for the Secondary Market

Two other issues that came out in the recent financial crisis was the lack of detailed information about the mortgages that made up the mortgage backed securities and the lack of skin in the game by the borrower, the mortgage originator and the mortgage backed security (MBS) issuer.

As for skin in the game we should require the combination of the borrower and the loan originator to cover at least twenty percent of the property value and for each to have covered at least five percent of the property value when a mortgage is originated if it is sold on the secondary market. Any second mortgage may not eliminate that five percent of equity for the borrower. (The ability to borrow from their Social Security XXI account will aid borrowers to reach both the five and twenty percent requirements.) The borrower will also be required to carry mortgage insurance until they have at least twenty percent equity in the property. The loan originator may cover their portion with capital or covered bonds.

Next we should require that the MBS issuer must retain at least five percent of each tranche of any MBS. This will make sure that all of the major players have a stake in a successful completion of the mortgage and that all try to accurately account for the risk.

The next step in the process is to make mortgage backed securities transparent so that the market can appropriately price them. Each mortgage and MBS should be registered in a common interactive database available online. The loan originator should begin the file on a mortgage. The loan servicer should have a file linked to the originator's file to show the continuing state of the mortgage. Each MBS should link back to each mortgage in the security. If a MBS contains other MBSs it should link back to the earlier MBSs. As the loan servicer updates the file, all of the linked MBSs should be updated. All of this information should be easily downloadable so analysts and investors can work with the data as they desire.

Some of the information that should be included in a file:

Unique Loan ID Number

Percent of the mortgage in the MBS

Original loan amount

Current balance of the loan

Original percentage rate of the loan

Current percentage rate of the loan
Loan originator ID code (Company not individual)
Initial down payment percent paid by the borrower
Percent retained by the loan originator
Percent retained by the MBS issuer
Length of mortgage (In months)
ARM, Yes or No?
Original ARM description
Maximum annual ARM percentage rate change
Average annual income of borrower for previous 3 years
Annual income for borrower for previous year
Credit score of borrower at time of purchase
Current credit score of borrower
Month and year of loan origination (MM/YY)
State where property is located
Subdivision of the state ID code
Type of property
Frequency of payment (W/B/T/M/Q/S/A)
Lifetime of loan missing payments
Past year missing payments
Lifetime of loan late payments
Past year late payments
Prepayment penalty (Y/N)
Description of prepayment penalty
Full recourse (Y/N)
Paid Off (Y/N)
Each current and piece of information should be retained in the file history along with the dates of updates.

If all mortgages on the secondary market follow the same reporting system on a common registry then it will be easier for investors to analyze mortgage backed securities. Annually the borrower will have to supply the loan originator or servicer with a copy of their tax return to verify their income. The loan originator will report the borrower's income information, missing or late payment information, current credit score and changes to the percentage rate of the loan to the registry. Failure to update or fraudulent updates should leave the responsible party subject to civil and/or criminal penalties.

Additionally, the MBS issuer will post all of the information on their website providing a listing of the current status of each issued security that includes even a portion of the mortgage. If another MBS issuer repackages

MBSs then the second MBS issuer can go to the registry.

Part of the agreement between the loan originator and the original mortgage buyer is designating who gets to make decisions about renegotiating the loan conditions with the borrower. The designee can make a foreclosure or workout decision. The options that are permitted or prohibited will be listed in this agreement. Any subsequent division of the mortgage will be subject to the conditions of this agreement. A copy of this agreement will be available on a link on the original mortgage buyer's website and the registry's website for review by subsequent buyers. If possible coding should be developed for these for the common options.

There should also be a deadline of perhaps two or three years for existing mortgages and MBS to be registered. This should provide more transparency and help the markets to price the existing supply of mortgages on the secondary market. A similar registry system could be used for securitizing other debt such as vehicle loans, credit card debt, and mixed debt securities.

## Mortgage Modifications

Government mandated mortgage modifications are dangerous for the economy and for borrowers, investors, and lenders. Mortgages are contracts and should not be interfered with by the government unless they are unlawful. Not because some people don't like the results. When the government exhibits a pattern of interference two things happen. Various interests will seek preferential treatment from the government. Lenders will raise the original cost to borrowers to guard against the risk that they will be forced to modify a loan. This raises the cost to all borrowers.

Mortgage modifications freely agreed to between the lender and borrower should be permitted. In fact when many homeowners are underwater on their mortgages it is a smart move for lenders to achieve stability and continued payments from their loan portfolios. At the same time it is difficult to do this without moral hazard. Homeowners may stop paying to try to force a modification. Lenders are reluctant to cut their interest income when there are many other bad mortgages on which they are losing money. This plan attempts to reach a viable modification plan.

This plan is for those who have adequate income to make the payments at a lower market interest rate. This plan may only be viable with mortgages that have not been sold on the secondary market.

The Agreement
1. Reduce the interest rate to the current market rate.
2. Borrower agrees to continue paying the difference between the old payment and the new payment or as much of it as current income

allows as principle payments until the borrower is estimated to have at least 10 percent equity under current market appraisal.

    a.      Borrower will have a new payment of up to 40 percent of gross income for PITI with up to a maximum total debt load of 40 percent of gross income or the old payment, whichever is less.

    b.      Borrower agrees not to increase their debt load over 40 percent without written agreement from the lender until the 10 percent equity target is reached. Borrower agrees to notify the lender of any increase in debt load. Notice of this agreement should be placed in credit reporting agency files.

3.   At the time of sale of the house the borrower and lender split the gain if there is a gain.

    a.      It must be an arm's length transaction and the lender should set some reasonable guidelines and time period for advertising.

    b.      The borrower should have the option to buy the lender out of their split of the future gain. This is beneficial to both. The lender does not have to wait for the sale of the home. The borrower can retain more of the future gain.

This is not a perfect answer for lender or borrower. These two stakeholders have the most at stake on any single house and by working together they can help each other. Both made mistakes in the initial loan agreement or misjudged the housing market. By each taking a small hit they have the chance to keep the borrower in the house and get to a point where there is enough equity to readily refinance on the secondary market.

## Federal Debt Arbitrage Elimination

There have been reports over the past few years that financial institutions have utilized their ability to borrow from the Federal Reserve and used these funds to purchase US Treasury securities. The current cost of borrowing from the Fed is much lower than the return from investing in Treasuries. This situation may allow these institutions to generate profits to offset their losses from other investments but is done at the expense of taxpayers. This is simply another transfer of wealth from taxpayers to big banks. It does nothing to improve investing in real economic growth activities.

Borrowing from the Federal Reserve and using it to purchase Treasury securities does not help the economy grow. It shelters the Federal government from the true cost of borrowing on the open market. It allows the Federal Reserve to bail out the Federal government with covert quantitative easing.

To eliminate Federal debt arbitrage by companies that can borrow directly from the Federal Reserve there should be a requirement that any company that owns US Treasury securities and has an outstanding debt with the Federal Reserve will forfeit to the Federal Reserve the full earnings of the Treasury securities. The forfeiture will be calculated on a daily basis. The financial institution will be exempt from this requirement for the portion of Treasury securities that exceed the amount borrowed from the Federal Reserve. The highest earning Treasuries will be counted against the forfeiture.

The purpose of this new requirement is to pressure the banks to make loans with the money they have to grow the economy. This will not prevent banks from borrowing from the Federal Reserve or from owning Treasury securities. They will simply forfeit the earnings from the securities that exceed the cost of borrowing from the Federal Reserve when they have an outstanding debt to the Federal Reserve.


## Gradual Revolving Credit Reduction

When the recession hit, many businesses and individuals with lines of credit had them cancelled or suddenly and greatly reduced. This presented many with a cash flow problem that exacerbated their already difficult financial situation. The solution that follows also applies when the borrower is in default on the revolving line of credit or a different debt.

The line of credit is gradually reduced to limit the creditors exposure to the debt. This is instead of cancelling or drastically reducing the line of credit immediately. Revolving credit for a small business is used to maintain cash flow. Credit cards can help individuals to maintain cash flow in the same way. Users can make payments greater than the minimum on the line of credit and still use much of that same income to make payments on other bills using the line of credit. While this is far from an ideal situation it keeps creditors satisfied for a little while longer until more income can come in.

For simplicity the example used is for a credit card. The same principle applies to other revolving lines of credit. By cancelling the credit card the user has to choose whether to pay the credit card bill or another bill. When this happens the credit card suddenly becomes the last in line despite the interest rate because all of the other bills are for current needs.

Rather than cancel a person's credit card, institute a gradually declining credit limit. For example, a card with a $5,000 balance. Put the card on a plan to immediately reduce the credit limit to just above the balance and then by $100 per month until the user is caught up on all debts. The creditor will receive $100 plus the interest incurred for the month or the borrower will likely be in default. The advantage for the borrower is in being able to pay as much additional money as they can and still be able to use it for other recurring expenses. Knowing that this borrowing window will not suddenly close will give people confidence to cycle their money through the credit card. It will allow the user to maintain cash flow and still reduce the exposure of the creditor. It will help the creditor keep their own revenue and cash flow higher by keeping the velocity of money higher.

If a credit card is cancelled during times of financial distress people struggle to meet the minimum payments and the creditor has to downgrade the quality of the credit card debt. Instead the creditor would have better quality debt in its portfolio with a credit limit and balance that has gradually declined but is still receiving larger than minimum payments. Creditors could greatly reduce defaults and collections cost by moving to a gradually declining credit limit plan over a credit cancellation plan or a single major decline in the credit limit. It encourages people to keep making payments rather than moving it to last in line. This allows individuals, businesses, creditors, and the economy to recover faster.

# 10 FOREIGN POLICY

"Diplomacy in general does not resolve conflicts. Wars end not due to
peace processes, but due to one side giving up."
**Daniel Pipes**

With so much of the world dependent upon the US for security our
strategy must be to be able to defend everyone. The threat of our military
restrains many despots and serves to head off many conflicts. **The USA is
the leader of the free world!** If we abdicate that responsibility there will be
others that fill the power vacuum. Countries like China, Russia, Iran, and
Venezuela and radicals from the left and right and Islamists. Many others will
align with them out of fear. Some will resist and have to fight to defend
themselves and others will become aggressive in their own right out of fear
about the future. We need to pressure our allies to step up and help much
more in defending freedom around the world. We cannot abandon our duty
even if they do. We do not owe all of these other peoples. We owe our
descendants the best, most peaceful world we can give them. We do that by
fostering freedom around the world.

We and our allies will not be safer if we pull back our forces and our
influence. Many of the allies we have now will not trust us in the future if we
abandon them now. It will make reengaging in the future far more difficult
and costly. We have lost faith with allies and other people's seeking freedom
in the past in Eastern Europe and China (1945), Hungary (1956),
Czechoslovakia (1968), Southeast Asia (1975), Afghanistan (1989), Pakistan
(1989), and the Shiites of Iraq (1991). We abandoned the freedom fighters of
the Arab Spring to be chewed up between radical Islamists and authoritarian
regimes. We have failed to adequately aid reformers in Ukraine and many
other countries around the world. Only by remaining strong and engaged can
we deal with conflicts abroad and keep them from becoming bigger
problems.

We need to have a freedom agenda for our foreign policy. The US is the lone superpower right now and we have the largest economy in the world. That will not last forever. There are several large nations that could over time also become superpowers. We need to help foster a world made of countries that respect individual rights comparable to our own Declaration of Independence and Bill of Rights. A world of republics where their citizens have a means to periodically change their leadership peacefully at the ballot box! A world of free market economies with private diffused ownership of all sectors of the economy. This is needed to give our descendants a better chance at living in peace.

Whenever possible we should conduct our foreign policy without the use of military force. That will not always be possible. When we do use force it needs to be decisive and with a plan to achieve victory! Not just a military victory but also a political victory. We have the most powerful military in human history but we have repeatedly failed to follow up their successes with a meaningful strategic victory. That is the responsibility of the nation's political leadership.

President Obama's decision to cut and run from Iraq and Afghanistan is reprehensible. It is another example of a politician putting himself before the country. He has snatched defeat from the jaws of victory. We still need to secure these countries and solidify our gains. Casualties in Iraq had been very low for some time before we left. Maintaining a presence that is a stabilizing influence like we did in South Korea, Japan, and West Germany would help democratic institutions and processes take hold and strengthen these countries.


### Political Evolution


In many countries that are just beginning as democracies there is too much expectation that they be ready to run a nation as a democratic republic right away. Democracy is about more than just having elections. It requires the development of coalitions and a functioning, effective, and responsive bureaucracy that can get things done according to the policies set by the elected officials. It also requires a judiciary that rules according to laws and not influence.

Especially after living under totalitarian and authoritarian governments people usually have unrealistic expectations about democracy. Democracy is by nature a slow change agent because compromises between many constituencies are needed in order to govern. It can be frustrating waiting for leaders to develop who understand the process and are effective in working the system. This can lead to desires by many for a return to dictatorship in order to provide stability. It is human nature to seek certainty over uncertainty. We need to come alongside these countries and help them through this transition. We can help provide stability during this transition.

There is a tendency among political elites to try to control their countries for their own benefit instead of in the public interest. They concentrate the power and wealth of the country in the hands of a small elite. We need to use our influence to block these unhealthy concentrations of power. We have the technical, political, diplomatic, and economic capability to exert the necessary influence. It must be done to keep these nations from being undermined by cronyism.

Cronyism not only undermines these other nations but makes it more difficult for US businesses to compete globally. It undermines the rule of law and encourages routine bribery and rent seeking. These corrupted governments usually align with major national businesses to control the local market and to gain competitive advantage internationally.

## Protectorates

It is time to revamp how we provide nationbuilding support in some developing countries. Some countries have just been spinning their wheels for decades as one group after another has come to power and milked the country for its own benefit. Rather than just give money and hope that the next clique isn't too bad it is time to set up voluntary protectorates.

A country like the US or a group like the EU or NATO could administer a protectorate for a generation so that the institutions for self-government can be built. This should only be done if the people of the country agree to it in a referendum. To do otherwise invites war. This would involve negotiating a specific constitution for this time period setting what the limits are for the protector and the timeline for the transition to independence.

It would start by bringing in a pared down book of basic laws and regulations to build upon according to the culture of the country. Bringing in advisors to mentor and develop the leaders, bureaucrats, and technicians that are needed to run an efficient civil society.

At the same time we start developing republican democracy at the local level. Over the course of the 20-25 years of the protectorate more and more is turned over to the local people until they are largely running their own country after 15 years and completely running their own country by the end. Running the country with clear and exercised checks and balances on concentrations of power.

During the term of the protectorate the senior levels of the executive and judicial branches of government will be from the US. Each level of courts will transition to locals from the bottom up over the first fifteen to twenty years. During the term of the protectorate the local court cases can be appealed to the US federal court system. Begin using external leaders in the executive branch and promoting locals on merit to move into these executive branch positions over time. The executive authority will gradually transition to locals but for the full term of the protectorate the representative of the US President will hold veto power that can only be overturned by the US President or Congress.

While developing politically we can rapidly bring up the educational and healthcare capabilities of the country. We can provide security for the people to go about their daily lives without fear. As in all areas we should be helping people to help themselves by providing training and mentoring.

As a protectorate they will benefit from increased trade and investment both from a favored status and because of the increased stability. This will amplify the efforts of the protector, create many local jobs, and generate tax revenues to offset much of the costs of development.

The greatest concern with setting this precedent is the possibility of it being abused by countries like Russia or China in order to control other countries for their own political or economic benefit. We need to be willing and able to block coercion even of countries on the periphery of these nations.

## Civilian Stability and Reconstruction Forces

In order to bring about the needed changes in many of the countries we are working with we will need a new force to achieve this in a timely manner. This will be a force that can operate alongside of the military. The primary purpose of the military is to defeat enemy forces. They are needed for security in stability and reconstruction operations. They should not be forced to be too many things and therefore lose their edge in their primary mission of defending the country. The Civilian Stability and Reconstruction Force (CSRF) will be the force to handle the primary reconstruction and development operations.

This is a capability we needed in place before Afghanistan and Iraq. The military has enough on its plate already. The US Agency for International Development and the State Department has tried doing some of this work. Unfortunately it has not been done well and it has not been done quickly and efficiently. This force will have discipline like in the military and go wherever needed and do whatever needed to get civil society up and running again.

They will be capable of going in even as the military is still securing the area and stay long after the military is no longer needed in the area. This force is not just for support of military operations. It will be the lead agency in support of disaster and humanitarian relief operations around the world. They will also have a secondary mission like the National Guard to help in the case of disasters stateside.

Each mission and each project team will be tailored to the needs of the project area. Capabilities should be in place for an immediate jump-start to an area followed by teaching and employing indigenous people to do for themselves.

At the national level the staff will be a cadre of operations management, logistics, and planning staff to coordinate with the State and Defense Departments, NGOs, FEMA, and local governments in the areas of operations.

Most of the force will be in the form of reserves ready to deploy at short notice to foreign and domestic areas of operations. The force should be built to a level of 200,000 screened and trained personnel prepared for deployment over the first ten years. This large of a force is needed because the stability, reconstruction, and nationbuilding operations last a long time. (Hopefully we can get our EU or NATO allies involved in this endeavor with us and take part of the load.) We need to be able to rotate people home regularly.

Whenever possible the teams should be collocated with military posts and reserve component armories to promote their ability to coordinate with each other. These team members will be trained to protect and defend themselves with small arms, hand-to-hand combat, first aid, and other defensive techniques.

The positions would range from general laborers to engineers, doctors, and attorneys. Most of these people will do work similar to their regular work at home. This provides a great depth of education and experience. There needs to be a capability to do everything within the force, if necessary, and transition to an increasing level of indigenous people trained and equipped to do for themselves.

This force should have reemployment rights similar to the military. This is essential for the teams to be ready to deploy on short notice. They can deploy and return to their regular jobs.

The first component of the force is Emergency Relief. This force will provide food, water, sanitation, and healthcare stateside or overseas. This is not necessarily different people than other components just a rapid deployment component.

Following close behind is the Infrastructure Reconstruction component. This is needed to solidify the gains made in the Emergency Relief phase and to add more permanence and local capabilities. These two early phases emphasize making rapid advances for the local population and then on developing local self-sufficiency. This is primarily an overseas component.

The third component will assist the local populace in developing for the long-term. In areas of governance, law enforcement, education, sanitation, healthcare, energy, commerce, infrastructure, and transportation, etc.

The goal is to develop self-supporting democratic republics that will join in supporting the freedom and prosperity of their own citizens and of the world. Building a global coalition of freedom.

## US Nuclear Umbrella

The world has been under threat from a nuclear power who uses the threat of massive nuclear attack as a way to try to get their way in the world. Others may repeat this behavior in the future. Some non-nuclear countries will be cowed into backing down from their legitimate positions. Some with the technical capabilities or the money will obtain nuclear weapons of their own to protect themselves. The world will only become more dangerous with more nuclear armed countries. Even for countries that now would only use them defensively, a far different government may come to power in the future.

The US needs to establish a bipartisan policy of placing our nuclear umbrella over all nonnuclear countries as a cornerstone of our national foreign policy. Any non-allied country that uses a nuclear weapon against a non-nuclear country except as a final defensive measure to prevent the country from being overrun will face a nuclear retaliation from the US. (A nuclear power invaded by a nonnuclear power is not sufficient for this exception. The nuclear power will have to largely exhaust its conventional forces to qualify for this exception.) It will be considered as an attack on the US.

It is expected that any US ally will only use nuclear weapons in retaliation for a nuclear attack. An exception is Israel using tactical nuclear weapons as a final defensive measure if the country is being overrun. It is expected that if small tactical nuclear weapons are used against a US ally that our ally or the US will only retaliate with small tactical nuclear weapons. The US and our allies will seek to minimize civilian casualties as with all other types of weapons.

This is especially important in the near future to our Arab friends facing off with Iran, the former Soviet Union republics like Ukraine, and our Asian friends like Japan, South Korea, Taiwan, and the Philippines. It includes other countries that face threats from the likes of Russia, China, North Korea, and Iran.

## Iraq

In Iraq we need to put together a plan to shore up their defenses and continue training their forces so they are capable of defending their country by themselves. Our commitment should continue for a considerable time, much like our support of South Korea. We will be able to gradually reduce our forces but as long as we are allied we should continue with joint training and networking. Our level of casualties was down considerably when we left and there was increasing stability.

With the departure of US forces from Iraq there was far less influence in favor of moderation between the various factions. The Iranians gained much more influence with the Shiites and ISIS was able to overrun much of the Sunni areas. There has been a general collapse of government control over much of the western part of the country.

After the removal of Saddam Hussein the best course was to try to maintain the unity of Iraq. More should have been done to undercut the forces of division and to build up the democratic institutions. Now there may have been too many sectarian attacks to bring the country back together.

The Kurds have certainly earned the right to their own nation. They have had a semi-autonomous region since after the Gulf War in 1991. The Kurdish areas of Syria should be joined with the Iraqi Kurdish areas. Turkey will not like this initially. A Kurdistan may actually be better for Turkey. With a Kurdish nation the Kurds will need to maintain control of their border with Turkey and work to prevent Kurdish violence in Turkey. Turkish reprisals against Kurdistan will not be as regionally destabilizing as attacks against Kurds in a unified Iraq or Syria. This will incentivize the Kurds to tame the separatists in Turkey. It may also be a magnet for Kurds to emigrate from Turkey and a place to exile undesirable Kurds from Turkey.

The Sunni areas of Iraq present a different problem. There is much intermingling with Shiite areas in the central part of Iraq. Making the division in these areas could lead to great violence if not managed well. It may be beneficial to join Sunni Iraq with Syria. It would be better if the Shiite and Sunni factions in Iraq could learn to work together to avoid the severe violence that would likely occur in a separation.

The preceding is focused on the future. Too often the question of whether we should have gone into Iraq in 2003 is brought up in political campaigns. Because of the demagoguery by opportunistic politicians many have become confused about the lead up to the invasion. Saddam Hussein had a history of using chemical weapons against Iran and his own people. After the 1991 Gulf War, Iraq was required to destroy their WMD capabilities. Saddam Hussein frustrated the efforts of UN inspectors for many years by hiding his chemical weapons and other WMD capabilities. In 1998, Hussein kicked the UN inspectors out of Iraq. At that time, it was believed that Iraq was still hiding large stockpiles of chemical weapons.

In 2002 renewed efforts were made to bring Iraq into compliance with UN resolutions and their agreement to destroy their WMD capabilities. The Iraqis again made it difficult for inspectors to inspect facilities. This gave the impression that the Iraqis were trying to hide their chemical weapons. There were also communications intercepts appearing to show the Iraqi military taking account of their chemical weapon stocks. There was evidence that Iraq was conducting research on biological and nuclear weapons, UAVs, and ballistic missiles. All in violation of UN resolutions.

We had the history of the Iraqi government in obstructing inspections and hiding their WMD capabilities. A strong belief that they still had large stockpiles of chemicals. There was no reason to believe that they had destroyed their stockpiles after UN inspectors had been kicked out of the country. It would have been irresponsible to assume that the Iraqis had destroyed their stockpiles. It would have been irresponsible to assume that if sanctions were lifted Saddam Hussein would not pursue WMD further in the future.

After the war it was determined that most of Iraq's chemical weapons had been destroyed during the 1990s. There were some remaining in small numbers around Iraq and in the remains of bunkers bombed during the first Gulf War. It was also determined that Iraq had active WMD, ballistic missile, and UAV research programs and that they intended to reconstitute these capabilities following the lifting of sanctions.

Between the two wars in 1991 and 2003 Iraq was restricted to selling only enough oil to pay for humanitarian needs such as food and medicine. They frequently circumvented these limits by bribing UN officials to sell more oil illegally. Sanctions limited the ability of Iraq to pursue WMD and limited their economy but the burden of the sanctions fell on the Iraqi people far more than the leadership. In 2003 there was already a movement to end the sanctions against Iraq. It was likely that if the US had not invaded Iraq in 2003 the sanctions would have been lifted soon after. Then Iraq would have been able to produce ballistic missiles and chemical, biological, and nuclear weapons shortly after this. Evidence discovered after the war showed that Iraq was less than five years away from being able to produce a nuclear weapon.

Besides the WMD argument, Iraq was the best candidate to try to bring a democratic republic to the Muslim Middle East. There was an enemy dictator ruling who was in repeated defiance of UN resolutions. He had repeatedly attacked his own people and neighboring countries. Iraq was centrally located in the region.

Until people have the political and economic freedom to have a reasonable level of say over their own life there will be instability and a susceptibility to radicalism. This is found around the world. In the Middle East the radical ideology is Islamism. In the 20th Century the scourge of socialism, both communist and fascist were prominent. Anarchists and street gangs are symptoms of the same sense of powerlessness over one's life.

The only thing that has been keeping radical political Islam at bay has been the authoritarian regimes in the Middle East. But the repression that these regimes use can only contain the pressure for a limited period of time.

Eventually this type of system will always collapse. While it is better if a gradual transition to a liberal democratic republic is done systematically there were no volunteers. Saddam Hussein in Iraq was a threat that needed to be deposed making Iraq the place to start changing the Middle East.

Unfortunately the US leadership had an unrealistic expectation that the Iraqi people would just spontaneously embrace democracy. A country that does not have a history of democracy or a strong opposition movement embracing principles of freedom needs at least a generation to make the transition. It requires the development of a new worldview among the people and the elites.

The US did not prepare for the aftermath of destroying the Iraqi military and political power structure. With all of the experience and education in the leadership of the Administration and State and Defense Departments it is difficult to understand how such a significant lapse could occur.

The decision to go into Iraq in 2003 was the correct decision. Unfortunately the political leadership of the US was not prepared for the time after the military victory. This has been a consistent problem for the US since the 1960s. The military delivers the wins on the battlefield but Washington does not achieve the overall strategic political victory. In many cases they do not seem to realize that is their responsibility.

## Syria

The Arab Spring supporters in Syria were initially protesting peacefully for months. They tried to have a nonviolent protest to obtain democratic reforms. The US failed to support these efforts even when Assad sent military forces to shoot, bomb, and gas unarmed civilians. Then President Obama doubled down on his failure to support the Syrian people by not preventing the rise of ISIS. Now the prodemocracy people of Syria are caught between the murderous forces of Assad and ISIS.

What we need to do is set up refugee camps separate from the UN and NGOs. In our camps we should be providing education for the children so they do not keep falling behind during the war. Alongside of the refugee camps we should set up training bases for a Free Syrian Army. We will then train and equip and lead a professional Free Syrian Army. These soldiers should have to have family and friend references from among the refugees in our camps.

The mission should be regime change and the creation of a democratic republic. It is in our national interest to have a stable, friendly, self-governing state in Syria and in every other part of the world. Whether it is Islamists or criminal syndicates, these areas are a draw to evil players. Lawless areas weaken freedom and create danger for locals and the rest of the world.

As a condition for help the majority of the Syrian refugees will have to agree to a basic set of minimums for a new Constitution and set of laws. We will establish our minimums and then those refugees who agree can move to our camps. They will then elect their own representatives to expand on the Constitution and laws as they see fit as long as it does not contradict the base minimums we set.

As we help establish free areas in Syria we assist in reconstruction and development of local government and institutions. Part of this must include civics education for all people in the details of being an active part of a republic.

## Libya

Muammar Qaddafi was a murderous dictator and terrorist. When the US and NATO intervened he was sending his army to attack prodemocracy Arab Spring rebels in Benghazi. That attack was thwarted and we continued to aid the anti-Qaddafi militias in fighting the government. In a short time Qaddafi was dead and various militias controlled different parts of the country.

When we went into Iraq it was political and policy malpractice to not have a comprehensive plan for the reconstruction and development of the country after they were defeated militarily. There has been enough examples from history showing the instability when nations lose wars and when authoritarian governments are overthrown. Given the recent experience in Iraq, the fact that Obama and NATO did not have a plan to help Libya transition to a democratic republic is malpractice of the highest order.

Now we have near anarchy reigning in Libya. Militias allied with different government factions, different tribes, ISIS, al-Qaeda, and criminal gangs rule parts of the country. Europe is being flooded by refugees from Libya and from other parts of Africa flowing through Libya.

We need to put together a Free Libyan Army under a plan similar to Syria to bring stability to Libya. Then work closely with the new Libyan government for the next generation to shepherd them into a developed democratic republic.

## Afghanistan, Pakistan, and Central and South Asia

We have been struggling in Afghanistan, Pakistan, and the rest of Central Asia because we have been taking too many half measures. We have repeatedly tried to get by with the minimum forces and effort. This has kept us from even dreaming of victory much less striving for it. We should not send our soldiers into combat without having a goal of victory. It is cruel and immoral. Through fifteen years and two Presidents our government has not convinced itself that it can achieve victory.

Victory is possible and should be our goal. We have to stop the half measures and go all out for victory. It will cost fewer lives and less money in the long run than half measures. We must return to the counterinsurgency strategy in Afghanistan but it needs to be fully resourced with sufficient military and civilian forces. In war we must press the enemy from every direction possible and keep on pressing until they beg for peace.

As Clausewitz said, war is a continuation of politics by other means. A political solution will be needed to end the war. But in order to reach the point where a suitable political solution is possible we need to exhaust the enemy without exhausting ourselves. Year after year of half measures is exhausting our endurance and patience even though we have used so little of our strength.

This matter of half measures includes our dealings with Pakistan. We have failed to find a solution to the sanctuaries in Pakistan. Pakistan has resisted eliminating them for their own political and security interests. We must present another way for them to meet their political and security needs without the Taliban, Haqqani network, and other destabilizing groups.

We need a "Marshall Plan" for all of Central and South Asia to bring stability and economic and political growth and liberty to the whole area. We did this kind of nationbuilding after World War II to rebuild Western Europe and help hold back the influence of communism. There are many isms seeking power in Central Asia. With a concerted effort we can help build an interconnected region that can easily trade with each other and the rest of the world. We can help them reach the point where they can manage and pay for their own security and grow their own prosperity. There is great potential for trade and development in the region.

The key country in this region is Pakistan. We must ally ourselves with those in Pakistan that will be good allies to us and isolate and help to diminish the power and influence of those who are opposed to us or who are playing both sides. By helping them with development and making them stronger with increased economic and political liberty we can give them the internal strength to take on groups like the Taliban, Haqqani network, and to secure the frontier provinces. It is in our national security interest to help Pakistan to become a stable, self-sufficient, and self-confident country that ceases needing to control or undercut its neighbors.

Along with the development and trade assistance to Pakistan we also have to make it clear that if they do not control their own territory we will. One of the core functions of government is to control and administer their own territory. We should do anything reasonable to help them to become capable of doing this on their own. Training and equipment for security forces and economic development will help but they have to have the will and the drive to do it themselves. If they cannot do this on their own within a reasonable amount of time then we will have to do it for them.

The other countries of Central Asia would benefit greatly by a stable trade route through Afghanistan and Pakistan. It would reduce their dependence on Russia or China. They would have more opportunities then to develop free republics instead of oligarchic puppets aligned by necessity to Russia or China.

## China

We have a very complex relationship with China. They are now the number two economy in the world with about half the economic output of the US. They are a major trading partner of ours and of many of our allies. They have been greatly expanding their military capabilities including stealth aircraft, an aircraft carrier, and a variety of improved missiles.

They have been more aggressive with their neighbors. Challenging Vietnam, Taiwan, Malaysia, Brunei, and the Philippines over control of the South China Sea, through which 25 percent of the world's shipping transits. China is trying to drive the others out and claim sovereignty over the sea both for the energy supplies underneath and for control of such a significant transit route. Like most bullies they are trying to get their neighbors to be conditioned to accepting their intimidation. The US is the only country with the strength to aid these countries in standing up to China.

China has been putting pressure on their other neighbors like Japan and India. They are competing for control over islands and the sea between China and Japan. They have had a long running dispute with India over the location of the border.

China is also trying to pressure the US into not supporting Taiwan. They regularly threaten Taiwan and have large military forces positioned opposite the island. Taiwan is a vital US ally that needs to be supported and not abandoned.

Our trade with China is enormous and likely to grow larger. We have some serious outstanding trade issues regarding intellectual property rights, other property rights, counterfeiting and product piracy. China also has major instability issues due to government subsidies causing inefficient allocation of resources, causing bubbles in housing and other sectors in China. We need to put pressure on the Chinese government to keep moving toward being a nation of laws and not connections. Protections and respect for personal and property rights need to be strengthened.

There is growing discontent in China with the Communist Party over arbitrary rule, suppression of political, religious, and cultural dissent, suppression of information, and preferential treatment of state companies.

Many Chinese are moving more of their wealth overseas to hedge against problems in China. We need to help facilitate change in China toward more economic, political, and religious freedom. It is better if these changes occur peacefully and gradually and not in a sudden collapse of the country.

There are frequent reports of Chinese computer hacking of US and allied government, industrial, and research databases. Public reports usually do not definitively show that the Chinese government is the hacker but it is highly likely. Regardless of who is doing it we must have cyber security forces in place to defend and to counterattack the attackers. As we have in other areas of warfare, we need to be a couple generations ahead of our enemies in this area as well.

China is not capable of going to war with us now. They are a prisoner to trade. They are too dependent upon outside energy and other resources to sustain a war with us. By using standoff weapons we can shut down their ports and power plants and bring their economy to a standstill. This will reduce their ability to sustain a major conventional conflict.

They do not have the naval forces to protect their trade routes. They can bring large forces to bear only near their borders. That is why we need to maintain sufficient air and naval forces to aid our allies that live near China. Without the US having their back diplomatically, politically, and militarily they could be overrun relatively quickly. We also need to keep pressure on China to try to bring liberty and democracy to the Chinese people before they become powerful enough to consider challenging us militarily away from their borders.


## Russia

(The first part of this section was written for the 2012 edition. It is left intact to provide some context for what follows.)

With Russia we have many similar problems as with China but to a different degree. They have the heart of a superpower without the body (economic strength) for it. They want to have undue influence upon their smaller neighbors. But if they did not have nuclear weapons the eastern half of Russia would be part of China.

The political power is concentrated in the hands of Vladimir Putin and his United Russia Party. Even with their disappointing results in the 2011 legislative elections the United Russia Party is still in control. Only time will tell if Putin will accept a loss in power or make sure that no one can challenge him with more repression.

We have to keep pushing a freedom agenda with respect for individual liberty, secure property rights, and the rule of law. Our relationship with Russia is important but it is foolish to think that there will ever be a good relationship without true liberty for the Russian people.

We need to support the other former Soviet republics in maintaining their independence. They do not have the strength on their own to resist an aggressive or even a merely assertive Russia. In the long run it will be better for Russia as well as their neighbors if clear boundaries in behavior are established where Russia is not trying to control its neighbors. A model more on the order of the European Union of independent nations freely joining together should be encouraged. It is most likely that the EU will expand to Russia's neighbors before Russia has matured enough to build a separate block. So the encouragement should be to proceed along both paths but not be married to either.

Russia can be a superpower again but it will have to trust in the free market, respect property rights, and develop the institutions of a truly free representative democracy. Among the Russian people there is too much pessimism to really grow the country without serious reforms. The country is dying right now. The backlash against corruption this year is hopefully the start of the necessary reforms. Russia needs the West. We should help them evolve into a strong federal republic that respects the rights of its citizens. A country we can be allied with. This will frequently be done with diplomatic tough love.

**The preceding Russia section was written in 2012. Much has happened since then.** Russia under Putin has embarked on an effort to undermine the European Union, NATO, the Ukrainian reform movement, the post-World War Two international order, and the US relationship with the rest of the world. Given the weak hand that Russia holds they have done remarkably well.

Putin is very much an opportunist. He has recognized the weak leadership in the US and EU. He has exploited this weakness to achieve gains and will be seeking to lock them in before the new US president is elected in 2016. He will continue to look for opportunities to exploit. The only way to stop him is to confront every move, roll back his gains outside Russia, and contain him.

In Ukraine he has seized Crimea and part of the Lugansk and Donetsk regions in the east. He continues to undermine the political process in Ukraine with the war and promotion of corruption. Russia does not have the combat power to occupy much of Ukraine but they do have enough to lay waste to large parts of the east.

The Russian government is like an association of mafia families aligned for the purpose of acquiring power and wealth. They do not want to end that. Right now Putin is the "Boss of Bosses". They will put a bullet in the back of Putin's head when he goes too far and it will just be "business". They will let him push forward as far as he can take them. When he becomes a liability he will be gone and they will regroup to try another way. Their own version of a "reset."

The Russian government and economy are brittle. The US and EU need to have plans for when both collapse. It will be a very dangerous time but an opportunity to help guide the Russian people to freedom.

## Ukraine

There is a dual war in progress. The first is the war with Russia. The second is the war to reform Ukraine into a nation without systemic corruption and with political freedom and free markets. It is in this second area that Russia and Ukraine's oligarchs are allies. Both have a strong interest in preventing reforms. They will lose substantial influence and power over Ukraine.

To the extent that the oligarchs "fought" for or sided with Ukraine over Russia it had more to do with trying to keep control over their personal empires. With Russian domination the Ukrainian oligarchs would have been subject to Putin and their business rivals, the Russian oligarchs. This would be a step down from their control over substantial segments of Ukraine. They can be counted on to work to counter a Russian victory but also to counter reforms.

Having studied how Putin and the oligarchs have operated in the past it is likely that there is an understanding that if the oligarchs can derail the reforms sufficiently Russia will come to an accommodation with them over control of Ukraine. This is likely one of the factors keeping more extensive Russian military advances from occurring. Much like feudal lords supporting a foreign king in order to maintain their fiefdom.

### Ukrainian Economy

The economy of Ukraine is held back by five major interrelated forces:

1. The war with Russia.
2. The power and corruption of the oligarchs.
3. The arbitrary power and corruption of the judicial, prosecution, and overall legal system.
4. The arbitrary power and corruption of the bureaucracy manipulating excessive and conflicting government regulations.
5. The transfer of the national wealth from the Ukrainian people to select insiders through manipulation of the government.

These forces must be attacked systemically and simultaneously. The relationships or points of connection between the oligarchs and other "clusters" of corruption should be hit hard. Squeeze their sources of revenue and freeze their assets so they cannot pay off politicians and bureaucrats or hire thugs to intimidate. Much as in a military campaign, breaking up the enemy's cohesion and ability to be mutually supportive.

In the US military there is a concept known as using combinations to cause the enemy dilemmas. It involves the use of complementary and reinforcing means of attack that overwhelm an enemy by only allowing him bad options for response. The strategy for aiding reformers in Ukraine should include a plan to defeat the centers of power that are in opposition.

A significant part of this will include linking reforms to targeted support from the US, EU, IMF, and other foreign supporters. It is better if this is done at the request of Ukraine than forced by outside powers. The Ukrainian leadership needs to find a way to do this to block the anti-reformers.

Another essential component is getting the sequencing of reforms right. The constitutional reforms, division of power reforms (In the Constitution and in the supporting laws), judicial reforms, and legal system reforms have to be done first. These are the areas which could allow anti-reform forces to undercut or reverse the new legislation in other areas. Reforming these areas will also open up many avenues of attack in the courts on corrupt powers involving criminal and contractual accountability.

With an ongoing war, military and security reform is just as vital. The very survival of the nation depends upon it. This reform has already been moving too slow. The national political leadership has to force the military leadership to greatly expedite the transition to a modern doctrine, tactics, and force structure. New equipment needs to be brought into service faster. A clear path has to be laid out to reach a regionally dominant level of combat power within two years. This is entirely possible, the will to do it just has to be there. The US can support this with modern training and equipment. Ukrainian soldiers have shown great courage and stubbornness in defending the country even when outnumbered and outgunned. They can defeat the invader themselves if properly trained, equipped, and led.

Beyond these areas the next vital areas to address are tax, energy sector, regulatory, media ownership, and election reforms. These will have the greatest negative impact on the power and finances of the corrupting powers as well as having a substantial positive impact on the economy and foreign investment. The economy needs to be greatly improved for Ukraine to afford to make the changes and to pay for the war. This hierarchy is not to say that any area should be left to wait. The urgency of all of these areas is such that they should be prepared and implemented as quickly as possible.

The US needs to work with others who seek to bring more freedom and liberty to Ukraine. Especially in working to develop an actionable plan and then executing the plan. Most important is working with the many reformers and reform groups in Ukraine. The EU needs to renew its belief in the values of freedom and self-determination and join in aiding the Ukrainian people in achieving freedom from war and corruption.

## Ukrainian Unity

The Ukrainian people need to find a way to unify. The Russian invasion has actually helped to unify large sections of the country in defense of the country. But it has also resulted in greater differences with those who identify with Russia and the separatists.

Significant progress on reforms will show people that the government and the people from other parts of the country care. Until then this is just a power struggle between different factions that seek to exploit Ukraine. There will never be unity as long as that belief holds power.

Develop and employ precision weapons such as enhanced fiber optic guided missiles to attack Russian artillery and other weapons in close proximity to civilians. Stop firing "dumb" artillery and rockets into civilian areas.

The government needs to start emulating the many church groups and NGOs in the country that are coming to the aid of IDPs and those in the war zone. In the front line cities have people organizing unemployed people to take care of their cities. Rebuilding damaged homes, clearing rubble, distributing food and water, and providing medical care, etc. Restoring services such as water, gas, electricity, and schools as soon as possible or arranging some type of local solution. Prepare comprehensive evacuation plans that allow people to be quickly evacuated when major attacks occur.

Provide daily mass communication by television and radio in the east to counter the Russian propaganda.

Decentralize issues and authority that does not need to be handled by a central government. Empowering people to have a say over local issues will reduce their frustration with the central government. It will reduce the effectiveness of political factions pitting regions against each other over allocation of government resources.

## Breaking The Oligarchs

Breaking the oligarchs requires disrupting their revenue streams and depleting their cash reserves. Much of their legitimate business operations are inefficient compared to US, EU, and Japanese businesses. The profit margins from many of these operations are small or non-existent. It is from the corruption schemes that much of the "profits" come from. Depleting their resources will make it more difficult to buy support and influence.

There are several things that need to happen to break the control by the oligarchs.

1. Take away the corrupt revenue streams from government coffers.
2. Replace the entire judiciary and prosecutor system. Revamp the whole legal system.
3. Prosecuting according to the law and not the bribe.
4. Honoring contracts and property rights.

5. Break up monopolies. Pass laws that no more than 20 percent of any major industry can be owned by the same owner or syndicate. Some sectors may need to be limited to 10 percent or less.

6. Diversify mass media ownership. Limit an individual to five percent ownership of a single television station and a single radio station in each media market. Require that at least ten people are needed to achieve 25 percent ownership, that at least 200 people are needed to achieve a majority of ownership, and that at least 1,000 beneficial owners are needed for each company.

6. Banking reform. There needs to be a separation between financial institutions and nonfinancial institutions. Prevent self-dealing.

7. Require a review of all past privatizations of public property. Require that fair market value was obtained or reclaim all or part of the property for reauction.

8. Privatize most of the property owned by the Ukrainian government. This includes the defense industry, energy infrastructure, agricultural land, and forests. These nationalized enterprises are overrun with rent seekers working in collusion with the oligarchs and other corrupt people. Privatization will put owners interested in protecting and profiting from their investments in control of these assets instead of bureaucrats and their cronies who profit from exploiting the enterprise.

9. Over the next few years foreign countries need to aggressively investigate and prosecute the oligarchs and organized crime groups that are fighting against reforms in Ukraine. This will be a great way to occupy their time and consume their resources. Reducing their effectiveness at fighting the reforms during this crucial time period. As part of these prosecutions, their assets should be frozen when possible.

### Russia and Ukraine

Putin will try to take advantage of any opportunity that he believes will benefit Vladimir Putin. In Ukraine his preference is to swallow Ukraine whole if he could do it without making Russia unstable. So the continuing open defiance of him by Ukrainians along with improving capabilities to resist his forces can prevent this. He does not consider Ukraine to be a country but a part of Russia.

Since he could not keep political control over Ukraine with the ouster of Yanukovych Putin tried to carve off the eastern and southern regions from Ukraine. He will continue to try if he can do so at a reasonable cost. Here again, Ukrainian resolve to fight any attempt to take the eastern oblasts will likely give him pause.

Continuing to keep Ukraine unstable is Putin's most likely course of future action. By sending small forces into the east he can keep the country from unifying. Over time it has driven out the more pro-Ukraine people who want to feel safe again. (A New Russification.) This will change the makeup and sentiment of the remaining population. This strategy will also drain away resources and focus of the leaders and people of Ukraine, slowing down improvements in other areas such as the economy and anti-corruption reforms. Maintaining a "disputed area" will prevent any attempt to join NATO or become full members of the EU. If the east is not recovered it will make the rest of Ukraine more susceptible to further Balkanization.

In the future it will be necessary for Ukraine to secure the border with Russia and prevent continued artillery attacks on the country from Russia. Because even if Ukraine can defeat and drive the Russian forces out of Ukraine it will not likely end attacks from Russian territory without a proven capability and willingness to strike Russian forces inside Russia.

As Ukraine becomes more capable, Russia will ratchet up the pressure to try to keep Ukraine down. In the military area this currently involves the continued pressure on the front lines to slowly push further into Ukraine. This will likely continue indefinitely because it is working. Ukraine has not been able to control the whole line of contact so there are weak points that the Russians take advantage of. Additionally, the West is not increasing sanctions when they do it.

The exception to this is the possibility that Putin will believe he has to break the reform movement in Ukraine and force a new government in 2016 before a new President is elected in the US. This new President may be more active in aiding reforms and in arming Ukraine. If this becomes more likely Putin is more likely to dramatically increase the pressure on Ukraine. Only time will tell if he decides he needs to break Ukraine and lock in his gains before 2017.

In the future when Ukraine goes on the offensive again to recover the occupied areas Russia will keep increasing their forces to the level needed to defeat the Ukrainian forces. And they will "justify" it in the world press by claiming it is to prevent ethnic cleansing by Ukrainian forces. They are likely to be able to minimize any further sanctions by claiming that Ukraine is violating the Minsk Agreements.

Politically and diplomatically Putin would prefer to wait for Ukraine to try to retake the occupied areas in order to have an excuse for a massive attack into Ukraine. Militarily he needs to have that happen before Ukraine is strong enough to defeat the Russian military. He can be counted on to periodically try to instigate an attack by Ukraine while at the same time working to undermine reforms in Ukraine. Not responding to provocations will be demoralizing to the Ukrainian military and people. Ukraine needs to prepare the military to achieve an offensive victory as soon as possible before inaction in the face of provocation brings down the government.

On paper the Russian military appears massive with a lot of equipment. Especially in comparison to Ukraine. But Russia suffers from many of the same constraints as Ukraine does plus some of their own. Their system is riddled with corruption which makes efficiency impossible. While they have small numbers of newer, advanced equipment, most of their equipment is old. Much of their force still depends upon short term conscripts. Their military operations are still largely centrally planned and controlled. They have a huge territory to control and many forces that would welcome a weakness in the control from the central government. They have real security issues in the Caucasus and Far East in terms of maintaining their control. They believe they have to be concerned about NATO from the west. This forces them to spread out the forces they have available.

That last issue plays a major part in leveling the playing field for Ukraine. Russia is not likely to be able to muster more than 150,000 trained ground troops for use in Ukraine and along the border. Even to achieve that will require a serious depletion of the contract soldiers in other areas or the reliance on more conscripts. Rather than thinking in terms of the whole Russian military, Ukraine only has to concern itself with what Russia can actually bring to bear against Ukraine. This makes for a more manageable problem.

The Russian Navy has a limited ability to cause damage along the coast but very little capability to project further into the country. There is a small number of vessels that could actually land troops amphibiously. The Russians are not known to have strong capabilities in suppression of enemy air defenses making airborne and airmobile assaults unlikely.

The US needs to support Ukraine with training and equipment. Many observers believe that Russia has escalation dominance in Ukraine. That is true only up to a certain point. They have limited resources as well. Ukrainian soldiers have proven courageous and tenacious fighters in defending their country. With US quality training and modern equipment they can defend their own country.

The US can keep strong pressure on Russia in ways that do not involve combat. The US and EU sanctions are more of a political statement than an economic impediment to Russia. The greatest economic issue for Russia is the low prices for oil and natural gas. The US can aid in keeping these prices low by fully opening US oil and gas for export. This will continue to drain Russian cash reserves.

Another method to put pressure on Russia is demographically. Russia already has a declining population. It is only the Muslim population that is growing. The ethnic Russian population is dropping dramatically. This is already considered a strategic threat by Russia. We could put on additional pressure. Set up a special emigration program for ethnic Russian women aged 20-35. There are about 750,000 women entering this age group each year. Allowing 350,000 women to emigrate each year would cut the ethnic Russian population in half in less than a generation. We could enhance the impact by prioritizing those with a university education. We could further enhance this by only considering unmarried women without children. Any women interested in emigrating would avoid marriage and pregnancy to maintain their eligibility. This will depress the birthrate of those who remain in Russia. Ideally our European allies will join us in inviting Russian women to emigrate to their countries as well. We will not have to wait for a generation to get results. The Russians and any potential investors or lenders know the damage this will cause to Russia. There will be an immediate reaction to downgrade Russia's economic prospects. Russia would have to react to such a threat but it would be difficult to do so militarily. It would be impossible to keep these women from leaving the country. They will show their lack of faith in the future prospects of Russia under Putin by voting with their feet. It could provide considerable leverage to push for reforms in Russia. Putin is not the only one who can think asymmetrically.

## Russia and Syria

There has been much speculation and concern about the goals of Putin in Syria. Many commentators, including President Obama have said that Putin is making a serious mistake getting involved in the mess that is Syria. From the perspective of a Western politician that would certainly be true. But for an authoritarian country like Russia winning is measured differently.

The first and most obvious benefit to the Russian intervention in Syria is to prop up the faltering Assad regime. Syria, a longtime client state of Russia and the Soviet Union is a valuable foothold for Russia in the Middle East. Russia is supporting Iranian development of a Shiite power arc that stretches from Western Afghanistan to Lebanon through Iran, Iraq, and Syria.

Keeping Assad in power is the preferred result for Russia. It is necessary to prevent either ISIS, a Turkish client state, a Sunni-led authoritarian state or a Western backed democracy from coming to power in Syria. Of these four options, an ISIS state would be the preferred outcome for Putin. But it would only be temporary because it would force the West to become much more involved in removing ISIS and installing one of the other options. Stability and nonalignment with Russia would eventually result in gas and oil pipelines from the Arabian Peninsula to Turkey and Europe. Undercutting the Russian efforts to control the European market. For Putin, Assad does not have to win, he just has to survive. Putin needs to prevent anyone aligned with the West from winning.

The Russians call all of the anti-Assad forces terrorists and consider them all legitimate targets. Putin does not respect the Western Allies enough to even blame a lack of cooperation for the attacks on western backed rebels. He thumbs his nose because he understands the moral weakness in the current Western leadership.

The West is spending billions in Syria and Iraq with few signs of success. Russia can spend far less to prevent a Western victory in the Middle East. While the Obama administration is not likely to change course and work for a victory the next administration is likely to be far more assertive in achieving some type of success in Syria and Iraq. Regime change in Syria will have to be a part of that. With Russia and China providing protection for Assad any efforts in Syria will have to be worked out with them. In addition to their veto in the UN they now have a veto on the ground. As long as the West cannot stabilize the Middle East they will not be able to shift more attention to Ukraine or East Asia. This will give Russia and China more space to maneuver in areas that are even more important to them.

The other significant opportunity that has fallen into Putin's lap is the refugee crisis in Europe. The world has witnessed the strain on European cohesion. The EU has already been under strain from many issues including; differences between the creditor and debtor nations, a sluggish economy, austerity measures, unemployment, separatism, sanctions on Russia, and numerous sovereignty issues.

In the near future the pressure to do something about the refugee crisis at the source may have resulted in an operation to create safe areas and/or regime change in Syria. The Russian forces in Syria certainly complicates such a scenario if not making it impossible. They will most likely insist that any safe areas be under the authority of the Syrian government. Any attempts at regime change will run the risk of incidents between Allied and Russian forces.

Two-thirds of the Syrian refugees are displaced internally. Putin can influence and facilitate their mass migration to Syria's neighbors and then on to Europe to cause more disruption. Already Turkey, Jordan, and Lebanon are under great strain from the large numbers of refugees on their territory. Pressuring the Sunni internally displaced persons to flee Syria will make the country's demographics more favorable for the ruling Alawites. With another huge influx of refugees Syria's neighbors may close their borders or facilitate the movement of refugees to other countries. Russian intelligence working through organized crime groups can use the flow of refugees to put pressure on the EU. This is another front in Putin's war to fracture the EU and NATO for strategic advantage. By driving those IDPs that are undesirable to the Syrian regime to Europe they can further destabilize the EU.

Putin has already been quite successful in fomenting division in the EU. He has long manipulated CEOs and government officials with differential gas prices. In 2015 he was able to get Germany to betray Ukraine and much of Eastern Europe with the Nord Stream Two agreement. There is division in the EU about sanctions against Russia. Many want to restore trade with Russia to help the EU economy. Russia and their European apologists are using Russian proposals to fight ISIS as another excuse to normalize relations with Russia.

Putin has provided funding to fringe political parties on the left and the right throughout Europe. Many of these parties already have an anti-EU platform. The rightwing parties also tend to be anti-immigrant and nationalist. Putin can further aid these groups by flooding Europe with refugees, especially Muslim refugees. These parties are already using the refugee crisis to stir up a populist backlash against immigrants and the EU system. Even if these fringe parties do not come to power it puts pressure on the mainstream parties to adopt some of their positions.

European countries have already closed some of their previously open borders. When several million more refugees show up on European shores the crisis will become much worse. Extreme left and right wing political parties have already been gaining support in Europe due to the economic stagnation and perceptions of loss of national sovereignty to the EU. Millions of Muslim refugees will only exasperate this problem. As public and political resistance to the immigrants builds the humanitarian situation of the refugees will worsen.

In the midst of the refugees there are Islamist radicals. They will use any humanitarian problems in Europe to help radicalize more refugees to continue their war against "infidels" in Europe. The alienation that many of these immigrants will feel because of the increasingly unwelcoming reception they receive, especially among young men, will drive more into the arms of the Islamists. This will increase the terrorist threat, further destabilizing Europe.

While Russia did not start the refugee crisis they have found a way to exploit it to further their hybrid war against Europe! While the direct benefits of intervention in Syria are valuable to the anti-West coalition that Russia is forming, the far greater benefit could be a devastating flank attack on European Unity!

## Israel

Israel is our best friend in the Middle East and we need to continue to support them. It is outrageous that President Obama is undercutting the Israelis with talk about going back to 1967 borders and criticism for new construction in Jewish areas. We need to make our continued support of Israel and its right to exist clear.

The Palestinians have repeatedly rejected reasonable two state solutions. We should still try to influence change in the West Bank and Gaza to promote liberty, rule of law, education without hate, and trade. Parents need to be encouraged to stop the hatred that is holding back their children. They should not get any support for pressure on Israel to forgo adequate security assurances.

Those that still attack Israel need to be put down. Israel has the right to self-defense and should exercise it as needed. The US needs to back up that right and encourage other nations to support it.

## Iran

Iran cannot be allowed to have nuclear weapons. The apocalyptic world view of the Islamic Revolutionary leadership makes it too likely that they will use it if they have it. It is foolish to think that others will not live by their values and act according to their worldview. We are the only country that is equipped and capable of stopping them from getting nuclear weapons. It is clear that they will not be induced to stop themselves. Unless they are overthrown internally we will eventually have to use military force to stop them from getting a nuclear weapon.

The nuclear agreement will not stop them. Germany has already reported that Iran is trying to purchase new equipment for their nuclear program. There are too many flaws with the agreement. Every suspect site must be searchable by independent inspectors at any time without exception. Every infraction of the agreement should be responded to immediately and without exception to drive the point home that we will not let up. This will keep their infractions in front of the world even without sanctions. It will create enough instability that much new investment will be held back. Over time they will comply or we will get more sanctions reinstated. If that is ineffective we must go in and destroy their nuclear and ballistic missile capabilities, Revolutionary Guards, and regular military.

US and EU banks and corporations should not be permitted to lend to Iran. This will put them at risk of losing these funds when sanctions are reimposed. Even worse these corporations will put political pressure on their governments not to reimpose sanctions in order to continue getting paid.

In the meantime we have to make every effort to slow them down in every area possible until a true secular democratic republic exists in Iran. We can help keep oil prices down by fully opening US oil to the world market. We have to restart sanctions when they violate the agreement. This will limit their economic capabilities. We have to be assertive with reconnaissance, covert actions, sabotage, cyber-attacks, etc. We can undermine their influence in Iraq, destroy their forces in Syria, undermine Hezbollah and Hamas, and support the Saudis against the Houthis in Yemen.

## Korea

South Korea is our ally and we should generally work for a unified front in dealing with North Korea. The regime in North Korea is a worthless bunch of thugs that are destroying its own people. There should be continuous pressure on the regime until it collapses or reforms. No aid should be given except in direct exchange for weapons grade uranium or plutonium. If they sink a navy vessel we should sink five of theirs. If they shell an island we should destroy a couple artillery batteries. Attacks should never be tolerated. Again, the South Korean government's position has to be respected because any escalation will affect them the most.

In the meantime we should get the six-party talks going again. We should encourage change that could lead to reunification under the South Korean model. Offer a truth and reconciliation model like South Africa for crimes against humanity committed in the North. South Korea could offer that any sentences for lesser felonies would receive amnesty and serious felonies would receive reasonable sentences served in house arrest with work release privileges. The serious felons should also be barred from holding political office, working for any government entity, and not be allowed to vote for the duration of their sentences. Any crimes not confessed to the truth and reconciliation commission should be prosecutable with regular penalties for guilty verdicts. Anything confessed should be able to be used against the person if they commit a similar crime after reunification. If there is a war that results in reunification then anyone who aids the quick collapse of their military unit or the regime or actively prevents the use of weapons of mass destruction should be granted amnesty for other crimes. These proposals should be prominently advertised and promoted by all possible means in the north.

In order to maintain stability there should be martial law for the first couple of years in the north. This will be a time of great change and as history shows there will be a degree of chaos and criminality by many in a population immediately following release from repressive governments. The moral fabric of society is eroded by these types of governments as people struggle to survive. It is better to have tight security initially and ease it off gradually as people learn a new way to live. We failed to do this in Iraq and it put us on the defensive for many years.

In a similar vein political freedom should be brought about gradually. This is mostly because they don't have experience in self-government. Also in part it is because of the cult of personality present in the north. The last thing we would want is to win the war and have much of the north vote for a member of the Kim family. After the initial relief phase and people are starting to build new lives then everyone should undergo civics education to learn about democracy and representative government and their rights and responsibilities in this system. As soon as possible, this will vary by locality, local leaders should be elected to run things at the local level. A few years later regional/provincial leaders should be elected. A few years later advisory representatives should be elected to the national legislature with the power to participate in debate but not yet vote on legislation. A few years later full members of the legislature should be elected. A few years after this the northerners should be able to vote for the President. Depending on the situation on the ground this full transition could be done in fifteen to twenty-five years.

If there is reunification then we and the rest of the free world need to support the South in stabilizing and rebuilding the North. We should offer to China that any US military forces that are left on the Korean peninsula would only go so far north. We could set a boundary about 100 km from the border. Then they won't have US forces sitting directly on their border but we can still have a presence to promote stability.

### Election Process When Electorate is Factionalized or Parties are Immature

In Egypt the Muslim Brotherhood dominated elections because they were better organized even though they did not constitute a majority. This is similar to the Hugo Chavez victories over a divided opposition in Venezuela.

Here is a process that allows a factionalized electorate a chance to form coalitions preliminary to the formal building of parties. If parties are sufficiently strong enough to achieve fifty percent of the vote in an election then it will not matter if this process is in place. On the other hand, this has the potential to allow an ad hoc coalition to form between smaller parties that are more closely aligned in values in order to not be overrun by a large minority party winning with less than a majority of the voters behind it.

**Step 1:** Require each candidate to get nominating signatures from the electorate for their district. (One percent of the district electorate.)

**Step 2:** First election in which all candidates qualified under step 1 are allowed to run. If a candidate receives more than fifty percent of the votes, the candidate wins the election. If no candidate receives fifty percent of the votes go to step 3.

**Step 3:** For two weeks after the results of the first election are certified, the candidates may throw their support and their votes behind another candidate in order to achieve fifty percent. If there is no coalition that can reach fifty percent behind a single candidate then the second election is held. The candidates from the first election with the most votes are added to the ballot for the second election until eighty percent of the votes cast in the first election are accounted for. Candidates who formed coalitions short of fifty percent may formally join their votes behind one candidate for the second election in order to improve their position or make the cut for the second election. If a candidate receives more than fifty percent of the votes from coalition building, the candidate wins the election. If no candidate receives fifty percent of the votes go to step 4.

**Step 4:** For two weeks after the results of the second election are certified, the candidates may throw their support and their votes behind another candidate in order to achieve fifty percent. If there is no coalition that can reach fifty percent behind a single candidate then the third and final election is held. The two candidates from the second election with the most votes are placed on the ballot for the third election. Candidates who formed coalitions short of fifty percent may formally join their votes behind one candidate for the third election in order to make the cut for the third election. This final election will determine the winner of the election if the first or second did not already.

It allows developing parties to put their best candidate forward then consolidate for the second and third round of voting based on the feedback from the electorate. This is better than ceding elections to an organized radical party that is only capable of attaining a plurality in the early stages of a transition to democracy. It takes time for coalitions to develop. A democratic republic requires consensus building to be successful.

This method is preferred to instant runoff voting (IRV) in the case of immature political parties and coalitions. IRV does not require the small parties to cooperate with each other. It encourages differentiation and undermining other parties. By forcing the candidates and parties to communicate and work out coalition agreements parties can be built around a range of issues. By joining forces for an election they can develop relationships for the long term. Over time they will find it more stabilizing to join forces earlier and unify behind candidates who can win in the first round. Until that time moderates can unify on an ad hoc basis to outpoll radicals.

## Trade

Trade with other countries is a significant part of the US economy. The changes in the tax structure and the reform of Social Security and Medicare will go a long way toward improving our trade imbalance by reducing structural drags on our economy. Instituting the VAT will increase the cost of imports while reducing the costs of US made exports. Some other issues we need to deal with include negotiating more free trade agreements, reductions in government ownership of the economy, reforms in currency exchanges, and promotion of a liberty incentive.

Free trade opens up more opportunities for US exports and reduces costs for US consumers. As an incentive for other countries to negotiate free trade agreements with us we should have a reciprocity policy to raise the cost of imports from countries without agreements with us. We should not submit to predatory trade practices by other nations.

There is a dangerous consolidation of power when governments control too much of the economy whether it is here or abroad. These enterprises distort markets. They are a consolidation of power which have an unfair advantage over free market competitors and threaten democracy in the world. There is substantial concern that these connected enterprises will manipulate markets to their advantage and to create instability and other disadvantages for competitors.

For example, a country with great resources could buy huge amounts of a commodity such as iron ore; driving up the price of iron. Then when the price is high start dumping large amounts of iron and steel products back onto the world market. Their competitors buying in smaller quantities are stuck buying at a higher price and then when the dumping occurs their prices are undercut. This cycle could last for a couple of years. In the meantime other companies decide to invest in mining operations that have suddenly become viable with ore at higher prices. Then when the price drops the investment is lost. This will delay or kill future investment because of too much uncertainty.

This situation involves state run industries in China, heavily supported industries in Europe, South Korea, Russia, Egypt, Brazil, and sovereign wealth funds in the Middle East. This also includes the US Postal Service, Tennessee Valley Authority, and government supported enterprises (GSEs) like Fannie Mae and Freddie Mac in the US. We need to negotiate trade rules that push all the countries of the world to greatly restrict the size and nature of GSEs around the world. They need to be limited to less than five percent of the GNP of each nation. They need to be restricted to operations that are primarily internal to the country, constitute less than twenty percent of an industry, or are limited to helping to start an industry in the country. There will be great difficulty in setting hard and fast guidelines but we need to work at it to build a framework over time. These reforms will help allocate resources more efficiently, help limit the theft of a nation's resources by the political leaders, allow for fair free trade, and limit the unhealthy consolidation of power.

We need to encourage the transition of China and other countries to floating exchange rates. Floating rates automatically adjust the balance of trade. While fixed exchange rates can offer some stability advantages for a while, eventually an adjustment needs to be made to bring it into its proper relationship with other currencies. Countries need to transition to floating pegs and then floating exchange rates to properly relate to other currencies. The larger the nation's economy the more important it is. China is in most need of this change. They will have no choice but to eventually make this transition. They want the renminbi to be an accepted reserve currency so they need it to be fully convertible in a free market with other major currencies.

Smaller, immature economies that would be unstable with floating currencies can peg their currency to a reserve currency or a basket of reserve currencies, or adopt one or more major reserve currencies for use in their country. After getting their economic house in order they can reestablish a national currency if they wish or continue with the reserve currency.

We need to have favored trade relations with countries that share our values or are making strong progress toward achieving similar governing values and institutions. There are huge reforms in progress in many developing countries. As we come alongside these countries to help them develop governing institutions we should come alongside them with help in developing their economies so they can pay for their own development. This will help to promote our values, help the people of these countries, and help our own economy.

# 11 MILITARY POLICY

"War is the continuation of policy by other means."

"The first and most important rule to observe...is to use our entire forces with the utmost energy. The second rule is to concentrate our power as much as possible against that section where the chief blows are to be delivered and to incur disadvantages elsewhere, so that our chances of success may increase at the decisive point. The third rule is never to waste time. Unless important advantages are to be gained from hesitation, it is necessary to set to work at once. By this speed a hundred enemy measures are nipped in the bud, and public opinion is won most rapidly. Finally, the fourth rule is to follow up our successes with the utmost energy. Only pursuit of the beaten enemy gives the fruits of victory."
**Karl von Clausewitz**

Of all the Executive Departments of the government, the US military is the most important. They have been consistently accomplishing the military missions assigned to them. Unfortunately the political leadership of the country has not done their part. The military provided the wins on the ground. It is the responsibility of the President to use the advantages that the military provides in order to complete the win with a favorable political solution. Too often this does not take place. The military is wasted if the President does not have a plan for securing the peace or fails to execute the plan. This usually requires domestic and allied nation support and a strong economy.

When we decide to use the military we need to use it relentlessly! When we declare an enemy we need to make every effort to destroy it. Wars are won by exhausting our enemy before they exhaust us. We should attack them in every way possible until they beg for peace or are completely destroyed. While we should always be ready to negotiate a peaceful settlement we should wait until the enemy is begging for it. There is no point otherwise. Most of our adversaries only use negotiations or truces as a means to regroup and prepare for future attacks upon us or our allies We should make sure that they are incentivized to seek peace by making continued war unbearable.

## No Defense Cuts

The idea of any defense cuts with so many security issues outstanding is ridiculous. We still have wars to finish. We need to refit our forces and modernize our equipment after the combat is completed. We still have major security challenges to deal with around the world. We are tracking and killing al-Qaeda and ISIS leaders and associates. China is becoming more aggressive in Asia. Russia is trying to dominate its neighbors. North Korea has a volatile regime with nuclear weapons. Iran is even more volatile and is actively trying to build nuclear weapons. Pakistan is unstable and has nuclear weapons. There are many other failed and fragile states in the world that can become flashpoints very quickly. We need to be prepared for them.

Even if we do not send forces into action in these other places we need them to believe that we are capable and willing to go in so we have a chance to deter them from being aggressive. As long as the enemies of freedom believe we are incapable or unwilling to intervene they will not be swayed by our non-military pressure. This is why Russia, China, and Iran have been so aggressive lately. It is better to win a war before any shot is fired. This can be done in two ways. The first is with deterrence due to perceived strength. Deterrence is not simply the avoidance of armed conflict. It is winning the conflict without force of arms. The second is to have such overwhelming strength due to superior people, equipment, doctrine, and training that we can devastate any opponent when war begins. Regardless of the type of war we have to fight.

This preparedness requires that we restore funding to 4-5 percent of GDP. The size of our navy and air force are shrinking to dangerous levels. We need to restore some of their lost funding without diminishing the funding for our ground forces that are involved in combat. We have seen that our force structure is not large enough to sustain two regional conflicts at one time. This needs to be remedied with larger reserve component forces.

## Balanced Force Structure

There needs to be a balance of different types of forces in the military to meet and defeat all potential adversaries. Stressing one type of unit or one branch of service will potentially leave us with a capability gap that an enemy can exploit or leave us unable to exploit an adversary's weakness.

Our strategy needs to dictate the specific force structure. This is based on what we need in capabilities to meet our potential adversaries on the battlefield and what we need to discourage them from trying to meet us on the battlefield. We either need to commit to meeting this standard or we should just disband the military and give up our leadership position in the world. Half measures are a waste of lives and money. I think most Americans would agree that we need to meet the challenges in the world and not cut and run.

## Increase US Military Strength

An increase in total forces will allow the US to maintain increased force levels in Afghanistan to bring stability and security until the Afghanis can provide for themselves. In addition, these forces will provide more leverage with Iran, North Korea, Syria, China, and Russia and the forces to deal militarily with those countries if necessary. The past few years have clearly shown that the US does not have the forces in place to deal with two regional conflicts at the same time. Our enemies know this and are taking advantage of this situation.

Our current volunteer forces have the training, attitude, and equipment to break the back of any conventional standing army. We need additional forces for stabilization and nationbuilding operations over an extended period of time.

We need to stand up 60 additional Army brigades (based on the pre-2013 downsized levels). Bring the Active duty Army to 45 Brigade Combat Teams (BCT) and 75 Modular Support Brigades (MSB). Bring the National Guard to 45 BCT and 135 MSB and the Army Reserve to 62 MSB. Most of the new BCTs should be infantry brigades in order to provide more security for stability and reconstruction operations. Support brigades with MP, CA, engineer, transportation, EOD, PSYOPS, logistics, and intelligence units to enhance capabilities for stability and reconstruction operations. Support Brigades also include aviation and artillery. The light BCTs are to increase local manpower density and may have sufficient organic artillery or be able to share aviation and artillery support if used in proximity to other BCTs.

There are benefits to the new units being light brigades assigned to the National Guard. They cost less than heavy brigades. They are better for stabilization and nationbuilding operations but given modern weapons are still very capable of fighting a conventional battle. National Guard units cost less because pay and benefits costs are reduced to essential training and deployment time. There are reduced on-base infrastructure requirements. The units can be used for missions when needed but the soldiers can be home when not needed for a mission.

We have a chance to keep experienced soldiers in the service longer if we have more opportunities at home in the National Guard when soldiers want to leave active duty. As a personnel issue it would be helpful to allow servicemembers to shift between Active, Reserve, and National Guard on temporary duty without leaving their original organization. Active duty officers and NCOs could shift to Reserve and National Guard positions in order to further their education or to live in the same location for an extended period. They would then automatically return to active duty based upon a prearranged agreement. Complementary to this would be allowing Reserve and National Guard soldiers to go active to be deployed overseas more often than their owning unit or to take the place of an active duty soldier on temporary duty overseas or at school. Leaders experienced with these other components of the Army can be helpful in integrating them during wartime.

**Executive and Contractor Security**

There has been a huge expansion in the use of contracted private security forces in dangerous parts of the world. These have been used to protect State Department and contractor personnel. These private security personnel have had to be paid much more than US soldiers are paid and they do not have the same protections under the law or the oversight that the US military has. While many of these security personnel are former military they do not work seamlessly with the military nor do they have the right to take offensive action to preempt an attack or to make counterattacks. This was a major deficiency during the Iraq War. Attackers were emboldened by the purely defensive private security forces on convoys and reconstruction sites. This set back our stabilization efforts and cost us huge sums of time and money.

It would be better to develop a force within the military to handle these duties. Parallel to the Special Operations Forces they would become specialists in security. They would be integrated into the overall military operations in order to be able to call on extra support as needed and to provide support by providing site and project security and key personnel security within war zones and other dangerous areas. There would be interoperability of personnel, equipment, communications, and intelligence. Logistic support would be easier.

The number and types of skills needed could be left flexible so that the DOD can make adjustments as needed. The number that is typically needed would be in the active force and the remainder to reach expected peak needs could be placed in the reserve components.

This force would also be able to provide a cadre of training expertise for training other types of units to a higher level of security training if they are needed for additional security needs. Many units were tasked with convoy and other security duties, especially in Iraq, when that was not their specialty beforehand. The hard won knowledgebase developed by these security specialists would be retained by the services and more easily passed on in the future. That will not happen with the continued use of private security forces.

**Language Training**

Have all US servicemembers with military occupational specialties (MOSs) likely to have personal contact with foreign nationals participate in language training. Select the fifteen most likely languages that our servicemembers will find helpful on deployment. Have 2-4 members of each platoon learn each language. Obviously if a unit is scheduled for deployment it would be advisable for the whole unit to concentrate on the languages of the area of deployment.

There are such a tremendous number of options available with current technology. We can use a combination of classroom, internet, DVD, phone app, satellite TV, and cable TV based instruction. With fifteen different languages there would be five to ten soldiers learning each language in each company. This would provide opportunities to create some degree of immersion in the language.

Each language should be broken down into individual tasks to aid unit trainers in teaching the language. Have unit leaders and education centers proctor exams. Have progressive levels of proven proficiency earn promotion points. Arrange for college credit for proven levels of proficiency. Over time unit NCOs and officers will be qualified to teach languages as part of regular unit training.

An additional use of the official list of languages is as a foreign policy tool. Adding a language that is common in a country we are having trouble with could be used as a warning that we may be considering "visiting" them. Increasing the number of new soldiers that learn a particular language could likewise be used as a signal.

Even if this does not become a mandated type of training the capabilities to learn these languages should be easily available for all servicemembers. Incentives such as promotion points and college credit should be available to learn languages on their own.

## Soldiers Pay and Benefits

The base soldier pay and benefits should be related to the average civilian pay. The country should make sure their soldiers have a standard of living comparable to the civilian sector. Each soldier should get this base pay plus extra pay for several categories of duty.

Combat Pay
Hazardous Duty Pay
Field Duty Pay
Foreign Service Pay

These other categories of pay are to compensate soldiers for more dangerous duty and for time away from family. Both are high sources of stress. This increased pay will never fully compensate for what they do but it does serve to differentiate those in the service who take on these jobs from those who serve their time in a stateside military office.

**Retirement Pay**

Establish a new point system for service members to accumulate retirement points to determine the amount of retirement pay they will receive. Any new system would only apply to servicemembers who join after the new system is established. All prior servicemembers will remain in the current system.

1.  One point for each day of service.
2.  Two additional points for each day in a combat zone. Replaced by three additional points for each day after four continuous weeks in a combat zone. Replaced by four additional points for each day after six months continuous in a combat zone. Prisoners of war would also qualify for this.
3.  Two additional points for each day performing a hazardous duty outside of a combat zone.
4.  One additional point for each day of field duty, cruises, or other duty away from home.
5.  Maximum of five points per day. Reasons must be documented. Soldier must be provided with a copy of documentation.
6.  Bonus points could be awarded in conjunction with high level awards.
7.  A bonus could be awarded for lengths of time in service over a certain minimum. These soldiers are typically leaders and have a lot of experience. The amount should be enough to help retain quality soldiers but not enough that everyone wants to stay for the benefits.

Set the base value of 20 years of service without any extras for combat, overseas, hazardous duty, awards or field duty at 75 percent of the wages and benefits for the soldier's highest rank. This would be 7305 points plus any bonus points for length of service. Set the standard starting age for the military retirement at the standard civilian federal retirement age. Soldiers would be able to begin taking their retirement early. They would then get a reduced monthly amount such that the value of the benefit received through to retirement age plus 25 years would be the same.

A servicemember with 20 years of service who entered service at age 18 would need 11500 points to receive a fifty percent pension from the time of leaving service. That is a 1.573 points per day average for twenty years. This is comparable to the current retirement. This will not be difficult for servicemembers deployed to a combat assignment for three of those 20 years and otherwise deployed away from family for a quarter of their service time. The typical active duty combat arms soldiers will earn more than this.

Twenty years will not be required to earn a retirement benefit. The servicemembers who only serve a short time but serve it in combat will be able to rack up a significant retirement benefit. The stress will be placed on combat duty over time served.

### Service Connected Disability

A service connected disability pension will be related to the standard pension. A 100 percent disability pension will be equal to a 20 year base pension of 7305 points. Added to the base will be any additional points earned by the servicemember. If the servicemember has more than 20 years of service, their actual points for service will be used instead.

### Veterans Health Services Reform

The current veterans' health services system needs to be restructured. The current model is not efficient and is not responsive to the needs of veterans. For decades there have been repeated issues with the Veterans Administration handling of healthcare. Here is a proposal to change how veterans' healthcare is financed. It will make it possible for veterans to choose where they get their healthcare services. They will be able to choose the VA or private providers as they believe best serve their needs.

At the core is a monthly contribution to the veteran's Medicare XXI HSA account related to the number of retirement points the veteran received during their service. This money is combined with the contributions from post service employment. This core contribution should be set to provide a benefit to secure healthcare services comparable to what is currently available for non-service connected issues. Current beneficiaries will receive their HSA contribution from current general revenues. Current servicemembers will receive the net present value of previously earned benefit and receive contributions as they earn retirement points into their HSA.

Added to the core is additional contributions or focused insurance or a combination for service connected injuries or illness. The focused insurance will be able to be used at any healthcare provider.

The VA will receive some direct funding to care for veterans dealing with service connected injuries and illnesses. These are the areas that the VA needs to take the lead in finding the best treatments and creating new or improved treatments. Veterans will still be permitted to use non-VA providers at their discretion for service connected issues. Most of the funding that currently goes to the VA will be redirected to the contributions to the veterans' Medicare XXI accounts. The VA hospitals and clinics will have to compete with the mainstream healthcare providers to receive this funding from the veterans. The VA will have to provide superior service and earn the patronage of veterans or downsize. Whether the VA reforms itself to meet the needs of veterans or the mainstream system steps up to meet their needs the veterans will receive more timely, efficient, and responsive care.

# 12 IMMIGRATION AND BORDER SECURITY

**"When a foreigner resides among you in your land, do not mistreat them. The foreigner residing among you must be treated as your native-born. Love them as yourself, for you were foreigners in Egypt."**
**Leviticus 19:33-34**

When discussing immigration reform, three things must be stressed. First is sovereignty and security. This is our country and the federal government has a duty to protect the American people. Second, the illegal immigrants we are dealing with are human beings and we need to act morally and justly with them. Third, we need legal immigrants to keep growing our economy.

On a personal note, if I was not born in the United States and could not get a visa to be here legally, I would likely be here illegally. There is a reason so many people come here both legally and illegally. This is a great place to live, work, and raise a family. That is a good thing. I would want this opportunity and future for my family and so would you. Most of us have ancestors that sought this opportunity.

The US government has an obligation to protect our sovereignty both at the border and internally. At the border we need to restrain illegal access to the United States. It is a national security, economic, humanitarian, and law enforcement issue. From a national security perspective, we must stop terrorists, spies, smugglers, and other criminals from entering and from leaving the country.

From an economic perspective we must control the number of people we allow in to keep wages from being depressed. At the same time we also need to allow an appropriate number of people linked to specific jobs or job categories to fill positions where needed. We need to reduce federal and state government services costs and the amount of uninsured healthcare costs that are passed on to US citizens and businesses. Also, there are high costs from crime and incarceration when criminals find a way into the country.

From a humanitarian perspective, there are many people who are injured or killed trying to cross the border. Families are divided with some that are citizens living here and some living in their home country. Many illegals are taken advantage of because of their precarious status, by both Americans and criminals in the illegal immigrant community.

From a law enforcement perspective, there is the initial problem of violating the law by illegally entering the country. Many are forced into illegal activities to pay off their cost of being smuggled into the country. When criminals enter the country they are victimizing Americans and other members of the immigrant community. This costs communities and law enforcement time, money, and lives.

**Border Security**

We need a multi-layer border wall along the border with Mexico completed as soon as possible. There must be control of our border and transit across it. Obviously we need some flexibility along rivers and environmentally sensitive areas but there is no rational reason why all land borders with Mexico should not have a multi-layer border wall. In animal migration areas there can be gates opened periodically and monitored more closely just during normal migration periods instead of keeping the gap all year long. Similarly where there are seasonal water drainage paths there can be gates to allow the water to pass through.

The point of barriers is not ironclad security because certainly there will be people who go over, under or through the walls. The point is to increase the relative cost of entering the United States illegally and to slow people down when they try. By increasing the difficulty of entering illegally and decreasing the difficulty of getting a work visa, fewer people will try to enter illegally which will give the Border Patrol a better chance at apprehending those who do try. The decreased flow of illegal workers will make it more difficult for smugglers and other criminals and terrorists to hide in their midst. Slowing illegal entry down with barriers will allow the Border Patrol more opportunity to reach these people in the border area.

We need more Customs and Border Patrol officers to control the border and to promote timely transit of commerce and people at regulated border crossings. We have frequently called upon the National Guard to help secure the border. That would be fine for an emergency situation. The National Guard should not be used for routine, continuous border work. Customs and Border Patrol officers are the appropriate forces for this. Don't take National Guard members away from their families, regular jobs and college for this; it is not an appropriate mission for them.

Any gaps or weak spots in our defenses will eventually be found and exploited by smugglers. By being flexible and innovative we can keep countering the evolving tactics that smugglers use. We will never completely eliminate smuggling or illegal immigration but we can and should greatly reduce it. Strong border controls combined with a responsive work visa program and legalized drugs will go a long way to securing the border. The relative cost for those crossing illegally will rise dramatically.

## Visas, Permanent Residency and Naturalization

We need realistic quotas on visas, permanent residency, and naturalization based on the type and number of workers needed across the country. Congress needs to set guidelines but leave the actual quota flexible based upon the needs in the various categories. This should increase when the unemployment rate is low and decrease when the unemployment rate increases. Putting this number for each year in the hands of a bipartisan commission with equal numbers of Democrat and Republican members would allow for frequent adjustments as the country's needs change.

Some of the relevant categories are highly educated/skilled people, farm workers, construction workers, food service workers, political and religious persecution victims, people who supported the US, and general workers.

Employer sponsorship of foreign employees must be simplified and affordable. Workers sponsored by employers should have priority over those who receive an open ended work visa. The open ended work visas are for primarily low skill workers brought in when the unemployment rate is low to fill the jobs than many Americans will not do, especially during good economic times. Many small employers will not have the resources to navigate even simplified sponsorship procedures to find foreign workers.

We need to expand visas for those suffering from helping the US overseas or from religious or political persecution. This group should be a priority over economic immigrants. The Christians being persecuted and murdered in the Middle East should have a priority. Not only are they in extreme danger but they have skills that will help to defeat terrorists. They are native speakers and know the culture of the Middle East. Our intelligence agencies and the military are perpetually short of native speakers to translate communications intercepts and other material.

An online jobs database should be established by the federal government (preferably contracted out) and maintained by fees from registering employers. All employers seeking employees needing a visa and all employers with employees working under a visa will post all of the company's job openings on this site. This will ensure that US citizens have the opportunity to apply for these positions.

Enable employment agencies to fill this employment marketplace by developing a pool of workers in other countries and connecting them to jobs in the US that US employers cannot fill. They will be able to help both workers and employers to maintain compliance with the law. These agencies should have to register with the government. Foreign workers need to be able to go to a US government website to find links to the registered agencies to keep them safe from smugglers and slavers. These agencies should not be permitted to charge application fees. All fees, commissions, and other compensation should be from the employer. This is normal for employment agencies in the US. This will make the exploitation of foreign workers more difficult.

People should be able to get work visas for up to three years at a time. When they have resided in the US continuously for the past three years and accumulated at least ten years of residency in the previous fifteen years they should be able to apply for citizenship and not before. Each arrest for being here illegally should earn a penalty of two additional years of waiting to apply for citizenship. (Example: reside in the US twelve of previous seventeen years.) Only legal years of residency will be counted.

There should be a maximum annual limit on naturalizations of 50 percent of the previous year's growth in naturally born citizens. This should be somewhat flexible and allow for doing some smoothing of the natural variations in the size of each age group. This will aid us in mitigating the effects of population troughs between baby booms.

English language proficiency and the equivalent of a US high school education/GED should be required for adults to get citizenship. Minors will automatically be granted provisional citizenship when a parent receives his/her citizenship and automatically be granted full citizenship upon completion of high school/GED. If provisional citizenship is not converted to full citizenship by the age of 21 then it will be rescinded and the person will be deported or have to enter the work visa program. There will be an exception or exemption for cases of past or current disability that prevents or delays completion of high school/GED in this time frame. There must be some minimal requirements for becoming a US citizen and these are reasonable. Hopefully it will decrease the school dropout rate in immigrant neighborhoods.

Those here on a work visa should not be eligible for more than three months of unemployment compensation or welfare benefits in a three year period. This will give the worker up to three months to find another job or have to leave the country. No benefits will be available during the first year.

Felons should be ineligible for citizenship except under special circumstances. (Example: Prosecution witness, honorable service to U.S. government, some cultural differences that result in criminal conviction here and not where the person is from—but no more than one conviction) Exceptions should be rare. The time needed in residence in the US to apply for citizenship will not include time prior to a felony or misdemeanor conviction or time serving a sentence. Their visa time requirement starts over and only their time after completion of their sentence is counted.

Alien felons should be required to serve their full sentences without the option for probation or parole. When the sentence is completed they should be deported. Any alien felons whose country will not except them back will be required to be incarcerated until there is a country who will accept them. They should not be permitted back on US streets. Pressure needs to be placed on foreign countries who do not accept their felons back. The federal government should be required to reimburse the states for the costs of incarcerating alien felons or transfer them to federal prisons to serve out their state sentence.

If an alien felon returns to the US after deportation there should be more severe penalties. Simply being caught in the US should incur a federal sentence of six months at hard labor. An alien felon deportee convicted of a crime should have to serve six months plus a penalty enhancement of 50 percent of their sentence at hard labor in addition to the normal criminal penalty. These penalty enhancements are to discourage the return of undesirable aliens. We have to make the penalty high enough that they will not risk returning. While it may be costly to imprison those who do return, the damage they can cause can be severe. Simply deporting them is likely to result in their return in a short time.

If their home country will not take them back then we must keep them incarcerated. They are not entitled to live freely in the US. The onus for freeing them is on their home country. If physically possible we should deliver these convicts to their home country even against the wishes of their country.

While family connections are very important, there should be limits. All else being equal, family members should get priority, but not otherwise. Visa holders with two good years in the US should be limited to sponsoring their spouse, children and stepchildren. Naturalized citizens should be limited to parents, stepparents, spouse, children, stepchildren, siblings, half-siblings, spouses of siblings and half-siblings, and children and stepchildren of siblings and half-siblings. These adult family members should need to meet the same work (unless homemaker, disabled, etc. in self-supporting household), time, education, and other requirements on their own merits to become citizens.

## Guest Worker Program

As part of immigration reform we need to set up a Guest Worker Program geared toward foreign workers who do not intend to seek permanent residency or citizenship. They intend to earn money then return home. This can be a good foreign policy tool to be used with people in countries we are actively trying to aid. They get experience living in a republic. They can aid their families back home with remittances. This can be a great form of foreign aid that is not diluted by bureaucratic programs. It goes to people who work instead of filtered through government officials.

## Dealing with Illegal Aliens Already Here

While in principle I believe that those who are here illegally should not be granted amnesty it is impractical to require them to leave the country voluntarily to apply for a work visa. Most are likely to be employed and would jeopardize the welfare of their families by leaving their job. The only people who would benefit if illegal aliens need to return home to make their application would be the smugglers. Many would continue trying to live here illegally rather than risking repeated border crossings and likely losing whatever current job they have. If they are caught here illegally before they receive legal status under the plan below they should have the consequences outlined below.

People should be allowed to apply online or through the mail even if they may actually be in the US. Require a mail and physical address and as part of an application the complete disclosure of place of residence and employment for the past ten years, under a penalty of perjury. Everyone will receive a conditional immunity from the use of this application for prosecution dealing with being in the country illegally during the transition period. ICE will not be allowed to use this information for arresting illegal aliens unless their visa application is denied. The information collected can be used by ICE to find patterns for better enforcement in the future. An application for a visa from people already here illegally will be considered on an equal basis with all others. If denied, the person's information will be turned over to ICE and the person will have to leave the country within 30 days. If they do not leave on their own they can be arrested and then have the penalty normally incurred for being in the US illegally.

If someone is here illegally after the two year transition period or the denial of a work visa the information may be used against the person. Employers who have hired illegals in the past will receive conditional immunity for disclosures by illegals on their applications. If the employer knowingly hires an illegal after the two year transition period the immunity is voidable by the government and the prosecution is allowed to submit records of a pattern for consideration at sentencing.

There will be no preference from the government for those who are here illegally now to receive the work visas that become available under the new program. The only preference that may be present is from employers who elect to hire specific people. People already connected to their community and employer have the best chance of being able to stay in the US. They are essentially selected by the people who personally know them. That is not a perfect solution but it is the closest we can realistically get to no amnesty and make it work in the real world.

Arrests for being here illegally after this new law is in effect will earn a penalty for visa application. During the two year transition to this program there will be no penalty for the first year. After the first year this will include arrests during the transition period unless the person applied for a visa and has not already been denied.

> 1st Offense - 1 year bar to apply
> 2nd Offense - 2 year bar to apply
> 3rd Offense or more – 5 year bar to apply
> All bars to application are consecutive

Aliens with more than one arrest for being in the US illegally during the ten years prior to the passage of the new law will have a bar of 1 year for each offense which will be counted from the time of the offense and multiple offenses will be consecutive. This will penalize those who have cost the most money by repeated attempts to sneak in and be returned.

Bars due to illegal entries prior to the new law should not prevent receiving a short–term visa for up to 30 days for a significant family event such as funeral, wedding, or birth of their own child. It is important to try to strengthen family bonds. Failure to comply with the terms of the short-term visa will be considered an offense and will incur the penalty listed above and a bar to a future short-term Visa. Failure to comply will also bar the sponsoring relative from sponsoring anyone else for three years and delay the sponsor's eligibility to seek citizenship by two years. If the sponsor was sponsoring more than one relative that failed to comply with the terms the penalties will be cumulative.

An especially irritating situation is immigrants and groups that advocate that some part of the US should secede and become independent or part of Mexico. All non-citizens that advocate for succession should be deported. Any group that advocates this should be shut down and prosecuted for treason. Any US citizen who advocates the same should be barred from sponsoring immigrants or workers as a danger to national security.

## Illegal Alien Business Owners

There should be a program for illegal alien business owners to self-sponsor and obtain a work visa. If people have created a business and supported their family with it then we should encourage them. They are the kind of people we want as citizens. There must be documented evidence of this self-supporting business enterprise. This must be a continuing business operation. They will need to continue self-supporting or enter the regular work visa system for the time needed to get their citizenship. This should only apply to those already in the US without the option for future illegals.

## Penalties for Living in the US Illegally

Many people who have lived in the US illegally will need to pay penalties for the past ten years. Any unpaid taxes and the appropriate interest and penalties need to be paid. This will include any unpaid payroll taxes. A fine of $175 per adult for each month present in the US illegally. This is for those who are still here illegally and for those who have been here illegally in the past. Both groups need to pay for their time here illegally.

Employers who failed to submit payroll or other taxes for illegal alien employees will be required to pay these back taxes along with interest and penalties.

The IRS will work with the employers and the workers to determine who owes what amounts.

## US Business Limits on Using Foreign Workers

While it is beneficial when US employers are able to use foreign workers when US workers will not do the job, some businesses want to use foreign workers to cut their costs at the expense of US workers. There need to be some limits.

Except for agricultural manual labor, a company should not have a work force that is more than 25 percent foreign workers in people or payroll. Foreign workers may not be paid less than the minimum wage. An employer's foreign workforce average pay must be at least the local prevailing wage based on experience and type of work. (Prevailing wage as calculated according to the author's recommendations in the Government Reforms chapter.) Benefits for foreign workers should be the same as for US workers. There should not be any opportunity to undercut wages and benefits for US citizens from the hiring of foreign workers.

## E-Verify

E-Verify needs to continue to be improved to provide a reliable and efficient means of verifying workers' right to work in the US. Employers will have to identify all employees and confirm that they are legally permitted to work in the US. Anyone erroneously flagged has plenty of opportunity to prove they have a right to work here. This process should still be improved further to be easier for workers and employers to get resolution in a timely manner. Workers that are appealing a flagged record should still be allowed to keep working without penalty to them or the employer.

Here are some proposed penalties for employer violations. If the employer is fooled by good fake documents there should be no penalty. If the employer has poor procedures in place or reasonably should have known this should be an administrative violation with fines to pressure the employer into implementing better procedures. If the employer intentionally overlooked or disregarded the law on a small scale this should be a misdemeanor offense with fines of double the median national wage for the time period each illegal is employed. If the employer intentionally overlooked or disregarded the law on a large scale this should be a felony offense with fines of triple the median national wage for the time period each illegal is employed. If the illegal alien earned a wage greater than the median national wage then the employer will be subject to fines double or triple the actual wages paid. Whistleblowers should get 20 percent of fines collected. Misdemeanor convictions should result in a six month bar for the employer to hire new foreign workers. These should be cumulative up to a maximum of two years. Felony convictions should incur a one year bar to hiring new foreign workers with a cumulative maximum of five years. These penalties should keep most employers honest.

## English Official Language

I believe that our forefathers have effectively established English as our de facto language of government and mainstream life. I have nothing against someone knowing and using another language. I wish I was more fluent in other languages and I believe our children should all become fluent in a second language to help us as leaders in the world in business and world affairs. But I also believe that for contracts and government documents we need a standard official language and it should be English.

## Dream Act

It is a difficult decision about what to do about children who were brought to the US by their parents and who grew up here. Many think of themselves as Americans and of the US as their country. If they did not this would be an easy decision. I am generally supportive of young people who are patriotic for America. I don't want to diminish that spirit. Hopefully most will recognize the need to jump through some hoops because of the long term need to provide secure borders for their families and descendants. Serving in the military is the best way to show that they think of themselves as Americans.

Offering amnesty or state residency college tuition rates or other benefits to these young people is problematic. It creates a moral hazard that encourages parents to illegally bring their children here in the hopes that they can evade deportation long enough for their children to get an education and to get amnesty. The reality is that under the proposed work visa program these young people will benefit because of their education in the US and their increased ability in English and their potential personal connections to sponsoring employers. It is wrong to explicitly provide a pass because of the likelihood that it will encourage more people to bring their children here illegally.

# 13 SOCIAL ISSUES

**"God created man in his image; in the divine image he created him; male and female he created them"**
**Genesis 1:27**

### Abortion

There are many of us who desire that the government becomes smaller and less intrusive in our personal lives. Many believe that the government should not have a say about the health care choices of women. For the most part I completely agree the government is far too intrusive into our personal lives and has overstepped its rightful boundaries. But in the area of abortion the government and all of us as citizens have a vital interest in ensuring the right to life of all people in our country. Currently unborn babies do not have the right to life according to our laws. They are considered part of the body of the mother without their own rights. Right now only the mother is afforded rights. We know that babies are clearly a separate person. Therefore babies should have their own unalienable rights recognized apart from their mother. Rights need to be balanced between mother and baby and rights need to be balanced with responsibilities.

Unless a crime is committed against the mother she is responsible for the baby being conceived. She can choose whether or not the baby is conceived. The baby has no choice in the matter and is therefore blameless. It is essential in a free society to expect people to be responsible for the decisions that they make. When the consequences of decisions are avoided people will not take as much care in the decisions they make. It is better that people have to deal with the natural consequences of their decisions and not be artificially protected from them. When abortion is illegal then men and women will have to take more care to not create a baby.

This is true not just in the area of pregnancy and abortion but in all areas of life. When we do not take personal responsibility and police ourselves, it becomes necessary for the state to increase its policing of us to prevent anarchy and vigilantism.

I believe that abortion is murder and for that reason I believe it should be illegal. I support a constitutional amendment that states that life begins at conception. Throughout history the point that life begins has been legally established at different points in the development of a baby. Determining when rights begin has frequently been tied to this understanding. In the past life has been considered to begin at birth, at quickening, or various other moments. All of these past standards were based upon the understanding at the time. As we know now from scientific research the single non-arbitrary development point that divides life and no life is at the point of conception. To continue keeping the legal beginning of life anywhere but the moment of conception would be an arbitrary standard. Because our understanding is much greater now than it was under earlier legal precedents the law should be changed to set the right to life when life begins at conception.

Many people believe that there should be exceptions to the prohibition on abortion for cases of rape, incest, and the life or health of the mother. While I care greatly for the victims of rape and incest and I am concerned about the pain and difficulties of dealing with the crime committed against them. I do not believe that the murder of their baby is appropriate or justified. With regard to the life or health of the mother exception, this should be limited to only the life of a mother. While I still believe it to be murder I do not believe that the state should be in a position to choose one life over another. In this situation the mother alone should make the final call without legal consequence. A court order from family court should be required to adjudicate that the life of the mother is in danger. In this case the baby should be assigned a guardian ad litem to protect his or her interests. The hearing should be conducted without delay to minimize the damage that the mother could incur from delay. Thankfully these types of cases are very rare and these situations are not a factor in most abortions.

When abortion is made illegal the criminal statutes need to be crafted with care. There are many babies lost in miscarriage due to unknown circumstances. It would be a great hardship on women if they have to go through an inquisition after such a grievous loss. Investigations and prosecutions should be limited to cases where there is a reasonable belief that an overt action was taken to illegally end a baby's life.

Most of us have seen the great pictures in Life magazine and elsewhere that were taken in utero. Many of us are also aware of the great advances in laparoscopic surgery techniques. We should support research and development into making it possible to transplant an embryo or fetus from one woman into another. Especially in the first few days following conception before the embryo attaches to the uterine wall it seems like an opportune time and easier procedure to remove the embryo and place into another woman. In cases of rape or incest when it has been reported quickly this could make things easier on the victim while sparing the life of the baby. Other women who want a baby could be prescreened and on a waiting list for these babies. Research and development into finding cures or other treatments for conditions that make it difficult or dangerous for women to carry a baby to full term should be promoted. There have already been many tremendous improvements in saving the life of premature babies and we should continue to support further improvements.

For those of you who do not share my convictions concerning when life begins or about abortion and hold back supporting a candidate for President because they hold a conviction similar to mine on these issues but would support him based on his other positions and attributes should still seriously consider supporting the candidate. Unfortunately there is little chance that the constitutional amendment I desire will be passed any time soon nor will comparable statutory legislation. Most politicians will not lead on this issue. They will not get far out ahead of their constituents. Presently there is not enough drive in the electorate to push their elected officials to pass this legislation. The American people will have to overwhelmingly support it before it will happen. So if you support a candidate on the other issues please consider supporting him completely to be your President.

For my fellow Christ followers, the legislation to end or limit abortion will not happen without your help. You are needed to run for office and help other believers run for office. But most important is sharing the Gospel and your lives with those who do not have a relationship with Christ. Not only in the area of abortion but many other problems in our nation will only be solved by a moral revival in our culture. This cannot be accomplished through politics, only by loving God and loving others around us. Political leaders can help by restraining evil as elected officials but renewing our culture will only come person to person by sharing the love of God. As I've mentioned before most politicians are not leaders. You will need to lead them to where we want to go. Lead them to the end of the holocaust of abortion!

We need more Supreme Court justices and other Federal judges appointed that are strict constructionists or textualists and are likely therefore to reject a right to abortion. I believe the preferred long term remedy is the passage of a constitutional amendment stating that life begins at conception. Without a constitutional amendment, abortion may come and go based upon who is on the Supreme Court.

I challenge the pro-abortion/pro-choice special interest groups to write their own constitutional amendment stating what they want in the constitution. Then we could have the Congress pass both of our constitutional amendments on the same vote. The instructions would contain a provision that the first of the amendments that is passed by the required 38 state legislatures will become the law of the land. I suspect they will not consider this until the Supreme Court decides against abortion. The sooner this happens the better. The American People need to make a definitive decision about abortion. This can be done when the debate is energetically engaged as it will be with this competition of amendments.

Let us all join together to provide safety and liberty to the unborn while protecting and preserving the lives of the mothers.

### Conscience Clause

A key reason for the First Amendment is to keep the government from forcing people to violate their beliefs, their conscience. Laws and regulations that attempt to force people to act against their moral beliefs should be avoided.

The attempts by liberals to force all health plans to include abortion, birth control, and abortion inducing drugs is a current example. No employer or individual should be forced to make purchases against their beliefs. Nor should doctors, pharmacists, and other healthcare workers be forced to perform procedures or dispense drugs that violate their conscience.

Another example is public and union funding of political campaigns. Any taxes diverted to political campaigns have to be replaced by taxes imposed on others, including other citizens who oppose the beliefs of the receiving campaigns. Most union members do not have a realistic say over how their dues are spent. They are forced to support political campaigns against their will.

There are many recent incidents of businesses such as bakers, florists, and photographers being forced to participate in same-sex weddings. We do have to be careful that businesses do not discriminate against a group of people for who they are. That could potentially Balkanize our country. On the other hand these businesses should be permitted to limit their participation to activities that will not violate their conscience. For example, a baker should be required to serve any customer with the basic production of their normal products. But they should not be required to include a message that violates their beliefs such as two same-sex figures on a cake or written messages they find objectionable. These businesses should not have to be present for an activity that they object to such as a same-sex wedding. Delivery of material products prior to the activity should still be required. People who want to have a marriage celebration should not want to have people who object to their marriage present. These cases in the media seem to be intended to push a political agenda or an attempt to cash-in with a lawsuit instead.

Another example that has been occurring in Canada, Europe, and on US college campuses is speech codes that seek to bar speech some people do not like. This has been especially common around the issue of homosexuality. It has resulted in civil and criminal charges against pastors and others that say that homosexual behavior is a sin. On US college campuses, student groups, students, and faculty have been penalized by similar speech codes.

People need to be allowed to act, speak, and think according to their own beliefs. The free exchange of ideas is a cornerstone of our liberty and necessary for a thriving democratic republic. Public debate saves our society from resorting to violence to settle disputes. When a people get pushed into a corner and are unable to live according to their own conscience and have a say in their own government it is only a matter of time before they strike back to achieve this freedom.


## Protection of Marriage

Intact families are the building blocks of a strong, stable society. Healthy marriages are the basis of an intact family. As I was writing this in the first edition in 2011 Charles Colson sent an email that said it better than I can. Here it is:

> It should be an open and shut case. Study after study shows the beneficial effects of marriage and the self-inflicted harm that people experience when they ignore this evidence. Marriage is good for us in so many ways.
>
> Here is a tiny sampling: People who have been continuously married have 75 percent more wealth at retirement than those who have divorced or were never married. Children in married, two-parent families experience two to three times more positive life outcomes than those who do not. Married people even enjoy better and more frequent sex!
>
> Yet the statistics also show our culture heading in the opposite direction. In 1970, 89 percent of all births were to married parents. Today, unfortunately, it is only 60 percent. In 1960, 72 percent of adults in America were married. Care to guess the number in 2008? Fifty percent. How did we get here, when it makes no logical sense?
>
> My friend Tim Keller at Redeemer Presbyterian Church in New York and his wife, Kathy, have written a brilliant new book that explains why marriage is in such dire straits, and how to rescue it. Their book, **The Meaning of Marriage: Facing the Complexities of Commitment with the Wisdom of God** … You need to get a copy!
>
> The Kellers diagnose this cultural disconnect. It's the natural fruit of the West's slow redefinition of marriage: from an institution where duty and mutual sacrifice are expected for the good of children and the larger society to one in which the marital partners primarily ask,

"What's in it for me?" "In short," Keller writes, "the Enlightenment privatized marriage, taking it out of the public sphere, and redefined its purpose as individual gratification, not any 'broader good' such as reflecting God's nature, producing character, or raising children."

As a consequence, this new understanding, which is supposed to be so liberating, he says, "actually puts a crushing burden of expectation on marriage and on spouses that more traditional understandings never did."

Because marriage is now all about me, no one is ever good enough, so we hang back, afraid to commit, waiting for the non-existent perfectly "compatible" person—meaning he or she is well-adjusted, beautiful, and can help us find sexual and emotional fulfillment. Or we drop the person we married when someone "better" comes along.

So how can we get out of this?

Well, their book, The Meaning of Marriage, lays out the solution in great and encouraging detail. It is written for singles, those in successful and stable marriages, and for those in the midst of marital crisis. The book is too rich to encapsulate in this brief commentary, but suffice it to say that the secret of marriage is grounded in the self-giving example of Jesus laying down His life for the Church.

If more of us in the church understood this and lived it out in our marriages, perhaps we could stop the decline and rebuild a culture of marriage in our country.

This is a book Christians need to read. It's a great resource to equip you to speak with your secular friends; to show them why the Christian understanding of marriage is not only a tremendous blessing, it's the only one that works.

This book resonates well with what I have learned in my own study and experience. We are all selfish to varying extents. Happiness and loving relationships depends upon our giving of ourselves to our spouse. (The book, **The Meaning of Marriage**, should be the basis of a primetime TV show. Break it down into 10-20 episodes. The content is so valuable that everyone in the world needs to hear it.)

No one is born without a sin nature. We all have temptations that are hard for us to resist. For some this is sex outside of marriage. This includes premarital sex, extramarital sex, and homosexual sex. All of these are sins against God and against ourselves and our current, former, or future spouse. To God all sin is evil and separates us from Him.

One of the things I realized in life was that God's instructions make practical common sense and that there are usually natural consequences to not obeying them. Trust is very important for relationships, especially for marriages. When someone has sex before marriage they are telling their future spouse that they don't need a marriage commitment to have sex. When someone waits to have sex until marriage they are telling their future spouse that they can be trusted to be self-restrained and only have sex within the marriage. This is largely only likely if they waited because of a personal relationship with Christ. Waiting just because of societal pressure may not be an internalized value. Some may be thinking that someone can have sex before marriage but then adhere to their vows after getting married. But what evidence is there that that is the person's true values? Their word? It is safe to say that everyone has lied at some time in their life. Will your spouse believe that you will never lie to him or her? Do you want your spouse to always have to wonder about your faithfulness? Which engenders more trust, actions or words? Not having sex before marriage will help your spouse to develop trust that you will be faithful. This will bring peace to him or her and add to the peace in your home. The Gift of Trust that can be given to our spouses is of immense value, far greater than money.

## Strengthening Marriage

We know the attributes of strong marriages. I am no expert on marriage but there are some other books I recommend for you to check out.

**Happily Married for Life** by Larry J. Koenig, (Copyright 2006) Published by Life Journey, an excerpt for which was on cbn.com at http://www1.cbn.com/family/what-makes-for-a-happy-marriage%3F in November 2015 that resonates well with what I believe about strong successful marriages. In Koenig's book he references a study by Judith Wallerstein and Sandra Blakeslee who undertook the task of interviewing successful couples across America to find out how people define a happy marriage. From this came their book called **The Good Marriage**.

Some other books to check out are **Love & Respect** by Dr. Emerson Eggerichs, **The Love Dare** by Stephen and Alex Kendrick, and **Wait for Me** by Rebecca St. James.

Too often the problem of bad marriages and too many divorces is due to the failure of couples to communicate respectfully and being unwilling to continuously work at reducing their own selfishness. Much of the success we have in our relationships is only possible by dealing with these two issues. We all need to be involved in helping those in our life to approach marriage with more seriousness and selflessness so that our families and our culture are strengthened and our children feel more secure and loved.

Another book to read is **The Five Love Languages**. Here is a quote by the author Gary Chapman from an article on the Focus on the Family website. (http://www.focusonthefamily.com/marriage/communication-and-conflict/learn-to-speak-your-spouses-love-language/discovering-your-spouses-love-language)

"It is easy to love your spouse when your spouse is loving you. It is easy to say kind words to your spouse when he or she is treating you kindly. But even if your spouse is unwilling to try or to reciprocate, unconditional love means that you will choose to love your spouse in his or her primary love language.

Although unconditional love is difficult, it is the kind of love that God has for us. Romans 5:8 says that God loved us "while we were still sinners" and sent Christ to die for us. Scripture also says that we love God "because he first loved us" (1 John 4:19). Therefore, when you choose to love your spouse unconditionally, you are following God's example. And if you ask God, He will give you the ability to do it.

In Romans 5:5 the apostle Paul says, "God has poured out his love into our hearts by the Holy Spirit." Likewise, when you pour out your love by speaking your spouse's love language, you are doing the most emotionally powerful thing you can do. Your spouse desperately needs emotional love from you. As your spouse's love tank begins to fill, there is a good chance that he or she will begin to reciprocate.

A full love tank creates a positive atmosphere in which you and your spouse can talk about your differences more easily and negotiate solutions to your conflicts. I have seen many hard, cold men and women melt when they begin to receive love in their love language. Love is the most powerful weapon in the world for good. It can thaw the coldest of winters and bring the blossoms of spring to your marriage."

## Dating and Marriage Preparation Ministry

For many Christian singles it is difficult to meet other singles of the opposite sex in an environment conducive to getting to know each other well enough to consider dating. In small churches there is a limited number of singles. In large churches it can be difficult and time-consuming meeting other singles. Even when participating in a small group or in a ministry there are limited opportunities for meeting other singles.

Even when there is a traditional singles ministry it is not always an effective venue. They are usually run by singles and when the leaders get married or step down there is many times a leadership vacuum. Scheduling can be a problem for a traditional singles ministry. Meeting times are set by the leaders based on the availability of the initial core people. Until there is a large number of people involved it is not possible to get a variety of meeting times. When there are limited meeting times it can be difficult to grow the number of people. Singles ministries are usually geared toward social activities.

Single people attend church less frequently than couples. When this happens it is more likely for these singles to drift away from the church and a relationship with Christ.

In the online dating venues there are many Christians with profiles but there are many inactive accounts. Many of the same people are on multiple venues. Many are discouraged by the lack of options on any particular site at any particular moment in time. This discourages people from paying to keep accounts active. When proximity to other Christian singles is limited there is temptation to date and marry non-Christians.

## New Ministry Recommendation

This ministry should be focused on equipping singles for dating and marriage and facilitating opportunities for singles to meet and get to know each other, and eventually get married. Help people to become the person that the person they want to marry would want to marry. Ideally a large number of Christian churches within a region would be involved in this at the same time; with several thousand singles involved. Each church (or a group of churches) would have their own single men's and single women's ministry for their singles to participate in.

The ministry should be led by married people who are trained to help prepare the singles for dating and marriage. These ministries will create small groups to help the singles to prepare themselves for dating and marriage. It would be better for separate men's and women's groups because there are some different issues that each need to deal with. These groups should be a place of preparation not for meeting singles of the opposite sex. That will come later. As the participants start dating they will hold each other accountable in maintaining purity, continuing to prepare for marriage, help with issues that come up, having realistic expectations, communicating better, etc. Ideally after they get married the relationships built in these groups will result in the formation of couples groups.

There should be a means for the ministries at different churches to share ideas and resources. An organization like Focus on the Family could build training modules that churches can pick from to aid in this preparation.

After several months of preparation the participants from all the churches in a region will all activate a profile in the same online dating venue. The local interdenominational steering committee for this could negotiate with the available online dating venues for a reduced price for participants and select a single venue for all to use. Ideally the singles groups should plan to activate their accounts around the same time. Different churches can then decide when to start their small groups based on what they have planned for preparation. The small group members can help each other prepare their profiles with ideas and advice.

After the initial round, new rounds of small groups could be organized once or twice per year to continue the ministry. Ideally this would be synchronized between the region's participating churches.

With regard to doctrinal differences between the participating churches it would be best for each church to provide its own guidance to its participants. The steering committee should make participation by churches relatively unrestricted. Ultimately each individual is responsible for their own decisions. With continuing participation in the small groups, issues that come up can be addressed within the group or brought to the church's pastors for discussion and guidance.

There are several expected results and benefits. Many more marriages (hopefully many thousands) among Christ followers. Given the tremendous benefits that marriage has for the individuals involved, their communities, and the culture this alone would be worth the effort.

Selfishness is the opposite of Love. The people involved in this will receive in-depth preparation for loving another. Whether they get married or not they will be learning to recognize and address their specific areas of selfishness and to love others well. Hopefully this enhanced preparation for marriage will result in far fewer divorces than their peers.

It will help to grow the Church by drawing singles back in who are drifting away. More marriages will likely result in more children. Drawing in seekers and non-believers who are attracted to what they hear about this ministry. Even if they initially participate just to expedite their goal of getting married the exposure to the Gospel and Christian worldview will be life changing for many of them and their descendants.

Growing the Church will help to change the culture. A restored Christian culture will transform the politics and policies of our country. This is not about growing the Church to improve political prospects. It is a recognition that followers of Christ have a different worldview and will support and advocate for different policies than others. Much like doing good works does not bring salvation but a good relationship with Christ will result in doing good works. We are all better off if more of us are being guided by God.

## Homosexuality and Same-Sex Marriage

According to the US Census Bureau in 2014 there were only 783,100 households with same-sex couples in the US. That is about 1.24 percent of households with couples. The total LGBT segment of the US population is about 3.5 percent. Around 1.7 percent identify as gay or lesbian, 1.8 percent as bisexual, and 0.3 percent as transgender. (Gates, Gary J., How many people are lesbian, gay, bisexual, and transgender?, Williams Institute, UCLA, 2011) This is far less than the 20-25 percent that many Americans believe.

According to the US Census Bureau only about 0.5 percent of married couples are homosexual couples. This is not surprising; the homosexual lifestyle has generally been about lust and promiscuity. It is not marriage that most want. It is for society to say that their behavior is acceptable. I don't believe that any level of acceptance will be good enough because much of the conviction that they are feeling about their behavior comes from the Holy Spirit. There is no legislation that can get rid of that.

We all have sinful impulses or behaviors that we are especially tempted with. Whenever possible we need to minimize the damage that our sin does to ourselves and to others. This is best done though a personal relationship with Christ.

There has been much debate about the cause of homosexuality and whether or not it is genetic. There are several studies from Europe where homosexual marriage and civil unions have a longer history than in the US. They are showing that well over forty percent of gay men report being sexually abused as a child. When the questions are rephrased to ask about their age of first sexual experience it becomes clear that well over 60 percent had early sexual experiences. Since many people resist being considered a victim or cannot admit the possibility that the abuse they received as children may be responsible for their sexual orientation the actual percentage is likely even higher.

There does not appear to be strong evidence of large percentages of lesbians having been abused by adult lesbians when they were children. It is more likely that most were sexually abused by males.

Statistically the vast majority of homosexuals do not sexually abuse children as some have feared. What is clear is that those who do sexually abuse children, in most cases men, likely influenced the homosexual behavior of their victims. It is possible that for gay men the familiarity with gay sex from the abuse overcame the societal taboo. Many probably believed they were gay due to being stimulated at times during the abuse. Another factor may be an attempt as men to take control of their sexual lives.

For lesbians the opposite appears more likely. Few were molested by women. Overwhelmingly the sexual abuse was from men. This may have caused a deep distrust and rejection of men.

The sexualization of children and teens in today's culture through widespread availability of pornographic materials, peer pressure, drugs and alcohol, and a lessoning of teaching of moral absolutes may contribute to part of the occurrence of homosexual activity. Rebelliousness against mainstream authority, pushing against societal norms, and experimentation may be contributing factors.

Childhood physical, emotional, and mental abuse and neglect may also be contributing factors. More likely these children are more vulnerable to pedophiles who offer attention and give the appearance of caring for these children.

It is important that we protect our children from sexual abuse. Eighty percent of child sexual abusers victimized children of family, friends, or neighbors. These were usually victims of opportunity. These offenders should have to serve their prison sentence and be required to live in a work release "apartment style" detention facility for the remainder of their lives. These should be electronically monitored. They would be able to work, shop, go to doctor/dentist/counseling appointments, and go to social activities with friends or family under the supervision of an approved adult. They should be able to marry and live with their spouse in the detention facility. Children should not be allowed in the facility. There can be a supervised meeting area where children related to the offender may visit.

The other twenty percent victimize children unknown to them. These offenders could be classified more clearly as predators. These offenders should be put in prison for life. They likely cannot be trusted to be in public. Some offenders that may appear to be opportunistic victimizers may actually be predatory. They may maneuver themselves into lives that give them access to many potential victims such as teachers, counselors, scout leaders, coaches, pastors, and living with women with children. The history of the offenders and the number of victims may serve to reclassify some apparent opportunistic offenders as predatory offenders.

There may be some who try to discredit this as an attempt to eliminate or reduce homosexuality. Certainly I want to eliminate homosexuality. It is a sinful behavior. This method should not be discredited. Many in the gay community do not want to believe that they have been influenced by the abuse they received. Instead they prefer to believe that they were victimized because of their sexual orientation. It can be disturbing to their sense of identity. But that is a mighty coincidence that such a huge proportion of homosexuals were abused as children. The percentage of heterosexual men who were sexually abused as children is one-tenth that of homosexual men. If this theory is wrong there will be no reduction in homosexuality in later generations. If the theory is correct then we are giving millions of children the freedom to choose their own future. Either way we are reducing the number of children who will be sexually abused. Compounding the benefit, many people who were sexually abused as children are more likely to use drugs and alcohol, commit suicide, drop out of school, and get into trouble with the law. No one should try to protect sexual abusers in order to protect their homosexual sense of identity.

Many will wish to contest the accuracy of the percentages above. Fine, let's commission a comprehensive study to determine the truth. Randomly select 100,000+ homosexuals from the population and compare to 100,000 randomly selected heterosexuals from the population. The first team in the study will select the participants. The second team will interview each person selected for the study without knowing which group the person is in. The third group is investigators who will do a deep background on each participant to find any evidence that the person leaves out that could distort the results. In each team the researchers are paired with one that is supportive of the homosexual lifestyle and one who is against. In a study like this there will always be accusations of bias. By having every decision made and every piece of evidence collected by people with opposing biases hopefully we can achieve an accurate and accepted study. This will be an expensive study but many lives are affected by this issue. Major public policies are affected by this. Right now many decisions are being made on the basis of opinion and not facts. The culture is being radically changed based on these opinions. Let truth win out!

In the area of homosexuality it should not be made illegal but it should not be endorsed either. Especially by the government! Violence against homosexuals should never be condoned and should be prosecuted just like any other crime. We need to treat everyone respectfully and with dignity and love as fellow image bearers. Out of love we cannot endorse sin and we must try to reach out to every sinner with the truth found in the Gospel. How can we not given the horrific consequences in the afterlife.

There is no compelling reason for the state to allow homosexual marriage, civil unions, or the like. Just because two people live together or have sex does not provide sufficient justification for the state to endorse and provide benefits to the relationship. The only relationships that have statistically provided strength and security for its participants has been heterosexual marriage. It provides the greatest chance of success and safety for children. We have to end the subsidization of the breakdown of the family.

There are some rights that should be ensured for people whether they are homosexual or not. People should be able to choose their own heirs. Aside from the need to ensure that dependents are fully protected and resourced the state should stay out of the decision. All people should be able to choose who receives their power of attorney, who can visit them in the hospital, make life or death decisions for them, be their caregiver, handle their estate, etc. These are basic issues of autonomy.

Unfortunately there are many in the homosexual and liberal communities who want to force everyone else to endorse their lifestyle. They are trying to outlaw even making the statements I have made in this chapter. That is un-American and a danger to everyone's liberty. History shows that it is dangerous for all involved when someone tries to prevent others from having and expressing their own beliefs and values.

### Foster Care and Adoption

The children in foster care are in great need of love. The Christian community should be volunteering in such huge numbers that there is a long waiting list for receiving children to care for. While most are not orphans they all have needs similar to orphans whether they are true orphans or temporary orphans. The Church is called to care for the orphans in our midst.

Children are best served by a father and a mother. It helps them to learn how to relate responsibly to other males and females. If the natural parents and relatives are unavailable then they should only be placed with a heterosexual couple until there are no more available. Other households should be in line behind them. After that female households (single and couples) are statistically safer than male households in terms of sexual abuse. Physical and emotional abuse and neglect are more closely balanced between men and women.

For all households, relational stability should be a major factor when considering placement. Physical abuse, sexual abuse, emotional abuse, neglect, substance abuse, and abandonment are more likely when there is instability in the home. Couples married for more than ten years should be preferred. Single people that reject cohabitation should be preferred over singles that support or engage in cohabitation. Cohabitation is inherently unstable. The couple has not even reached the point of making a lifetime commitment to each other. How do they commit to a child. LGTBQ couple households tend to be less stable than married heterosexual couples. The highest risk of child sexual and physical abuse comes from unrelated males living in or frequenting the home. With the highest risk coming from those who were sexually abused as children.

Some pedophiles will try to find victims in this system. The state has an obligation to monitor the living situation of all children placed in its charge. This should involve monitoring even after adoption to ensure that a child has not been placed with an abuser. To be clear, the overwhelming majority of foster and adoptive parents, both heterosexual and homosexual, will not abuse or neglect the children placed with them. We all owe them a great debt for the efforts they make to care for children. But there are enough cases of abuse and neglect that we need to be ever vigilant to protect these vulnerable children.

## Transgender Bathroom Laws

Women and girls need to be protected from men and teen boys using their bathrooms, locker rooms, and other such facilities by requiring that people use the facilities corresponding to their sex at birth. Liberals and the LGTBQ community try to frame this as discrimination against transgender people.

The reality is that less than 0.3 percent of people identify as transgender and some are heterosexual and some are homosexual. Some have had surgery to change their appearance to the other gender. The fact is most real transgender people who look like the opposite sex will not be noticed in a toilet stall. Locker rooms are another matter.

If transgender people can use the facilities based on how they identify themselves instead of by their biological status then there is nothing to keep men from pretending to be transgender in order to use women's facilities legally. Whether they are sincere transgenders or fakes, if they have male anatomy and are sexually attracted to women then they pose a threat to women in these facilities.

Another aspect is going to be the teen boys who will go into girl's locker rooms individually or in packs on a dare. That is the way teen boys think and act. Especially if they know they cannot get into trouble for it. Teen girls should not have to live with this uncertainty about their privacy.

One of the key aspects of freedom is that it has to be balanced against an infringement upon the freedom of others. There is a serious chance of harm from allowing males in female facilities. Transgender people are making a choice to act and dress as they do. The women and girls forced to share these bathrooms and locker rooms with men would have their freedom curtailed significantly through no fault of their own. The onus must be on transgender people to accommodate the safety and privacy needs of women and children.

## Pornography

Pornography is a scourge to loving relationships. It causes people, mostly men, to focus on lust rather than love. It gives people an unrealistic expectation of relationships by focusing only on body features and sex acts. It is especially important that children be exposed to as little pornography as possible.

It is unconstitutional to ban pornographic depictions of consenting adults. But there are ways that the use and availability of pornography can be reduced and limited in society. The most effective is to seek help from the Holy Spirit to provide the strength to resist this temptation. Legislatively there are means as well.

### Porn Tax

There is an incredible amount of pornographic material that is available for free, especially online. It is used as a marketing tool to get men to purchase pornographic materials. It has been a very effective tool. It is especially problematic that minors can easily view this huge volume of pornography. The Porn Tax is designed to require payment to view pornographic materials.

The tax to view a picture is one cent for each. The tax to

download/purchase a picture is ten cents. The tax to view a video is one-half cent per minute. The tax to download/purchase a video is five cents per minute. The tax will apply regardless of the medium used to convey the images.

The tax will apply any time female nipples, and male or female genitalia or anuses are shown. Any free to view advertising will require these areas to be covered. An exception will be made for medical and breastfeeding images that do not offer any images for sale. Another exception will be made for images of art that is older than 100 years.

Setting a tax is easy. Enforcement is more complex. There are thousands of websites available for viewing and purchasing pornography. The key to enforcement will be to require these websites to have an approved web analytics program monitoring the website under the supervision of an outside accounting firm. The accountants will file a report with the tax filings attesting under oath to the accuracy of the filing. The use of accountants provides a type of firewall between user identifiable information and the government.

Any website not complying will be shut down in the US market until their taxes are paid. If necessary, the government can sue to seize the business and the website and auction them off. Foreign websites will have to comply or be blocked from the US market. Ironically this law will probably strengthen the business model of primary pornography producers by weeding out thousands of low margin resellers and amateur porn sites that rely on advertisers for revenue.

To aid in the enforcement of this tax and to aid parents in blocking pornographic websites all such sites should be transitioned to .xxx and .porn internet domains.

## Copyright of Pornographic Images

The default ownership of pornographic images and videos that are not produced as work made for hire should be changed to the person or people in the image. Currently it resides with the photographer. Assignment of copyright can be made to photographers and others if desired by the people in the image. Dissemination of these images, either free or for a fee, should require the written consent of all owners of the images. This will aid in stopping vindictive former spouses, boyfriends, and girlfriends from legally releasing pictures and videos in their possession. It will make ownership of hidden video recordings and upskirt pictures belong to the victim. It will provide a legal basis for going after websites that make these available.

Here are some additional considerations. Someone performing a sex act will be considered a co-owner even if no private parts are visible. Licensed investigators and others may retain ownership of images and videos from infidelity or other investigations. These videos and images must be registered within ten days with a court and may only be disclosed to clients, in discovery, and in court proceedings. They may not otherwise be made available to the public. Releases and contracts should be held invalid unless signed by a disinterested witness and the person being filmed or photographed is completely sober at the time of signing. These contracts should specify the activities to be recorded.

### Pornography Registry

The registry would be a voluntary repository of ownership information, consent forms, proof of age, identification and contact information for those in the pictures and videos, and contracts related to the images. It would be overseen by the FBI. It should be paid for by fees from those who register their pictures and videos. But only enough to cover the actual needs. Pornography producers and copyright owners can register all of their images to reduce the need to be audited by the FBI for compliance with age requirements.

Some of the benefits for the owners of the images is that it allows the FBI to concentrate their investigatory resources on other purveyors of pornography who also happen to be competitors in the business. The FBI can more easily identify child pornography in contrast to barely legal pornography. The same with other types of pornography that would be illegal if real but are not if staged by a production company such as some "hidden videos." When copyright, consent, and contract information is registered then illegal distributors are easier to detect and the FBI can prosecute them.

As an aid to users of pornography every picture and video will have metadata attached that indicate copyright ownership, names and proof of age data of the people in the images, and will reference the registry file if it is registered. If registered, the real names of the people in the images can be replaced in the metadata with an identifying number assigned by the registry. This will make it easier to identify legal from illegal pornography. As part of this law it will become illegal to distribute pornographic pictures or video without this metadata attached. It will take some time to accomplish this administratively so the law should provide two years before the metadata requirement is enforced.

## Prison Rape Prevention Reform

As a society we have an obligation to protect everyone from rape. Just because someone has been convicted of a crime does not mean that they cease to be human beings. They are still image bearers of God. We cannot expect them to have respect for authority when they are not protected when they are prisoners of that authority. They have a greatly reduced level of control over their lives when they are incarcerated.

The corrections system has to be responsible for ensuring the safety of its prisoners. Many times this will involve ridding facilities of blind spots, installing more security cameras and replacing solid doors with bars. That is not sufficient. There have to be an adequate number of rotating corrections officers continuously patrolling the facilities to ensure that there is not enough privacy to facilitate a rape. This will cost more money but it is our responsibility to protect our prisoners.

The emphasis has to be on prevention because of the fear and stigma related to reporting being raped. It is not sufficient to wait for a rape to be reported and then to prosecute. There is simply too much damage being inflicted from unreported rapes.

A significant number of the reported rapes involve corrections officers. While some of these are likely false accusations there are sufficient numbers of proven cases to agree that this is a serious problem. Ninety percent of these reported cases are heterosexual rapes. The easiest way to reduce this is to only have female staff at female prisons and male staff at male prisons.

# 14 CAMPAIGN FINANCE AND ELECTION REFORMS

**"The true principle of a republic is, that the people should choose
whom they please to govern them."
Alexander Hamilton**

## Federal Campaign Finance Reform

Campaign finance needs to be reformed because career politicians are
able to accumulate huge war chests of contributions left over from prior
campaigns that make it difficult for opponents to run against them. This
makes it harder to hold them accountable. There are too many loopholes that
can allow non-citizens to contribute and there is a great deal of out-of-district
money swinging elections.

The ideal would be unlimited contributions only from individual US
citizens. No contributions from corporations or unions. Contributions would
only come from the citizens of the state or district for Congressional races.
Time limits for candidates to retain contributions. What follows is the closest
I have been able to get to this and still work in the real world with sinful
people and with prevailing Supreme Court decisions. It is not nearly as neat
and pure as above.

The intent of these reforms is to empower the citizens of a district with
more local control over political campaigns. Provide an easier means for a
small number of people to jump start a campaign but then set reasonable
limits that require more popular support to sustain a campaign. It sets limits
to prevent excessive influence by a few very rich people. It provides an easy
way for people to determine who supports each candidate financially and with
how much money when large sums are contributed. At the same time it
provides a process for anonymity for small contributors to avoid intimidation
for their contributions but also screens out non-citizens trying to contribute.

Here are a couple of definitions used in the plan. **Dynamic activities** are
active promotion and advertising, travel, voter identification, and get out the
vote activities, etc. **Static activities** are activities where people have to

voluntarily choose to receive information. Examples: website, copies of information/materials requested by individuals, staff people, database management, and educational and outreach programs that only deal with issues and not candidates or officeholders.

**General Rules**

All contributions must be from US citizens, corporations, or unions. There are specific sections later that deal with corporate and union contribution rules.

All contributions must be reported to the FEC and on the candidate's, party's, or organization's website five business days prior to being spent and no more than forty days after being received. Some exceptions include gifts in kind, contributions received in the final five days before the election, and contributions received as the price of admission to a fundraising event. Gifts in kind may be used immediately but must be reported within forty days of receipt. Contributions received in the final five business days before the election may be used immediately following posting on the campaign website. Contributions received as the price of admission to a fundraising event may be used to pay for the expenses of the event immediately but must be reported within forty days of receipt. All excess contributions from the event must be reported and used under normal rules.

Currently only the name, address, and amount are required and occupation and employer information must be requested by the campaign but does not have to be required by the campaign. The following information should be collected, reported, and posted for all contributions. This information would allow for more accurately linking contributions to the correct person.

Complete name
Address
Phone number (Campaign and FEC only, not on the website)
Date of birth (Campaign and FEC only, not on the website)
Driver's License or State ID number (Campaign and FEC only, not on the website)
Occupation
Employer name and address
Amount of contribution

All contributions must come from individual US citizens, corporations or unions. For purposes of residency, the individual must live or work in the district for at least 30 days. Military service members on active duty may use their last place of residence in their home state until such time as they establish residency elsewhere.

All information, online and offline must be presented in an easily searchable, sortable, and downloadable (online) format. Unlimited contributions are permitted for static activities. Primary and general elections will be treated as the same election. Contributions will be limited based upon the fundraising phase, which will be explained shortly.

Funds may not be carried over from one election cycle to another. The funds must be expended within one year of being received or one-third of the term of office, whichever is longer, or returned on a pro rata basis to contributors, or donated to a political party, transferred to the primary winner, or donated to a nonprofit organization, or a combination of these. The candidate must provide clear notice to contributors at the time of contribution about how the leftover funds will be disposed of at the end of the campaign. The candidate may change the disposition plan at any time for contributions made after that point in time. Campaign signs, printed materials, office equipment and supplies, etc. may be retained from one election cycle to another.

Funds transferred to the primary winner must adhere to individual contribution limits in the recipient candidate's account. This option must have a backup disposition for nontransferable funds. The candidate may make this option conditional upon which candidate wins the primary.

A candidate may contribute an unlimited amount to their own campaign but is limited to fifty percent of total contributions during Phase I and twenty-five percent of total contributions during Phase II. If the candidate exceeded the Phase II limit during Phase I he/she will be barred from further donations until they are under the twenty-five percent limit but will not have to return the excess.

It would be nice to have unlimited contributions by candidates and contributors. Contributions equate with free speech and there should be no limits in political free speech. Unfortunately, over time we could develop cliques representing different parts of the political spectrum that could overwhelm the electoral process. They could pool their money and resources and select the candidates. Similar to the oligarchs in Ukraine. It could become difficult to build a competitive campaign from the grassroots.

For the first time, the value of volunteer work will have to be counted due to the limits on out-of-district contributions. This is intended to prevent the payment of "volunteers" to try to circumvent these rules. All volunteer hours must be documented as contributions and can be valued at the federal median wage unless the volunteer fits the conditions below.

If a person does more than 260 volunteer hours (combined if divided between multiple campaigns) in any running thirteen week period they must document the source of funds for their living expenses. The volunteer must document the source of funds received from the previous 24 months. Individual campaigns only need to track volunteer hours and the value of those hours in their own campaign. When the FEC identifies individuals over the limit when working on multiple campaigns, the FEC will notify the campaigns and the individual. The individual is responsible for documenting this provision in a timely manner. The value of each hour is calculated as the person's total income from the 24 previous completed months divided by 4160 hours; but not less than the prevailing minimum wage for the work location. Monetary valuation is based upon self-reporting by the volunteer.

The FEC and not the campaign is responsible for verifying the information. The FEC must establish simple accounting rules for documenting compliance to these rules. The FEC will have the authority to check information against federal employment and tax records and to request information from the states to verify the information reported.

## Contributions to Presidential Candidate Campaigns

Phase I is the period when total contributions for a campaign are equal to or less than ten percent of the amount spent by the Presidential campaign from the past elections that spent the most contributions. No individual other than the candidate may contribute more than one percent of this limit.

Phase II is the remainder of the campaign period after total contributions exceed the ten percent threshold. There is no maximum contribution limit, but an individual (other than the candidate) may contribute no more than 0.25 percent of total contributions. Any individual who exceeded this limit during Phase I will be barred from further donations until they are under the 0.25 percent limit. This provision will allow a small number of people to jump start a candidate's campaign but then make it necessary for the candidate to become popular with the public to sustain the campaign. Following the party nominating convention, the Vice Presidential candidate will be subject to the same limits as the Presidential candidate.

## Contributions to Senate Candidate Campaigns

Phase I is the period when total contributions are equal to or less than twenty percent of the amount spent by the Senate campaign in that state that spent the most contributions in past elections. No individual other than the candidate may contribute more than five percent of this limit.

Phase II is the remainder of the campaign after total contributions exceed the twenty percent threshold. There is no maximum contribution limit, but an individual (other than the candidate) may contribute no more than 0.5 percent of total contributions. Any individual who exceeded this limit during Phase I will be barred from further donations until they are under the 0.5 percent limit. At least eighty percent of contributions must come from residents of the state. This allows friends, family, and political allies of the candidate to make contributions but requires the bulk of the support to come from the state.

## Contributions to House of Representatives Candidate Campaigns

Phase I is the period when total contributions are equal to or less than twenty percent of the amount spent by the House campaign from the past elections in the district that spent the most contributions. In the first election cycle after district boundary changes the total contributions limit will be based on the highest amount spent by a campaign for a district that included part of the new district. No individual other than the candidate may contribute more than five percent of this limit.

Phase II is the remainder of the campaign period after total contributions exceed the twenty percent threshold. There is no maximum contribution limit, but an individual (other than the candidate) may contribute no more than 0.5 percent of total contributions. Any individual who exceeded this limit during Phase I will be barred from further donations until they are under the 0.5 percent limit. At least seventy percent of contributions must come from residents of the district and at least eighty percent must come from residents of the state. This allows friends, family, and political allies of the candidate to make contributions but requires the bulk of the support to come from the state and district.

## Contributions to Issue Campaigns

This section pertains to organizations that are not political parties. Unlimited contributions are permitted for issue campaigns that do not mention candidates or officeholders. Unlimited contributions are permitted for static activities by issue campaigns even if political parties, candidates, or officeholders are mentioned. Contributions for issue campaigns that advocate a position or purport to educate regarding a political or public policy issue may only come from US citizens and US corporations and unions.

Contributions for issue campaigns that mention Presidential, Senate, or House candidates must adhere to the same limits as the candidate campaigns, except for the following. While all contributions must normally be spent within one year of receiving them under this plan; unspent campaign funds may be segregated and saved for future non-campaign projects but may not be reintroduced into campaign accounts. A subaccount must be maintained for each candidate mentioned and the contributions and expenses must be assigned to assure adherence to limits. If multiple candidates are mentioned in an advertisement the full cost of the advertisement is counted against the limits for each subaccount.

## Contributions to Political Parties

Unlimited contributions are permitted for political parties at all levels—national, state, and local. Political parties may advertise without limit for the party or for issue campaigns without naming its candidates, against another party without naming its candidates and against other organizations or issue campaigns. Political parties may fund voter identification, voter surveying, voter registration, poll watching and get-out-the-vote activities and coordinate these activities with candidate campaigns.

Political parties may not contribute to or finance candidate advertising on TV, radio, newspapers, magazines, mailings, and by other unsolicited advertising until the final ninety days before the general election or the certification of the primary election winner, whichever is closer to the general election. When political parties make these dynamic activity contributions they are acting as conduits and must itemize the amount from each original contributor.

### Contributions to Political Action Committees (PACs)

Contributions to Political Action Committees should be classified and treated much the same as contributions to political parties or issue campaigns or conduits. They will self-select their classification to best meet their goals.

### Contributions by Corporations

Corporations have several options for how and who can decide if the corporation can make a contribution and how much of a contribution. The shareholders will be required to vote annually for the upcoming year to select option 1 or 2; option 3 or 4 can be put in the corporate bylaws as the default.

**Option 1:** The decision is delegated to the CEO or other executive, an executive committee, board of directors, or a committee of the board of directors.

**Option 2:** A supermajority of shareholders can vote to decide every contribution following a proposal by the CEO, Board of Directors, or shareholder.

**Option 3:** The majority of shareholders can vote to decide every contribution following a proposal by the CEO, Board of Directors, or shareholder. Those that vote in favor of the contribution will have a portion of the contribution taken from their next dividend. The vote would be for a set amount per share which would reduce the dividend to the shareholder.

**Option 4:** This is the default option if none of the others is approved. The shareholders can also make a positive election that the corporation can only spend corporate funds to promote issues and candidates to shareholders and employees and lobbying of candidates and elected officials directly, through trade associations, or chambers of commerce. A motion can specify any restrictions.

Options 1 and 2 require approval by sixty percent of the vote of the total outstanding shares or the corporation may only make contributions under option 3 or 4. No non-citizens may make a decision to make a contribution or make a contribution proposal motion. Therefore any individual included in option 1 who is not a U.S. citizen or is subordinate to a non-citizen may not have this authority delegated to him/her. Non-citizens may vote against delegation of authority under option 1 to try to prevent the company from making contributions. They may not vote in favor of delegating this authority.

Non-citizens are not permitted to vote in favor of making a contribution but may vote against making a contribution. This will allow non-citizens the opportunity to try to prevent their part of the company from making a contribution. Under option 1, 2, and 4, US citizens must have free and clear ownership of sixty percent of the corporation in order to be an exercisable option. Under option 3, non-citizens may not participate in the voting.

Corporations, funds, or other entities that own shares of a corporation as intermediaries between individuals and the contributing corporation must apply the same restrictions and process as a corporation in deciding their votes for the corporation shares. Under option 1 or 2, any individual that owns one percent or more of the corporation is required to include their part of the contribution under their personal contribution limits.

Under options 1 and 2, the corporation will be acting as a single person and have to abide by the same contribution limits. The corporation must include a listing of its political contributions on its website. Under option 3, the corporation will be acting as a conduit and the contribution will be linked to the individual. Individual limits will apply. Additionally, when reporting dividend information any reductions due to political contributions must be listed and described.

For purposes of residency, the corporation must have a physical presence in the district or have a documented supply chain presence in the district under options 1 or 2. Under option 3, the shareholders voting in favor of making contributions must be residents of the district or the corporation must have a physical presence in the district or have a documented supply chain presence in the district. For corporations not chartered in the state and not headquartered in the district there are additional limits to their contributions. Total annual contributions for dynamic activities to all entities covered by this law will not exceed the greater of: total after-tax profits generated in the district, ten percent of revenues generated in the district, or ten percent of corporate purchases made from the district.

All shareholders must be allowed to participate in the voting whether they can attend a meeting or not. The responsibility for the cost of contacting the shareholders is with the initiator of the motion. Motions may be made from the floor of an annual shareholder meeting and may not need to reach out to non-attendees if the required threshold is reached.

The corporation may voluntarily take on the cost of sending proposed motions to shareholders prior to meetings. If they do they must include all proposed motions. Not just those favored by management. The corporation may divide the costs between the initiators of motions.

All investors in mutual funds may set blanket votes for all of their holdings. They can choose one of three options. The first is a "no" vote to any contributions. The second is a "yes" vote only for Option 4. The third is a "yes" vote for contributions to a particular political party.

The fourth is to delegate their voting rights to the fund management. In all cases fund management must have a webpage where they list their positions on each political contribution vote. This listing must take place within 24 hours of the fund management making a decision or voting. The listing must be shown for at least seven years after the vote.

The final option involves the direct voting by mutual fund investors. With current technology mutual fund websites could provide a portal for investors to interact with corporate shareholder meetings. The investors can listen live and participate in voting if preregistered. This should be limited to shareholders who have at least a full share of the stock. The cost of this portal should be passed on to those investors who make us of it. Other investors who use one of the blanket options should not have to pay for this service. Most mutual fund investors will not make use of this service.

## Contributions by Unions

Regular union dues may not be used to make political contributions or issue contributions that mention candidates, officeholders, or political parties. There must be a separate itemized political/issue contribution fee. The union will be acting as a conduit and the contribution will be linked to the individual. Individual limits will apply. Each union member must make a positive election on what they want done with their political/issue contribution fee.

The union member may delegate the decision to the union leadership at the local, district, state, company, national, or other level. No non-citizens may receive this delegation nor may anyone subordinate to a non-citizen receive the delegation. The union member may choose not to make any contribution and absent themselves from the fee. The union member may elect to choose which campaigns recommended by union leaders to contribute toward. Non-citizen union members may not make political/issue contributions.

## Anonymous Political Contributions

The FEC will establish a program for contributors to voluntarily register to obtain an ID number in order to make contributions anonymously. This program will allow small contributors to make contributions without fear of retribution while also insuring that non-citizens are not contributing anonymously. A bipartisan team will oversee the program. The information collected will not be shared with other parts of the government or with others outside the government except in court proceedings if the FEC brings a case for fraud or abuse of the system against someone who is registered. Audits will be conducted to ensure compliance with citizenship, contribution limits, and program requirements. Auditors will be able to compare the contributions to the person's tax filings.

Under the program, the contributor may not contribute more than ten percent of their annual income (earned plus unearned) or more than $50,000 in a calendar year, whichever is less. If they wish to exceed this limit, all of their current year contributions will have to be publicly declared. Contributors may make contributions both anonymously and in the open. If their combined contributions exceed the program limits then all must be openly declared. They will be given a warning if they go over the limit and have ten business days to request a partial refund to come back down to the limit. This claw back must come from the most recent contribution(s). A contributor may obtain a new ID number each year to help aid their anonymity.

There should be penalties for unlawful disclosure. It should be a felony offense to intentionally or with gross negligence release this information unlawfully. It should be a misdemeanor offense to negligently, but less than gross negligently, release this information unlawfully. Contributors should be allowed to sue to recover actual damages resulting from the negligent or intentional unlawful disclosure of information from this program. There will be an independent auditing and prosecuting team from each major party with the power to prosecute violations by contributors, staff, and others. (Principle involved here is Mutually Assured Destruction if there are unwarranted prosecutions.) The priority will be to bring people into compliance. Prosecutions should be reserved for negligence and intentionally trying to circumvent the law.

The FEC will maintain a website calculator to help individuals stay within contribution limits. The FEC will provide a free downloadable basic program for individuals, campaigns, issue advocacy organizations and parties to track donations given and received and for the completion of required reports. There are already many advanced campaign recordkeeping software packages on the open market. That will work for larger campaigns. A simple EZ program should be sufficient for smaller campaigns. Common software, such as Excel, should be useable by campaigns to upload and download their filings.

## Voter ID Laws

There has been controversy in many states over requirements that people show a photo ID when they vote. The Democrat argument is that few cases of voter fraud have ever been proven and that some people do not have photo IDs. It is true that few cases of voter fraud have been proven. While some people do not have photo IDs there are far more people that have state issued IDs than there are registered voters. It is already very difficult to do most financial transactions in this country without a photo ID. Also, in order to not violate federal prohibitions against poll taxes, states have to make free IDs available to those who cannot afford to pay for one.

The Republican argument is that there is no way to make sure that the person voting is entitled to vote unless there is a photo ID requirement. It is possible the reason that few arrests for voter fraud are made is because people do not have to prove who they are when they vote. This disenfranchises all of us who legally vote.

It is rare that someone does not have a state photo ID. The largest group of citizens in this situation are likely to be senior citizens who are homebound or under care in a hospital or nursing home. Where I live it is already common for municipal clerks to visit these people in the weeks leading up to elections or send an absentee ballot if they want to vote. It would not be difficult for municipal clerks to be authorized to collect the necessary information and picture for obtaining a photo ID from these people and submitting it to the state. The state can then send the ID to the person for future years. This could also be done from municipal clerks' offices to offer more locations and less of a wait for people to get an ID. I bet that if a request went out to app developers there would be a dozen apps designed within a few weeks that would work. The government would likely need more time to write the request than it would take to write the app.

As someone who has spent time analyzing elections, voter turnouts and running poll watching operations I know first-hand about the huge number of people who are registered to vote who do not vote. This is especially high in neighborhoods where there is a high turnover like rental areas and college areas. Any group with a well-developed door-to-door operation can identify who has moved. That information along with voting histories and the list of registered voters can predict who will not show up to vote at the local polling place. The Democrats and many allied community organizing groups would have this information. (I do not have any evidence this has been done but it is easily possible for it to be done without a photo ID requirement. The extent that they have fought these measures leads me to be mighty suspicious.)

A photo ID should be required by everyone to vote. The results are too important not to protect the integrity of our elections.

When collecting nomination signatures, recall petition signatures, and other political petitions it would be helpful if the circulator was required to view and record the type of ID and the identifying number from the ID along with the other customary information of name, signature, address, municipality, and date. Everything except the signature should have to be legible. Additionally, the campaign should be required to submit an Excel file with all of the information from the petitions with the submission of the hardcopy petitions. Then the state elections board could easily compare the submissions to the ID databases. The collectors of signatures should have the burden of proving that the signatures are valid.

### Absentee Ballots

Absentee ballots need to be distributed more carefully. There are several requirements that need to be implemented to prevent the manipulation of an election through fraudulent absentee votes. There should be no open-ended application for absentee ballots. A registered voter should have to appear in person with a photo ID to sign up for the following two years. Military service members should be able to get additional extensions by submitting an affidavit from a designated authority on military posts or vessels or by submitting a copy of orders indicating their deployment overseas. Municipal clerks should have a program to visit the homebound or otherwise confined eligible voters in their district to verify their identity and sign them up for absentee ballots. Bipartisan teams of poll workers should visit hospitals, nursing homes and other facilities housing people who are unable to go to a polling place to ease voting by these people.

### Methods to Prevent Absentee Ballot Manipulation
1. Limit the reasons that people can vote by absentee ballot.
2. When received by the municipal clerk the voter's signature should be compared to the signature on file before it is accepted as valid. If they do not match the voter should be contacted to confirm that they completed their own ballot. When registering to receive absentee ballots the voter should have to designate several security questions and answers to confirm their identity when contacted.
3. Bar third party voter registration groups and individuals from maintaining copies of voter registration forms. They may only keep a separate record of name, address, phone number, and email of those people they register. It may not include a photocopy of the form, copy of their signature, or identifying information such as driver's license number, state ID number, social security number, etc.
4. Bar third party groups and individuals from collecting, copying, or submitting absentee voter forms. They may only distribute blank forms.
4. Bar third party voter registration groups and individuals from selling or otherwise transferring copies of the information they collect in the voter registration process to others.
5. Require that absentee ballots have a "DO NOT FORWARD" note on the envelope.

6. Require that the USPS enforce the rule of not delivering private mail box mail that does not have PMB in the address. Penalty for USPS workers should be the same as mail fraud.

7. Require that the USPS has an online database listing all private mail boxes that election officials can get a password to access to check addresses for free. Have it available for a fee like their other lists for all others.

8. Require that USPS maintain an online database of all change of address, mail forwarding, mail stoppage and restart requests for the past ten years. Require election officials to review the list for their jurisdiction to verify that the people are still at the address before sending an absentee ballot. The database should have an automated process for election officials to do this check in bulk and not have to key in every name to complete a check. The system should record when a check is made.

9. Require that all voter registration and absentee ballot request documents ask if the address is a private mail box address. Require a physical address also.

10. Require that when a voter registers they have to provide their previous addresses for at least five years. The municipal clerk will notify the election officials of the previous addresses of the change in registration. This will be easy if states have a system like My Vote Wisconsin that WI has. (https://myvote.wi.gov/).

11. Require that state driver's license number or state ID number be written on voter registration and absentee ballot request forms.

12. Require a distinctive envelope for absentee ballots to be sent to the voter and to be returned by the voter. When the mail carrier delivers the ballot to the voter they complete a return card similar to registered mail. The card will be returned to the election authority.

## Presidential Primary Absentee Voting

Given the dramatic changes that can occur from week-to-week in a presidential primary there should be a reduced window when absentee ballots can be sent to voters and returned. A standard time frame can be used for voters to request an absentee ballot. The municipal clerk's office should then mail the absentee ballots so that they arrive at the voter's home on the second Wednesday before the primary. In-person early voting should only begin on the second Wednesday before the primary. This reduces the chances of people voting for a candidate who has dropped out of the race. New information is brought to light about candidates weekly. They improve or make mistakes. With the proposed changes to Presidential primary voting procedures people will need to make decisions about more than just their favorite candidate. Haste and too early voting is not helpful for the country as a whole in making this decision.

## Electoral College

I am a strong supporter of continuing with the Electoral College for the election of the President and Vice President. Originally it was designed to mitigate some of the imbalance between small and large population states. It still has that affect. More important it helps to minimize the effect of voter fraud. Fraud that may be prevalent in certain parts of the country can only affect the outcome in the state where it happens.

For this same reason I support the Congressional District Method of distributing electoral votes within a state rather than the winner-takes-all method. It will decrease the effect of voting fraud in part of a state overruling the votes in the rest of the state. Political machines have played a part in politics for much of our history. Usually more prevalent in large cities where power is easier to concentrate. Frequently we do not know the extent of the influence until well after the election, sometimes decades after. There are still stories and rumors about political machines controlling various cities or states. This is a threat to our liberty and needs to be eliminated. While this will not eliminate the problem it can reduce a machine's power and effectiveness at manipulating elections.

Other benefits of the Congressional District Method include spreading attention from battleground states to battleground congressional districts. This will put more areas of the country in play. It will make the issues of more parts of the country relevant to the national campaigns. As attention is brought to battleground districts it will increase turnout in those districts; potentially putting more statewide electoral votes in play. When these statewide votes are put in play it can make the whole state a battleground state. The electoral and popular vote results should be close if every state used this method. This will make the votes of more of the country relevant in the Presidential elections. This is good for liberty.

The United States has become increasingly polarized. This is in part because certain states are no longer relevant for each of the major political parties. The other side is essentially in control of the state. In practical terms this means little effort is made by campaigns to influence the vote in the state. Instead of a contest of ideas as happens in the battleground states there is one side simply reinforcing a single viewpoint. It pushes the lone powerful party in the state further to the left or right. This is dangerous for the unity of the country. We need a vibrant contest of ideas in every state and district for our republic to thrive. Without it we get the gridlock that has gripped Washington.

Much of the electorate only vote at the time of the Presidential election. Many Republican districts in blue states and many Democrat districts in red states will become relevant to the presidential race. This will increase the voter turnout in these districts. Because media markets do not follow congressional district boundaries other districts that neighbor these newly competitive districts will hear the competition of ideas. Over time this will make these neighboring districts more competitive.

The opponents of the Electoral College frequently cite the times when the popular vote was out of sync with the result of the Electoral College. When a Presidential race has already been decided before voting ends on the West Coast Republican voters are discouraged from voting. This diminishes the voter turnout and the strength of the Party in these states. With the Congressional District Method there will be more chance that a Presidential race will not be decided until the West Coast finishes voting. When these voters participate the popular vote will be closer to the results of the Electoral College.

When people do vote for President most also vote in the other elections held that day. This has an impact on these other races. Making more of the country relevant in the Presidential Election will make more local races competitive.

Besides the political advantage bias the primary arguments against the Congressional District Method of distributing votes are the problem of gerrymandered districts, increased campaign costs, and uncertainty by all parties in how to run their campaigns. With regard to reforms to the redistricting process to minimize the ability to gerrymander districts check out the next section. Increased campaign costs will work themselves out by increased fundraising or spreading out the many campaign commercials among more media markets. Uncertainty about how to run a campaign under the new conditions will shake out over the course of a couple of election cycles. Overall this method will give more people a real say in who gets elected to be President and Vice-President.

Getting the Congressional District Method implemented nationwide will take a constitutional amendment. In theory it could be done individually by each state but politically that will never happen. There needs to be a way found where both Republicans and Democrats can see benefits to passing the amendment. The best strategy may be to start with the Republican legislatures in purple states changing their states to the Congressional District Method. This will take many potential votes away from the Democrats in the next Presidential election. It will be difficult to get Democrats to agree to the constitutional amendment because the Congressional District Method puts them at a disadvantage compared to the Winner Take All Method. Overall the Congressional District Method will be closer to the popular vote than the Winner Take All Method. In 2008 Obama would still have won but in 2012 Romney won more congressional districts. Since 1960 only two times has a President been elected while not winning the majority of congressional districts; Obama in 2012 and Kennedy in 1960.

This has to be explained well to the American people as a means to more freedom. As a means to obtain a more responsive government. Passage in a single amendment along with redistricting reform may be the only way to generate sufficient nationwide support.

## Redistricting

Redistricting is always a volatile subject when it comes up every decade. Each party hopes to be in charge when it is redistricting time in order to favor themselves in the new districts. I want conservatives to have the greatest advantage but the people deserve to have the elected officials of their choice. Too little is done by the Republican Party to educate people on the issues and the platform. The Party needs to do the work to explain our principles and convince people that we are right. I firmly believe that in a head-to-head competition our values and ideas are best and will resonate well with most people. Too often people get hung up on misconceptions about the Republican Party and conservatives. We need to grow the Party through education and outreach. We need to stop only being concerned about elections and be concerned about solving problems with conservative ideas.

Many people in the parties just want to create safe seats for both sides as long as their side has the majority in order to not have to work as hard. Safe districts for a party tend to become safe districts for incumbents because there is great pressure not to challenge the party's elected officials. This situation, like all accumulations of power is corrupting. Liberty requires that people can readily and regularly replace their elected representatives when they do not feel like the officials are serving them well.

We need a constitutional amendment that sets some guidelines on redistricting that will provide more freedom for the people of the district than currently exists. Here are a few suggestions and are in the order of recommended precedence.

1. No more than a one percent population deviation between districts in each state. The split between districts should make the faster growing districts the lower population side of the split. (The faster growing districts will grow toward equality.)
2. All districts must be geographically compact.
3. Minimize the splitting of political subdivisions. No more than one municipality should be split in a district. No wards should be split in a district.
4. Minimize the splitting of school districts.
5. Minimize the change from previous district boundaries.
6. Minimize the number of media markets in the districts.
7. Natural geographical features and barriers should be respected.

An amendment like this should be done well before the next redistricting will take place in 2021. Amendments passed by the Congress have typically been given seven years to be passed by the 38 state legislatures needed.

I purposely left out any consideration for specific districts for minorities and any consideration of the Civil Rights Act. This amendment would serve to overrule any current laws that gerrymander to make specific set asides for any specific group. This is about equal liberty for all citizens. We have seen over the past decade many people of color getting elected in white majority districts and as President of the United States. Right now we have many districts across the country that are gerrymandered as required by law so that some districts can elect minority candidates. In some cases these set asides have actually helped Republicans lock in more seats by dividing black and white Democrats into different districts. It is time that we provide true equality in redistricting and set asides corrupt that possibility. This would be a truly post racial amendment. Officials should be elected based on ideas, values, beliefs, and ability rather than skin color.

These standards for redistricting should be applied at the state and local levels as well but this does not belong in the US Constitution.

## Apportionment of Congressional Representatives

Currently all people counted in the US Census are used to determine the population in each state for the purpose of apportioning Congressional Representatives and Electoral votes between the states. This means that non-citizens who are living in the US legally or illegally help some states to get more representatives in Congress. There are some districts with half the number of citizens as other districts. From 15-20 House seats and Electoral votes would change states. This is unfair to the citizen voters in other states. It takes political power away from other states.

Seven percent of the US population or about 23 million people living in the US are non-citizens. The highest concentrations of non-citizens are in California (13%), Arizona (11%), Texas (11%), District of Columbia (10%), Nevada (10%), New Jersey (10%), New York (10%), Florida (9%), Massachusetts (9%), and Hawaii (8%).

A constitutional amendment is needed to make apportionment based on the count of US citizens. This is the most fair for the citizens of the US. This is different than other proposals that want to change to apportionment based on the number of eligible voters in each state. This would complicate the apportionment because each state has its own rules on who is eligible to vote. Some states allow felons who completed their sentences to vote and others do not. States have different percentages of citizens too young to vote. Many of these minors will become adults before the next Census. It will be easier to apportion by a single criteria—citizenship.

## Citizenship At Birth

Following the Civil War and passage of the Fourteenth Amendment, it was appropriate to ensure recognition of citizenship for former slaves, Native Americans, and others living in US states and territories. Travel across our borders was much more fluid with people more easily coming and going. It was common that whoever was present was assumed to be able to participate in the community, including elections. On the other hand various groups of citizens were actively being excluded from participation in elections.

In the modern world there is much better documentation of births and citizenship. There are much better protections of voting rights. As a sovereign nation we have a right to decide who becomes a US citizen. The US Constitution should be amended to only provide citizenship to children born to a US citizen parent, either in the US or overseas, and children born to people who are present in the US against their will. (Ex. Children born to victims of human trafficking.)

By eliminating the "anchor baby" option we get rid of a temptation to illegal entry. This is a free, no law enforcement infrastructure needed method to reduce illegal immigration. This will keep a guest worker program honest. It will not be a backdoor immigration program. We do not have to be concerned about guest workers becoming pregnant in order to change their status. Regardless of a non-citizen's status, a pregnancy or childbirth will not be a factor that the government needs to be concerned with.

At the same time legal immigrants will have an incentive to complete the education and other requirements needed to become citizens quickly. (See the proposed requirements in the Immigration and Border Security Chapter.) They will need to become integrated better into the mainstream society to accomplish this. The result will be more stability and better economic prospects for immigrant families and the communities they live in.

## Term Limits

Term limits for members of Congress should be enacted but not as extreme as many limits being floated. Here is a proposed constitutional amendment with the following conditions.

No more than twenty consecutive years in any combination in Congress.

After a total of twenty years in office, the person is limited to holding Congressional office to sixty percent of the total years since reaching the age of eligibility for the office.

If a threshold is breeched during a term in office then the person can finish the term. No candidate may be on the ballot for an office in which he will reach the threshold before the midpoint of the term.

No years in office prior to the ratification of this amendment will count toward the limits of the amendment. (Personally I would like this section to be removed but I don't think we could get enough Members of Congress affected by it to vote for it without it.)

This method of term limits will allow people to move in and out of government as major issues attract them. It means they will have to live under the rules they make for the country. It still allows for development of expertise or institutional knowledge by members with seniority. It does not set a maximum limit only a relative limit. Combined with the campaign finance and redistricting reforms earlier in the chapter, this should lead to more frequent change in the composition of Congress. The goal of all of these reforms is to increase responsiveness to constituents and to return ownership of each office to the people. No office belongs to the officeholder.

Campaign finance and redistricting reforms will do the bulk of the work to make the Congress more responsive to the voters. Term limits may have little net benefit. While we may get some out-of-touch or corrupt legislators out of office we are also going to force some hard working, passionate, principled legislators out of office as well. Most legislators will not have difficulty finding jobs between terms of office. Few will truly live like the average person. It is the corrupt or most ideological who are going to be taken care of by cronies when between terms of office and may not have to face the true reality outside of politics. The principled statesmen and protectors of the public fisc and the Constitution who we want in the Congress will be less likely to be taken care of by cronies. But they and our Republic will still benefit from their time and experiences out of office.

## Primary Reform

### Sore Loser Contract

To avoid having a losing primary candidate make a third-party bid or otherwise undercut the nominee require all candidates to sign a binding sore loser contract in order to be eligible to receive bound delegates and participate in the debates. The contract will require that if they lose the nomination then they must endorse the nominee or remain publically neutral. The contract should require that they declare and pledge one-half of their net worth as bond. This will largely prevent sore losers from undercutting the nominee and the Party.

## Presidential Candidate Tax Forms

The concern about political image problems with the tax forms of Presidential candidates has been an issue for many election cycles. What tax loopholes have been used? What is their effective tax rate? How much was given to charity? The primary voters should have this information available when they vote. The Party should require that every Presidential candidate release a copy of their tax forms for the prior five years before they are eligible to participate in the debates. The candidate should not be eligible to receive bound delegates without disclosure. By the April 15 tax filing deadline in the election year their prior year's forms should be made available to continue to be eligible to receive bound delegates and participate in debates.

## Republican Delegate Allocation Reform

The allocation of National Convention delegates should be reformed to account for the implementation of the Congressional District Method of allocating Electoral College votes. The following reform gives greater weight to those states and districts that elect Republicans to Congress and provide electoral votes to elect Republican Presidents. It increases the number of delegates so that the winning candidates and the local party members each have a substantial number of delegates to send to the convention.

Each state should have eight state-wide at-large delegates, four for each US Senate seat. Each state should get five bonus state-wide at-large delegates for each sitting Republican US Senator. Each state with a sitting Republican Governor should get one bonus state-wide at-large delegate. Each state should get a bonus state-wide at-large delegate for each house in the state legislature with a Republican majority. That assumes a bicameral state legislature. If a state has a unicameral state legislature then they should get two bonus delegates for a Republican majority. The state party chairperson, national committeeman, and national committeewoman should be delegates.

There should be three district at-large delegates for each US House District. Each House district with a sitting Republican Representative should get three bonus district at-large delegates.

Each state should get bonus delegates equal to twice the number of electoral votes the Republican candidate received from the last two Presidential Elections. If the state electoral votes are allocated by the Congressional District Method, the bonus delegates are allocated to the districts and state based on the electoral votes that earned the bonus.

## Republican Delegate Selection Reform

Reform is necessary to insure that those who are selecting delegates to nominate the Republican candidate for President share Republican values. It is also valuable for the party to know who independents and other non-Republicans favor in order to take that into account for the general election.

In the 2012 and 2016 Presidential Primaries and in numerous other primaries around the country there has been a disconnect between the wishes of the Republican voters and the winner of the primaries. This has occurred in both directions of the moderate-conservative divide. We have multiple candidates on one side of the divide splitting their vote and resulting in a candidate with minority support in the party being nominated. What follows is a revision to the nominating process to select the candidate who most closely reflects the wishes of the party membership.

In each primary and caucus, rather than voting for their one preferred candidate each voter will place all of the candidates in order of preference. Each voter's top candidate would receive one whole vote. Their second place candidate will be awarded 0.50 votes. Their third place candidate will be awarded 0.25 votes. The fourth or greater placed candidates will initially be awarded no votes.

1. If a voter votes for the same candidate more than once only the highest placed vote will be counted.
2. As candidates formally drop out of the race the lower level remaining candidates will be moved up in their place on each ballot. The voter can have a say in the placement of these lower level voters or can leave the lower level votes blank.
3. The voter can leave the second and/or third place votes blank. This will deny votes to other candidates in the initial stage of the primary. In later stages their lower level votes may only move up into those places if there is a candidate that is removed from any of the first three vote levels.
4. It is reasonable to limit the number of vote levels. In the early stages of the primary season it could be limited to 10. At the midpoint of the primary season it is reasonable to limit the vote levels to 5. The reduction at the midpoint will be irrelevant most years because the number of viable candidates will be below that level by then.
5. Candidates can plan their departure from the race to strategically aid another candidate based upon the way the vote will be recalculated. Candidates can refrain from formally dropping out of the race until the national convention to block other candidates from moving up in the delegate count.

By using optical scan machine readable forms where the voter fills in an oval to select the candidates this should be easy to accomplish. The vote counts can be quickly calculated while retaining a paper copy for verification. By increasing the vote count of similar candidates they do not cancel each other out. The candidates who are less in touch with the current mood of the party will get smaller downstream counts and be forced out sooner.

The candidate campaigns should be permitted to select a slate of delegates for the regular delegates from the appropriate district and state to represent them based on the results of a primary or caucus vote. The party members from the state and district should select the bonus delegates in caucus to represent them. This is to incentivize the state and local parties to grow and develop their party. The regular delegates exist just for being. There should be no reward to the local party for simply being in a state or district. Their influence on the national party and picking the Presidential nominee should be based on their efforts to get Republicans elected, especially to Congress and the Presidency. In both groups the selected delegates must be members in good standing of the party and be residents for voting purposes of the state or district they represent.

Any candidates that drop out of the race will have their delegates replaced. The procedure will be to recalculate the state and district results with the omission of the dropped out candidate. This means that a slate of delegates for each state and district will need to be selected by each candidate campaign. The delegate breakdown will change as each candidate leaves the race. To provide enough time for delegate changes, candidates will only be able to officially drop out of the race until two weeks before the convention.

All of the delegates should be bound to their candidate for the first nomination vote at the convention. The state party chairman, national committeeman, and national committeewoman should be initially pledged to the candidate who won their state. Beginning with the second vote the delegates may vote for any of the top three remaining candidates as voted by the state or district they represent. Beginning with the fifth vote the delegates should be completely unbound.

Due to the potential volatility in the delegates who will go to the convention, the state party should arrange and pay for the transportation of the delegates to and from the convention and for a block of rooms for the state's delegates. An exception to gift rules for officeholders should be in place to allow them to be delegates.

## Presidential Primary/Caucus Calendar Reform

Given the jockeying over the order in the Presidential primary calendar by the states here is an idea for providing some variation. I have mixed feelings about leaving Iowa, New Hampshire, South Carolina, and Nevada at the front of the line. It does give them a disproportionate influence. On the other hand having some low population states where candidates can develop their message and are forced to interact closely with the people early in a campaign can be helpful. Candidates can build their campaigns in these states easier and at less cost than in most states.

If the concept described here is well liked, the majority can decide if these four states stay in front or if they are blended in with the other states. If they are blended in with their neighbors it would allow for some more breaks in the schedule or an earlier end to the primary season. More breaks would allow more emphasis on the other states.

Another issue is the problem of states far away from each other selecting the same week for their primary or caucus. This increases the travel costs for all of the candidates and the Secret Service. Large distances increases staff and advertising costs. It reduces the time that candidates can interact with voters. Grouping states will allow the candidates to save valuable time and money.

In this plan there will be a lottery to select the order in which states will conduct their primary or caucus. Other than the initial four states, they are divided into 16 groups based upon geographical proximity and their number of Electoral College votes.

It would begin the first Tuesday after January 15th and continue until the last Tuesday of June. Each group will have a Tuesday selected to hold its primary or caucus. Breaks would be taken the Tuesday after the first four states, the Tuesday after Easter, and the Tuesday after Memorial weekend and one additional Tuesday to break up the longest stretch between holiday breaks. The holiday breaks are left open because they are times for families to get together and it will be difficult getting many volunteers in the days leading up to these Tuesdays. States will not be required to hold their primary on the designated Tuesday. That is a target date. They would have a window from the Monday before to the Saturday following their designated Tuesday.

1. This plan rotates the order that states will hold their primaries/caucuses.
2. The groups of states will be drawn and placed in order and then the dates will be drawn for each group.
3. A group may trade with another group by mutual agreement.
4. Grouping states will reduce costs during the primary campaigns.
5. All non-participating states would have to schedule their primary at least one week after the final week of this plan or have their delegates reduced.
6. After the initial drawings for the next four Presidential elections, the lottery should be held sixteen years in advance to reduce the chance that someone will try to manipulate the process for their own benefit.
7. If possible, this schedule should be coordinated with the Democrats in order to reduce costs for the states.

Following is a look at what the primary calendars would look like under this plan in 2020, 2024, 2028, and 2032.

| 2020 | | 2024 | | 2028 | | 2032 | |
|---|---|---|---|---|---|---|---|
| 21-Jan | Iowa | 16-Jan | Iowa | 18-Jan | Iowa | 20-Jan | Iowa |
| 28-Jan | New Hampshire | 23-Jan | New Hampshire | 25-Jan | New Hampshire | 27-Jan | New Hampshire |
| 4-Feb | South Carolina | 30-Jan | South Carolina | 1-Feb | South Carolina | 3-Feb | South Carolina |
| 11-Feb | Nevada | 6-Feb | Nevada | 8-Feb | Nevada | 10-Feb | Nevada |
| 18-Feb | Break | 13-Feb | Break | 15-Feb | Break | 17-Feb | Break |
| 25-Feb | 1st Pick | 20-Feb | 1st Pick | 22-Feb | 1st Pick | 24-Feb | 1st Pick |
| 3-Mar | 2nd Pick | 27-Feb | 2nd Pick | 29-Feb | 2nd Pick | 2-Mar | 2nd Pick |
| 10-Mar | 3rd Pick | 5-Mar | 3rd Pick | 7-Mar | 3rd Pick | 9-Mar | 3rd Pick |
| 17-Mar | 4th Pick | 12-Mar | 4th Pick | 14-Mar | Break | 16-Mar | 4th Pick |
| 24-Mar | 5th Pick | 19-Mar | 5th Pick | 21-Mar | 4th Pick | 23-Mar | 5th Pick |
| 31-Mar | 6th Pick | 26-Mar | 6th Pick | 28-Mar | 5th Pick | 30-Mar | Easter Break |
| 7-Apr | 7th Pick | 2-Apr | Easter Break | 4-Apr | 6th Pick | 6-Apr | 6th Pick |
| 14-Apr | Easter Break | 9-Apr | 7th Pick | 11-Apr | 7th Pick | 13-Apr | 7th Pick |
| 21-Apr | 8th Pick | 16-Apr | 8th Pick | 18-Apr | Easter Break | 20-Apr | 8th Pick |
| 28-Apr | 9th Pick | 23-Apr | 9th Pick | 25-Apr | 8th Pick | 27-Apr | 9th Pick |
| 5-May | Break | 30-Apr | Break | 2-May | 9th Pick | 4-May | Break |
| 12-May | 10th Pick | 7-May | 10th Pick | 9-May | 10th Pick | 11-May | 10th Pick |
| 19-May | 11th Pick | 14-May | 11th Pick | 16-May | 11th Pick | 18-May | 11th Pick |
| 26-May | Memorial Break | 21-May | 12th Pick | 23-May | 12th Pick | 25-May | 12th Pick |
| 2-Jun | 12th Pick | 28-May | Memorial Break | 30-May | Memorial Break | 1-Jun | Memorial Break |
| 9-Jun | 13th Pick | 4-Jun | 13th Pick | 6-Jun | 13th Pick | 8-Jun | 13th Pick |
| 16-Jun | 14th Pick | 11-Jun | 14th Pick | 13-Jun | 14th Pick | 15-Jun | 14th Pick |
| 23-Jun | 15th Pick | 18-Jun | 15th Pick | 20-Jun | 15th Pick | 22-Jun | 15th Pick |
| 30-Jun | 16th Pick | 25-Jun | 16th Pick | 27-Jun | 16th Pick | 29-Jun | 16th Pick |

On the next page is a table that provides an example of the groups of states and their Electoral College votes.

| State | 2001-2010 | 2011-2020 | Total |
|---|---|---|---|
| Iowa | 7 | 6 | 6 |
| New Hampshire | 4 | 4 | 4 |
| South Carolina | 8 | 9 | 9 |
| Nevada | 5 | 6 | 6 |
| California | 55 | 55 | 55 |
| Texas | 34 | 38 | 38 |
| Pennsylvania | 21 | 20 | |
| New Jersey | 15 | 14 | 34 |
| Tennessee | 11 | 11 | |
| Alabama | 9 | 9 | |
| Mississippi | 6 | 6 | |
| Louisiana | 9 | 8 | 34 |
| Kansas | 6 | 6 | |
| Nebraska | 5 | 5 | |
| Arkansas | 6 | 6 | |
| Missouri | 11 | 10 | |
| Oklahoma | 7 | 7 | 34 |
| North Carolina | 15 | 15 | |
| Georgia | 15 | 16 | 31 |
| Arizona | 10 | 11 | |
| New Mexico | 5 | 5 | |
| Colorado | 9 | 9 | |
| Utah | 5 | 6 | 31 |
| Illinois | 21 | 20 | |
| Indiana | 11 | 11 | 31 |
| Ohio | 20 | 18 | |
| Kentucky | 8 | 8 | |
| West Virginia | 5 | 5 | 31 |
| New York | 31 | 29 | 29 |
| Florida | 27 | 29 | 29 |
| Connecticut | 7 | 7 | |
| Rhode Island | 4 | 4 | |
| Massachusetts | 12 | 11 | |
| Maine | 4 | 4 | |
| Vermont | 3 | 3 | 29 |
| Delaware | 3 | 3 | |
| D.C. | 3 | 3 | |
| Maryland | 10 | 10 | |
| Virginia | 13 | 13 | 29 |
| Alaska | 3 | 3 | |
| Hawaii | 4 | 4 | |
| Washington | 11 | 12 | |
| Oregon | 7 | 7 | 26 |
| Wyoming | 3 | 3 | |
| Idaho | 4 | 4 | |
| Montana | 3 | 3 | |
| North Dakota | 3 | 3 | |
| South Dakota | 3 | 3 | |
| Minnesota | 10 | 10 | 26 |
| Michigan | 17 | 16 | |
| Wisconsin | 10 | 10 | 26 |
| Total | 538 | 538 | 538 |

The states voting through the 9th Pick Week will award delegates proportional to the statewide vote. In the first stage the congressional district delegates will be awarded proportional to the vote in each district. Following this the statewide delegates will be awarded to achieve a total distribution of the state's delegates proportional to the statewide vote. Proportionality will give all candidates a chance to sustain a campaign long enough to give a sizeable portion of the country an opportunity to hear from them.

Beginning with the 10th Pick Week the delegates are awarded as winner take all by congressional district.

There are several US territories which do not have electoral votes but do send delegates to the conventions. Puerto Rico and the US Virgin Islands will be grouped with Florida. American Samoa, Guam, and Northern Marianas will be grouped with Alaska, Hawaii, Washington, and Oregon.

There is a high likelihood that the nominees would be known by early May as now but the parts of the country that get to narrow down the candidates will change every election. There will still be plenty of time for the prospective nominee to vet and select a running mate and organize a national campaign before the national convention. The whole process lasts 24 weeks.

### Instant Runoff Primary Voting

The primary races other than for President should be switched to an instant runoff system. The beauty of the instant runoff system is that similar candidates will not automatically block each other.

In instant runoff systems the voters rank the candidates in order of preference from first to last. After voting if no candidate has received a majority of votes the candidate with the fewest votes is dropped from consideration. The first ranked votes by the voters for this candidate are then dropped and their second thru last ranked votes move up a place and are assigned to the remaining candidates. The lowest ranked candidates continue to be removed one-by-one until a candidate receives a majority.

There are times, especially when people want change or reform when several candidates with similar beliefs make a run for an office. If the majority of the electorate support these beliefs there is a better chance with this system that one of these candidates will win. This prevents a candidate from winning with a plurality even when the majority of the party wanted someone else. The power remains with the voters.

### District of Columbia Representation

Regardless of how District residents are represented it will always be less complete than exists for residents of the states. Because the District is a federal district and the national capital the federal government needs to have a say over many issues in the District. These items should be the subject of negotiations to lay out some clearer and more consistent boundaries.

As for Congressional representation here is a recommendation:

1. The remaining portion of the District was carved out of Maryland. The residents should get to vote for and be represented by the Maryland U.S. Senators.

2. The residents of Maryland and the District should be combined to establish the population for representation in the House of Representatives. No more than one congressional district should include residents of both the District and of Maryland. The District should have population proportionate representation in the body that performs the redistricting.

3. The District should lose its independent electoral votes and share in the Maryland electoral votes consistent with their unified congressional representation.

4. These changes will require an amendment to the US Constitution. The Senatorial changes should take effect immediately following passage of the amendment. The House changes should take effect following the redistricting after the first census following the passage of the amendment. The District's current non-voting delegate in the House should be given voting status until the next reapportionment of Representatives.


## Voting Machine Reform

Touchscreen and other computerized voting machines have been shown repeatedly to be insecure and vulnerable to hacking. These need to be removed from service as soon as possible to ensure the integrity of our elections. Even when they provide a receipt to the voter that does not mean the vote was recorded the same in the hard drive.

The only type of system that can be trusted is an optical scan system where the voter fills in circles on a paper form which is fed into the scanner and "read." This allows for rapid counting on election night that can be verified within hours by a hard count from the paper forms. If there is a hack or defect with the machine the paper forms are there as a backup. If there is a discrepancy between the optical scanner results and the paper ballots there is justification for an investigation. Fraudsters would have to be able to compromise both at the same time and in the same numbers.

The integrity of our elections is too important to leave such vulnerable machines in place. People need to be able to trust that when they vote their vote will be counted accurately. There needs to be certainty that hackers cannot steal an election.

# 15 EDUCATION REFORMS

**"Upon the subject of education ... I can only say that I view it as the
most important subject which we as a people may be engaged in."
Abraham Lincoln**

Education in the United States needs to be returned to the local level. The
only legitimate roles the federal government has in education are student
loans for college, empowering parents, and evaluating the state of education
in the US and making recommendations for improvements. Most of the
activities and spending by the Department of Education should be eliminated.
States and local districts can assume responsibility for their own students. We
have to trust parents to empower their children by making sure they get a
good education.

For most of my life I have supported the public school system as a place
to get a good, "free" education and help build patriotism and national unity. I
was well educated in the public school system. But the public school systems
have changed greatly over the past decades and not for the better. The
teacher's unions, teachers and the administration seem to have priority over
students and their education and their development into good citizens.
Patriotism, good citizenship and conservative values no longer seem to be
taught and in many schools seem to be undermined. Over time this state of
affairs will destroy our country. Good education and good values are
necessary for our republic to thrive. I would love to see the public schools
return to a place of great education and great values at reasonable costs.
Places where our children can excel.

No school is going to be the best school for all students. Students have
differing learning styles, teachers have different teaching styles, school
districts have different cultures, families and the local culture have different
influences on the educational environment. I know parents that communicate
with each other and move their kids in and out of various public and private
schools just to avoid the poor teachers. They are trying to keep their kids
from having a dead or regressive learning year. There are good and poor

teachers in both the public and private systems. When the system does not do an adequate job of getting rid of the deadwood there will be avoidance tactics by the parents who can afford it. Unfortunately many parents do not have that option and it is sad that any parents and students need this option. It would be better if kids could go to school and grow up with the same group of friends and have this stability in their lives. Parents can exert the influence to force systemic change if they have the resources.

Parents need to have more freedom to obtain a good education for their children. The current public education monopolies have not been responsive to the concerns of parents and have frequently been dismissive of the beliefs of parents. The responsibility of educating children belongs to parents. They can delegate the authority to teach their children to teachers but the responsibility cannot be delegated. Therefore parents need to have the freedom and resources to make sure their children are educated properly. Universal vouchers are the only option that puts the power back into the hands of parents.

This chapter deals primarily with education financing. As accountability requirements increase and funding follows performance the education providers and parents will figure out what works best for each student. It is beyond anyone else's capability from a distance to make the right decisions for students as we have seen from federal education policies and programs over the past decades. No one solution is going to work for all schools, school districts or students. The following ideas put education back into the hands of parents where it belongs.

## Universal School Vouchers

While paying for preK-12 education should be a state and local issue, here is a plan that is far better than the current situation. Universal vouchers for every student are the preferred method so that parents can have their kids attend where they want. The greatest concern with this is allowing parents to take the entire amount currently spent in the public school system and applying it toward a private school. This will just drive up the cost of private schools and eventually create a combined public and private school lobby. A similar concern is politicians setting an arbitrary amount for the vouchers that will become an allure to corruption. This plan addresses that concern.

The percentage of state and local taxes that parents of school age children pay that are directed toward preK-12 education is available for the parents to allocate for their child's education. Any taxpayer in a state under this plan can allocate the portion of state and local taxes that they pay that is directed toward preK-12 education to support a child or children of their choice or to support the students of the school of their choice.

Here are some twists.

1. For parents and other taxpayers that support specific students. If the tuition at the alternative school is less than the per pupil average for their school district and their taxes paid exceed the alternative school tuition then they can keep the difference between the tuition paid and the full cost of tuition in the public school. They are effectively paying the full cost of educating the student and may keep the excess. This will help to keep downward pressure on costs because there is an incentive to consider cost when selecting a school for the children. The examples only use the school property tax but other taxes, such as the portion of income taxes, that go to schools should be included in the amount that taxpayers can direct to a student or school.

   Example:

   | | |
   |---|---|
   | Home school district cost per student: | $12,000 |
   | School property tax bill: | $10,000 |
   | School attended cost: | $9,000 |
   | Taxpayer pays school tuition: | $9,000 |
   | Taxpayer savings: | $1,000 |

2. Other taxpayers that assist parents may help multiple students. If the percentages of assistance adds up to 100 percent of a student the taxpayer may keep the excess that would have been due for their district.

   Example:

   | | |
   |---|---|
   | Home school district cost per student: | $12,000 |
   | School property tax bill: | $10,000 |
   | School #1 attended cost: | $9,000 |
   | Taxpayer pays toward #1 school tuition: | $3,000 |
   | Percentage of full tuition paid: | 33.3% |
   | School #2 attended cost: | $7,500 |
   | Taxpayer pays toward #2 school tuition: | $2,500 |
   | Percentage of full tuition paid: | 33.3% |
   | School #3 attended cost: | $12,000 |
   | Taxpayer pays toward #3 school tuition: | $4,000 |
   | Percentage of full tuition paid: | 33.3% |
   | Total tuition paid by taxpayer: | $9,500 |
   | Taxpayer savings: | $500 |

3. Taxpayers that support a school rather than a specific student can

assign up to the amount of tax they paid that is directed toward preK-12 education. This type of support will help those parents that do not have enough allocable taxes and income to pay for their children's tuition. In practice this will look like the previous example.

4.  Most lower income taxpayers do not pay enough school property tax to qualify for the 100 percent option. These taxpayers will receive credit for the percent of the full tuition that they did pay.

    Example:

| | |
|---|---|
| Home school district cost per student: | $12,000 |
| School property tax bill: | $3,000 |
| School attended cost: | $9,000 |
| Taxpayer pays school tuition: | $2,250 |
| Percentage of full tuition paid: | 25% |
| Taxpayer savings: | $750 |

5.  Renters will receive a statement from their landlord stating their share of property taxes paid on the parcel where they rent. The landlord will submit a copy to the appropriate taxing authority. The renter may use the property taxes paid in the same manner as a property owner.

6.  For home schooled kids, initially no more than one-quarter of the per pupil average may be retained or received by the parents unless verified qualified expenses exceed this. This is to guard against abusive or neglectful parents that choose homeschooling to stay under the radar or just to cut their taxes and do not educate their children. The remainder that they would receive if they were a private school would be placed in escrow and portions of it should be released as their children pass the competency based exams. Contributions may be made by other taxpayers to cover authorized expenses as with children enrolled in a regular school.

7.  Competency based exams must be established for each subject taught to K-12 students in the state. These will be used for public, private, and home schooled kids. An independent company will be used for the testing to guard against cheating. To permit flexibility in what is taught these tests are not set for a specific grade but rather are scheduled when the competency has been achieved in the classroom. There should be a series of exams in each subject with progressive levels of rigor. Every state should have dozens of approved tests for each subject. Any company should be permitted to submit tests to the state for consideration. Any that meet the curriculum standard should be permitted. These tests should then be available to any testing company to use for a standard minimal fee. No school or home schooled child should use the same testing company more than one out of every three years.

8. Participating private schools will be limited in the methods that can be used to select students using the voucher program. They can select by academic merit only. They can select by low-income status only. They can select by both academic merit and low-income status only. They can select by membership for religious schools only. For the membership criteria to be used exclusively at least one parent must have been a member since before the birth of the child or for ten years. Otherwise they just get multiple entries in a lottery for the remaining slots if there are any. One lottery entry for each two years of membership. All other private school slots must be filled using a lottery to select the students if there are more voucher students requesting attendance than there are slots for them. Students may be retained in later grade levels after originally entering a school under regular criteria even if they no longer meet the regular criteria. Younger siblings of retained students may be admitted without meeting the regular selection criteria.

9. These vouchers should be able to be used in other public school districts. Public school districts may refuse to take students from other school districts. If they open up their schools to out-of-district students they must use the criteria for student selection that the private schools use. The academic merit only basis may not constitute more than twenty percent of the total out-of-district voucher students for the district to prevent cherry-picking students to improve school ratings.

10. Because public school districts may need to maintain excess infrastructure to be ready for major fluctuations in student populations the public school district should consider renting out any excess space to alternative schools.

11. For students with learning disabilities (LD) there will need to be an independent evaluation system to avoid conflicts of interest. It may be financially beneficial for the local school district to provide a subsidy that follows the student for the difference between the average student cost and the LD student's estimated cost but less than the public school cost for these students. Otherwise the public school system will likely have a much higher concentration of LD students which could drive down the public perception of the school.

12. Schools will not have to tone down or eliminate their religious beliefs to participate. No participating school can advocate killing or physically harming other US citizens. No participating school may advocate sedition, succession, or violating the US or state constitutions.

13. Any school outside of the student's public school district may filter out students with a felony conviction and violent, drug, alcohol, and sexual misdemeanor convictions.

14. If the student's school district does not have a preK program, the state average cost should be used as the basis for the financial calculations.

15. Private exchanges can be established so that relatives, friends, or others can exchange support with other people in other school districts. The student or school that a taxpayer wants to help may live in a different school district than the taxpayer. The school districts have a different cost per student basis. The exchange allows people to account for this difference by exchanging the percentage of credit for each district.

Under this model much of the moral hazard of funding private schools with public money is eliminated. The parents and other taxpayers that allocate these tax dollars to these private schools have a vested interest in seeing kids educated well and in holding the costs down. It can be expected that if results are insufficient then kids will be quickly moved to a better school. Better education results but at a lower cost!

## Parent Trigger

There is a relatively new program that got its start in California that gives parents more control over their local school. The parent trigger forces change on their local school if the parents of more than fifty percent of the students at the school vote for change.

Parent triggers should give parents three options. The first option allows the parents union to negotiate with the school board for specific changes in personnel, curriculum, funding, and activities at the school. The second option would require the school board to replace at least fifty percent of the staff and negotiate on curriculum, funding, and activities at the school. The third option would close the school and require that a charter school is opened in its place with new staff.

Parents in all states should have this option but this is primarily a state and local issue. One of the few areas appropriate at the federal level is an intervention method in failing schools and school districts where states have not adequately addressed the failure. Schools and/or school districts that are in the bottom third in the country for five of the past ten years should be eligible for this intervention. A mechanism should be in place for ten percent of the parents of a failing school or school district to petition a federal court (As a Civil Rights issue.) to oversee a parent trigger vote and negotiation. The law should require that the state and local governments that normally provide money for the school or school district to have to continue at a level equal to what they did before the parent trigger or equal to the per student average provided to all students in their jurisdiction, whichever is greater. This will allow for intervention against entrenched local teacher and political interests but still keep the authority and responsibility local with parents and not with federal bureaucrats.

One of the issues that has come up is school districts threatening illegal alien parents that sign parent trigger petitions. They threaten to report them to immigration. This has a chilling effect on this mechanism for change. To remedy this the petition should be considered valid if ten percent of the citizen parents sign it or if ten percent of all of the parents sign it. Likewise the vote should be considered valid if fifty percent of the citizen parents vote for it or if fifty percent of all of the parents vote for it. This will neutralize the tactic.

## Student Loans

Loans for college students to pay for education are one of the few appropriate things for the federal government to do for education in this country. Loans provide the means for a significant portion of the college students in this country to pay for their education. Student grants from the federal government for college education should be limited to the first year for low-income students.

The loan program should be means tested so that the money is put to best use. There should be an expectation that the entire loan is repaid and that it is repaid in a timely manner. The Democrats and President Obama have moved in the opposite direction by reducing the amount that has to be paid back each year and setting a maximum number of years that a former student has to make payments. This undermines the responsibility to repay the obligation that our students owe to the taxpayers who earned the money that sent them to college. Another component of the requirement that education loans be paid back fully and timely is to put more pressure on students seeking loans to be working on a degree that allows them to earn enough to pay off the loan. If not they should consider a different degree or a different school. It will put pressure on colleges to keep their costs down better than they have been doing. It is well documented that as more money becomes available and at easier terms universities find it easier to increase their tuition and fees that they charge students. By making the student consumer of the education fully on the hook for the costs then they will be more likely to shop around for the best value. If the student does not, maybe mom and dad will for the student.

Grants should only be for the first year of college for low-income students to determine if college is the right path for them and to gain the confidence of passing college level classes. After the first year they should switch over to loans and be responsible for the costs of their own education.

Grants and loan forgiveness undercut the value of the education benefits of our veterans. It is an insult to what they had to do to earn their benefits to just give it away to those who have done nothing to serve their country. They serve to force the military to compete for recruits against free benefits. This costs the services and taxpayers much more, unnecessarily, to overcome what is already available for free.

In order to help hold down the inflation in college costs that far exceeds the overall inflation rate we need to set the amount of money available for student loans and grants on autopilot. We could take what was allocated in FY 2008 as the benchmark. From this benchmark we should adjust it based upon the ratio of the general population each year between 17 and 40 with the same age range in FY 2008. Additionally it should be adjusted according to the overall national inflation rate. This will require that colleges do a better job of controlling their costs or students or parents will have to pay more or shop around for a better deal or join the military. I am sure our best and brightest can figure out the best way for themselves.

Another option is to require that the increased amount of money available for future students comes only from the principle and interest paid on existing student loans. Appropriate new funds only for a limited number of years so that there is enough money circulating through this process to be self-sustaining. Put the responsibility and the peer pressure on recent students to replenish the fund for new students.

## Tenure

Tenure should be eliminated and in its place the employer and union should establish an annual evaluation system similar to the following. A system in which one-third of the weighting is from a peer evaluation, one-third is from an evaluation of the growth in knowledge and capabilities of the served students, and the remainder from an evaluation by the employer. It may be helpful to have an attorney or CPA or other consultant from outside the district and with no connection to any parties involved selected to receive the sealed evaluations. Then compile them into a single report for each person evaluated and convey a copy to the employer, the union, and the person evaluated. The union and employer will decide beforehand what threshold will result in termination and which will warrant remedial training. The union and employer should develop a remedial training requirement for those below average or unsatisfactory. At no time should an employer be required to continue employing an employee that receives a second unsatisfactory rating in their career.

When layoffs occur they should start at the bottom of the rating scale not by seniority. Remedial training should end immediately if laid off. Any employee with a single unsatisfactory or below average rating laid off for more than one school year should be able to be removed from consideration for rehiring.

## Balanced Education

In recent years there have been many people promoting Science, Technology, Engineering, and Math (STEM) education. These are very important topics and every student should get a good education in these subjects. But we cannot neglect other areas of education to do this. We need our students to be exposed to a broad range of subjects. This helps students to determine the direction that interests them. It provides a basic background that they can draw upon for the remainder of their lives.

Education needs to prepare students for work. But it also needs to prepare students for the other parts of their life. A thorough civics education is essential for a democratic republic such as ours. An understanding of our government and the basis of our liberty. This includes a detailed study of the Federalist Papers, the Constitution, Declaration of Independence and related constitutional philosophy. They need to understand how our government works and how to exercise their rights and responsibilities as citizens.

Economics and history are other essentials. Economics teaches about how the economy works, the benefits of free market capitalism, the crippling deficiencies of all other economic systems, and economic history showing how some countries prospered and others have not and why. History aids our understanding of how we got where we are now. But it needs to be more than memorizing names and dates. Learning cause and effect are crucial to truly understanding history. Perhaps it would help children to relate to history if they traced their genealogy back as far as possible. They can place their ancestors in the history they are studying.

We live in a global economy. Our students should have the opportunity to learn any of the top ten most spoken languages in the world. It should be mandatory that high school graduates are fluently bilingual in two languages.

Other areas of education that get shortchanged are art, music, and gym classes. These are needed as well. Art and music help us to appreciate the world around us. They are a part of our human experience. Gym classes are needed to promote physical fitness.

Practical daily life activities such as consumer banking, insurance, pension and other retirement accounts, annuities, investing, and understanding the value of compound interest should be taught.

## Year Round School Year

The summer vacation on most school calendars is too long for children to be away from school. It is an outdated schedule based on the farming calendar from the days when most children lived on farms and were needed to help their family. When children are away from school for such a long period of time they have to spend several weeks reviewing the old material before learning new material each fall.

The school schedule should be increased from 180 instructional days to 210 days per year. In additional to reducing review time with a year round schedule, 30 more days will permit more material to be taught each year. This still provides 50 days of vacation for children each year. Ten federal holidays and eight weeks spread throughout the year. Schools can decide if they want to have a single track or multi-track schedule based on their own circumstances. Neighboring schools can have different vacation schedules allowing parents to send their children to another local school that fits their schedule better.

Most teachers already make a full year's income under the current nine month schedule. Few should need to be paid more than they currently receive. They will not like this but there are many others willing to teach in their place. The key is to use the government employee average compensation formula described in the Government Reform chapter. This will set their average compensation in relation to the community average. That is the most equitable way to establish the compensation for the school district employees.

The longer schedule will aid lower income parents who struggle to pay for childcare. While this is not a primary consideration it is a significant cost to these families. It is also a significant cost for the government with programs to pay for childcare and in the form of childcare tax credits. It is better to pay for more education than more basic childcare.

**Foreign Students**

Many universities have been increasing the numbers of foreign students recruited to attend their undergraduate and graduate degree programs. There are many benefits for the university and the US to educating foreign students. The only major concern would be if the numbers of Americans is reduced at a school in order to accommodate foreign students. This must be discouraged. US universities need to maintain their numbers of US students in their whole range of programs. We need to continue training US students at current levels or greater in relation to the US population in the graduate degree programs. Especially in the STEM degree fields for economic and security needs.

# 16 CIVIL LEGAL REFORMS

"Freedom makes a huge requirement of every human being. With
freedom comes responsibility. For the person who is unwilling to grow
up, the person who does not want to carry his own weight, this is a
frightening prospect."
Eleanor Roosevelt

## Personal Bankruptcy Reform

Part of the reason for the recent economic crisis is the extension of too
much credit to people without the means to pay for it. This becomes
especially bad when people start losing their jobs or have their hours cut back
and they don't have much discretionary income or savings. All of a sudden
their monthly bills are more than they are bringing in. We need to realign the
rules for the disposition of debts in bankruptcy to bring about different
behavior by creditors in extending credit. Here are some proposed rules for
bankruptcy:

It is prudent to limit monthly debt payments to 40 percent of monthly
gross income. To encourage prudence in extending credit there will be severe
limits on the ability to collect a debt that was extended over this limit.
Forgiveness of debt should be rare when the debt load is limited to 40
percent of gross income. Only in cases of unexpected, unforeseeable debt or
new limitations on earning power should be considered. This is most likely in
cases of very high medical bills or disability. Implementation of Medicare XXI
should greatly reduce the chances of very high medical bills being the reason.

If when the credit was extended, the debt payments were less than 40
percent of gross income and at the time of bankruptcy the debt payments are
less than 50 percent of gross income then the debt may not be discharged in
bankruptcy. The bankruptcy court may only consider debts outside of these
limits for discharge or restructuring. In general, the greater the debt load was
at the time credit was extended the less recourse the lender should have at the
time of bankruptcy. The purpose of these rules is to restrain lenders from

extending too much credit to people.

In bankruptcy, debts need to be paid in the order they were initiated. When a new creditor offers additional credit they need to know that they will be in the back of the line and what place they are in the line. When some debts are paid it should be the newest first. If a borrower fails to include any of their current debt on an application for new credit and the amount of the omitted debt puts the new debt outside the 40 percent limit then the new debt may not be forgiven. It should still be placed in its appropriate chronological order.

Debt payments in bankruptcy may not be reduced below 50 percent of the borrower's gross income if it includes the home they still reside in. Rent plus debt payments may not be less than 50 percent of the borrower's gross income. Rent up to the median for their county of residence is all that may be counted for the limit.

Any revolving credit that does not have a definite time period will be considered three year debt for determining the monthly payment for the purposes of the bankruptcy law.

For purposes of seniority revolving credit should have seniority based upon when the credit was originally extended. If the credit limit is increased, the additional credit will have its own seniority based upon when the credit limit was increased. For clarity these dates and amounts should be listed on the online account and be part of a hardcopy statement at least annually.

Collateral for a loan should still be collateral first for the specified loan but any remaining equity should be available to dispose of other debts. The collateralized debt should still be placed in its chronological order for receiving payment from the available funds.

One exception to the income guidelines for the extension of credit is with student loans. For student loans that are not due until after the student completes their planned course of study the lender may use the median entry-level income that can be expected for a graduate of the course of study as the income basis. If there are existing debt obligations at the time the student loan is applied for then the borrower must meet income guidelines for the terms of the current and new debt. Any debt issued after the student loan(s) must take the terms of the student loan into consideration and will be junior to the pre-existing debt even if the start of payments is substantially later than the newer debt.

The implementation of Social Security XXI and the ability to borrow from their personal account will require that these loans be accounted for in the person's debt load. Loans from the Social Security XXI account cannot be discharged in bankruptcy but impact the ability of borrowers to repay other debts. The same requirement will be needed from other similar accounts.

By restraining how much credit is extended, people's debt loads will be more manageable when a recession occurs or there is an income loss due to injury, illness, or job loss. Over the whole society this is beneficial in helping to limit the damage from cascading losses from defaults. It also helps those early creditors by keeping their interest from being diluted by other creditors. This places the costs of risk with those who deserve it.

## Tort Reform

This can apply at the state and federal levels. Here is a reasonable set of limits.

Liability should be several; each defendant should only be responsible for the percentage of damages equal to their percentage of liability. No one should be held responsible for more than what they had the authority to materially affect.

There should be no limit to economic damage claims. Economic damage claims include compensation for long-term loss of wages and fringe benefits to the injured party, if applicable. This will be based upon the level of disability. It includes the cost to replace property losses and pay for medical care. Damages for medical care can include the immediate care and extend well into the future. Either for care related to the injury or illness or due to long-term or permanent disability.

While it is difficult to establish a dollar value for non-economic damages a reasonable compensation needs to be estimated. Non-economic damages claims should be limited to:

An amount equal to the remaining lifetime loss of wages and fringe benefits to the injured party.

Plus:

An amount equal to double the remaining lifetime loss of wages and fringe benefits to the injured party's spouse, parent or guardian who becomes a caretaker for the injured, or for intangible harms such as emotional distress, disfigurement, loss of the enjoyment of life that an injury has caused, including sterility, physical impairment and loss of a loved one, etc.

The minimum wage standard for 100 percent disability should be compensation consistent with the disability guidelines in the Chapter on Social Security for the duration of the disability or until death. If the person dies due to the injury before the average national life expectancy, the compensation will go to the person's estate or beneficiaries until the person would have reached the average national life expectancy. If the person can prove that they would have likely earned more than the national disability standard based on a combination of past compensation levels, education, and experience then a higher level of compensation may be awarded to compensate for the estimated loss. The absence of a past employment record or limited employment record should not reduce this below the disability standard.

No defendant should be able to erase their liability for damages through bankruptcy and these awards should become debt senior to all unsecured debt and all subsequently acquired secured debt. Based on the date of injury. Defendants should be required to carry insurance that will pay the damages if their income ceases before payment in full. For individuals this would likely be life insurance.

Punitive damages should be based upon the degree of negligence exhibited or intentional harm inflicted by the defendant. Punitive damages in cases of slight negligence should be limited to an amount equal to the total of economic and non-economic damages. In cases of gross negligence the punitive damages should be limited to five times the total of economic and non-economic damages. For cases of reckless negligence and intentional harm there should be no statutory limit. The judge and jury should have discretion to make a reasonable damage award. Beyond this, punishment should be removed from the malpractice insurance policy and from civil court. The place for additional punishment should be in the criminal courts. There are already laws dealing with negligence, and intentional harm.

## Divorce and Child Custody

This is a state issue and should remain a state issue. The ideas presented here should help provide more stability for families, especially children.

There are many who say that it is too easy to get a divorce and that it is harming families, especially children. The blame is frequently put on no-fault divorces. Certainly no-fault divorces can make it easier to get a divorce but forcing a finding of fault may not be the best way to try to keep people married. The divorce process even without a legal fault finding is contentious and amplifies the conflict between the couple. There should be a longer waiting period to get married, at least a one year waiting period before the divorce finalizes and at least two years before a new marriage can take place after a divorce finalizes.

It is better to encourage people to be more responsible before marriage than to pick up the pieces later. In order to get a marriage license, everyone should have to go through pre-marital classes and counseling. This should help head off many potentially bad marriages or help couples to communicate better and strengthen their relationships. As an incentive to being better prepared for marriage before getting married the waiting time should be shorter for those who go through the classes. With classes a waiting period of 30 days and without classes a waiting period of 180 days would go a long way to improving marital outcomes. Some may say that this will discourage marriage altogether. This should not be done in isolation. The reforms to welfare and tax policy, Social Security XXI, and Medicare XXI will encourage people to marry for direct economic reasons.

When a couple files for divorce they should have to wait at least a year for it to finalize. Two years if there are minor children. In the meantime they should have to go to a class about the effects of divorce on children if they have children. They should have to try mediation to settle the marital issues first, then to reach agreement on the divorce issues second if they cannot settle the marital issues. Obviously, the Judge should have the ability to suspend some of these requirements in cases of abuse, abandonment, or incarceration.

There should be penalties for game playing with scheduling mediation and other appointments related to divorce and custody. It is all too common for one party to fail to show up for meetings. This is costly and delays the process. The party who fails to appear should be required to pay for the costs of the meeting and any wages lost by the party who did appear as scheduled. This provision should be on the condition that the parties involved had a say in selecting and agreeing to the time and place of the meeting.

After the divorce is finalized there should be another waiting period before someone can get married again. The waiting period should be at least two years and at least five years since the previous marriage started. This will encourage people to get their lives in better order before they get remarried. It may also make people a little more careful about their marital decisions.

For too long child custody laws have not given equal value to both mom and dad. This needs to stop. Both are important for the development of children and for their learning to relate to both sexes throughout their lives. Children need and deserve the security of strong relationships with both of their parents. By default, both parents should have joint custody and as close as possible to equal placement. Child support should be minimal and only for the imbalance in placement.

There should be a minimum and maximum level of child support. There are two aspects to this. One is how much a parent pays out on a monthly basis. The second is how much is needed to support a child, even if the parent accrues a debt because current income is not sufficient. For the former twenty percent of a person's income is appropriate for one child and thirty-five percent the limit per parent. If they owe child support for more than one child then the thirty-five percent should be equally divided between all of the kids, in and out of their home. All of the children that a parent is financially responsible for are to be considered. The children living with the parent need support as much as those living away from the parent. More than this makes it difficult for the parent to pay their own bills.

For the latter each parent is responsible for half of the cost of raising a child. In my state, as a minimum it costs about $600 per month to raise a child so each parent should be responsible for $300 of that amount. (This does not include healthcare. Each parent should be responsible for half of their child's healthcare costs.) This amount will be different in other states. If they owe for more children than they can afford they should accrue a debt. The county child support agency should track these balances. Child support should not be dischargeable in bankruptcy.

Quadruple the minimum is a reasonable maximum per child limit to child support payments. The maximum is for cases where the parent's income permits such an amount. The actual amount owed is based on the number of children, the amount of time spent with the children, and the amount of income.

Parents should not be required to maintain a certain level of income based on prior levels of income. Many people have lost jobs and been forced to take lower paying jobs. This has placed many in a position of being in violation of child support orders for not paying enough or forced the parent to live in poverty because their remaining income is too low. The minimum and maximum amounts and accrual is a better method for determining child support obligations. One the low end each parent is obligated to provide half of the minimum level of support. On the high end each parent is encouraged to grow their income because at a certain level they no longer accrue an increased obligation.

For some families it may be necessary for welfare assistance to make up the difference. When this occurs a lien should be placed on the future child support payments for repayment of part of the welfare benefits. This allows the needs of the children to be paid when they are growing up.

These child support figures are for a parent who plays no part in their child's life. Child support should be reduced to as low as zero with an even split in placement. Obviously in these cases both parents are paying for their child and not paying the other parent to raise the child. Additionally, each parent should be responsible for half of the reasonable healthcare costs.

Parents should be required to carry life insurance to make up for at least the minimum child support requirements from the present until each of their children reach age 19. This insurance benefit should be paid out in monthly installments to assure that it is available to care for the child.

The reality of divorce and children splitting their time between two homes is a great expense and the greatest cause of poverty. The infrastructure costs that are incurred are difficult for many families to bear. Trying to maintain two households on the income of what should be a single family. Parents need to do their best to provide a stable home together for their children. Children have a right to expect their parents to put their children's needs first.

# 17 CRIMINAL LEGAL REFORMS

**"Without liberty, law loses its nature and its name, and becomes oppression. Without law, liberty also loses its nature and its name, and becomes licentiousness."**
**James Wilson**


## Torture

Torture should never be legal in the US or under US authorities. Especially not permitted by the government! In the Declaration of Independence we clearly recognize the unalienable rights of life, liberty, and the pursuit of happiness that are endowed by God. Rights from God are for all people not just US citizens or people we like.

There is some debate over whether waterboarding is torture. If someone came to you and forcibly took you and waterboarded you, you would feel tortured. Certainly many people have voluntarily been waterboarded and we do it to our own military personnel in SERE school but that is different psychologically than having it done by people you consider your enemy. It is definitely torturous.

Torture is dehumanizing. Not only to the person being tortured but also to the torturer. Cruelty employed as a state tactic is immoral. It diminishes the moral authority of the state to justify punishment for many crimes. The ends do not justify the means. The means must be justified morally and constitutionally.

Whether or not we can gain some intelligence value should be a secondary consideration. The primary consideration should be that we act morally. We need to limit our interrogation techniques to those that are effective within moral boundaries. As a Christian I believe that all people have immortal souls and are made in the image of God. All of our nations, governments, institutions and man-made creations are finite but peoples' souls are not. Even the old straw man argument about using torture to try to stop a deployed WMD is not supportable under this understanding.

One of the factors that can convince enemy fighters to surrender or to fight less desperately is the reputation of the US for treating prisoners well, with dignity and respect. Other nations we have fought have treated US POWs better than they have other nations prisoners due to our treatment of their POWs. This can save US lives on the battlefield and in the POW camps.

## Between Misdemeanor and Felony

We acquired the categories of misdemeanor and felony from English common law. It was meant to differentiate between less serious and more serious crimes. Misdemeanors are for less serious crimes typically with a maximum penalty of one year in jail. Felonies are for more serious crimes with potential penalties greater than one year in prison.

We need a new category between misdemeanor and felony. There are many crimes where there is a need for supervision extended beyond one year. Drug and alcohol abuse crimes, child abuse and neglect, and domestic violence are best solved through counseling, education, mentoring, close supervision, and behavioral changes. These changes take time. For many of these areas five years is a more reasonable period of time to make these changes into life habits. We do not want to convict these people of felonies in order to gain this time to change behaviors. The loss of constitutional rights and social and economic opportunities will be an unnecessary burden for these people and their families.

These are categories for which many states attempt to use deferred prosecutions. Even in those situations the amount of time available to make changes under the agreement is limited. This middle category will help to provide the time for these changes to take hold for the long term.

Initially people will say the words they need to say to finish their sentence. It is only over a substantial amount of time of living with new habits do they become incorporated into the person. The current 6-12 months of counseling or anger management classes are largely worthless. It is not enough time. People need this much time just to break through their denial. Much more time is needed to achieve real change. This can greatly help rebuild broken families. We can break the cycle of abuse and neglect in many families before it is repeated by the next generation of these families.

This category should allow for court ordered supervision for up to ten years. No incarceration time should be part of this category. If incarceration is warranted for the offender then it should be done under the regular misdemeanor or felony categories.

This category is not for all people in these categories of crimes. There will be some who are just too dangerous. The prosecutor will still need discretion in deciding whether to pursue this path or prosecute as a felony.

## Incarceration Reform

Here are some ideas for incarceration reform at both the state and federal levels. Many of these ideas can provide better outcomes for those who are incarcerated and for everyone who will be neighbors of these offenders when they are released. These ideas are likely to reduce the long-term costs associated with prison inmates. These ideas are far better than releasing inmates early as many states are considering because of overcrowding and budget problems.

**Use work release facilities to reduce the use of traditional prisons.**
Use work release facilities for those convicted of non-violent crimes, habitual substance abusers, violent criminals in the final 10-20 percent of their sentence and sex offenders on extended or lifetime supervision. Offenders can pay for a portion of their own living expenses. They can pay child support. Offenders can use their own insurance to pay for counseling and healthcare for themselves and their dependents. They have the opportunity for further education at their own expense. The offender's time away from the facility is tightly controlled and they have to spend the remainder of their time in a secure facility.

If there is construction to build new facilities or to add on to a facility there should be consideration for several things. The larger facilities should incorporate basic classrooms so that the local community colleges can teach classes without the inmates spending more time outside and to reduce the staff requirements needed for processing people in and out of the facility. Inmates permitted access to internet connected computers can take classes online or with video conferencing. Emphasis should be on GED and core classes for college level. Classes that do not require expensive infrastructure such as labs. Good behavior and successful completion of the core classes could be a way to earn the opportunity to attend the local college for the more advanced classes.

Provide meeting rooms for group and individual counseling. Again, it is easier to process one non-inmate in and out of the facility than to process many inmates at varied times. Station probation agents at the facilities to make it more convenient to make sure that inmates are progressing on their court ordered and probation ordered responsibilities and obligations.

Incorporate more family visiting areas that allow inmates to meet with their families, especially their children. An observation area should be incorporated to facilitate observation by social workers/parenting education professionals. This will help tutor better parenting techniques and communication skills to reduce inter-generational criminal patterns and to improve family relationships to keep families together and strengthen communities when the offender is released. Conversely, interactions can be evaluated to determine when or if an offender can be allowed to return to the home with their spouse and/or children.

## Mental Health Prisons

There are many prisoners who suffer from mental illness. These inmates should be grouped and segregated in specific facilities for dealing with their illnesses. This may involve completely separate facilities or different cell blocks in the regular prison facilities. Mental health professionals need to be on staff to work with these inmates to mitigate the effects on their lives, on the prison staff, and to prepare them to reenter free society as most will do at some point in the future.

There should not be a "not guilty by mental disease or defect" option in court. There should instead be a "guilty due to mental disease or defect" option for conviction. The offender will then be required to serve their time initially in a mental health prison facility. They may serve their whole time in such a facility or be sent to a regular prison if "cured" or placed on extended supervision to complete their sentence. They should not get a shorter sentence due to mental illness.

## Other Related Reforms

Require every offender in the system to have a high school diploma, high school equivalency diploma, or GED before they are released from supervision. This will help offenders' job prospects after release. Many community colleges have had evaluation services and classes available for many years for those with learning disabilities. Most offenders should be mentally competent enough to complete this requirement.

Remove any roadblocks that exist for Christian organizations to work with inmates. In particular the Interchange Freedom Initiative run by Prison Fellowship has proven very good at changing the attitudes and worldviews of offenders and greatly reducing recidivism. Those of us who are Christians need to step up and make sure there is an abundance of volunteers to work with inmates in our communities. We need to train up mentors for inmates and those on probation and parole and for their families. This will have a tremendous impact on their lives and be a blessing for generations for the whole community.

Whenever a juvenile enters the criminal justice system it should trigger a requirement for the county human services department to become involved with the family to address any problems. The stress should be on improving the situation. Some options that should be available include parenting classes for the parents, counseling services, substance abuse intervention, domestic abuse intervention, financial management counseling, and monitoring for abuse and/or neglect. The same action should occur whenever an adult with custody or visitation of minor children enters the criminal justice system with a second misdemeanor (First time if it is domestic violence.) or a felony.

Convicts should be required to pay reasonable restitution to their victims. Frequently, it seems that restitution is minimal or absent when sentences are handed down. It should be reasonable that offenders make their victims losses whole to the extent possible.

For work release inmates, parolees, and probationers there should be a requirement that they have jobs. If they do not have a job they should have reasonable job search requirements. There should be a database of community service work that needs to be done that they can call-in or log-in to sign up for. There should be an automatic requirement to complete 40 hours of work each week; either paid or unpaid. Although paid vacation should be allowed to fill this requirement.

## Habitual Offender Laws

Sometimes called, Three Strikes Laws. These laws appear to have helped bring crime rates down over the past couple of decades. In some cases people with low level or nonviolent felonies have been sent to prison for life under these laws. Some modifications should be made to these laws to find a balance that is more appropriate to the level and type of crimes being committed.

For a second felony the maximum sentence should be 150 percent of the standard maximum. The minimum sentence becomes 75 percent of the standard maximum.

For a third felony the maximum sentence should be twice the standard maximum. The minimum sentence becomes 125 percent of the standard maximum.

For a fourth felony the maximum sentence should be three times the standard maximum. The minimum sentence becomes twice the standard maximum.

Each subsequent felony after the fourth should have the minimum and maximum increases by 25 percent over the previous conviction.

Multiple felonies committed as part of the same crime should be considered as the same felony for the purposes of determining the minimum and maximum sentences under this law. Same with multiple repetitive low level nonviolent felonies like burglary or car theft. Part of the purpose of this is the deterrent effect. A first time conviction of multiple felonies could result in an extremely long sentence otherwise. Any offender convicted of multiple felonies will already be facing many years or life even without the habitual offender enhancements. To avoid arbitrary manipulation of the order felonies should be ordered by the date of the crime not the date of charging or conviction. In some cases this may require resentencing if newer felonies result in convictions before older felonies.

This is not conducive to an easy soundbite like Three Strikes. It will create a better balance by increasing the sentences of repeat violent offenders without sending low level repeat felons to prison for life.

## Statute of Limitations Reform

Usually statute of limitations are important because over time witness memories fade and become less reliable. It also has the benefit of not incarcerating people who reform their ways. Unfortunately some career criminals who should be locked up for the rest of their lives get a pass on old crimes.

An exception to the statute of limitations should allow prosecution for crimes substantially similar to a crime for which the person was convicted. The renewed window for prosecution of the old crime should be the statute of limitations that exists for the newer crime for which the person was convicted.

The most common prosecutions likely to benefit from this type of reform will be sex crimes. The nature of sex crime motivation is such that these offenders are more likely to be repeat offenders. DNA profiles do not get into the CODIS database until after an arrest in some states or after a conviction in most states. There may be earlier crimes that can be attributed to theses offenders that can then be prosecuted. A larger window of time is available with this statute of limitations reform. Many pedophiles have dozens or sometimes hundreds of victims before they are caught. Getting justice for as many of these children as possible will also help put these offenders away for much longer.

This reform may be a powerful deterrent to future crime. Someone who has already reached the statute of limitations for past uncharged crimes could face a substantial penalty if they commit a crime similar to a past crime.

## Sexual Assault Reform

Sexual assault can be especially devastating to the victims. The profound consequences to victims dictates that the penalties for offenders need to be great. Compounding this is the high recidivism rate of this type of offender.

Many states still do not have criminal penalties commensurate to the harm caused. Most of these offenders will get out of prison at some point. Many communities have rules about where these offenders can live, visit, and work. Many times communities make it nearly impossible for these offenders to live in the community. This forces many to live in other communities.

Increasing the concentration of offenders for these other communities. Over time it will become increasingly difficult to find a community that will allow the return of sexual assault offenders.

The solution to protect communities and provide a place for offenders is to establish secure long-term work release facilities in every county. After serving their traditional prison terms these offenders should have to live the remainder of their lives in these facilities. These inmates should have their own small apartment. When they leave the facility they should be wearing a GPS ankle bracelet. Their routes and locations should be prescribed when they are outside of the gate. There should be periodic drug and polygraph testing. Their money and assets should be monitored. All phone and internet connections should be monitored and recorded if permitted at all. The offenders should be required to carry a mobile phone and answer immediately when called by their monitor. All planned trips outside of the facility to work, counseling, doctors, etc. should require that the supervisor, counselor, doctor report when they arrive and depart the facility. This should be done with an automated system so they do not have to be inconvenienced. These calls need to allow Caller ID and location information.

Perhaps at some time in the future there will be a means to protect society from these offenders without lifetime supervision. We are not close to that day now. The overriding imperative is to protect others from being victimized.

One area where sex crimes have been over criminalized is sex between young people. While it should be illegal to have sex with minors, those close in age should not have a sex offender label and lifetime punishment for consensual sex. They should have a deferred prosecution and supervision for several years. The limit for deferred prosecution instead of felony prosecution should be an age difference of about 20 percent of the younger person's age. This will allow a larger difference for older minors and a smaller difference in age to protect younger victims. All of the minors involved should be under supervision until at least their 18th birthday. They are more likely to be victimized or victimize in the future. It is better to get these young people counseling, mentoring, and supervision to reduce future incidents.

## Human Trafficking and Prostitution Reform

Human trafficking and prostitution have been problems for much of human history. Unfortunately the numbers of people victimized in these ways seems to be growing here and around the world. This is an especially insidious group of crimes. Traffickers and pimps exploit the desperation of poor people and revictimize many people who were sexually abused as children.

The penalties for human trafficking and pimping should be greatly increased. The damage caused by these crimes is substantial. The penalties should be as well. Sometimes in the media pimps are shown as protectors of the prostitutes. If that is the case in a real life situation discretion should be used when sentencing. The reality is rarely, if ever, like that. Much of the time coercion, intimation, rape, and drugs are used to force people into prostitution and to keep them there. In these cases they should be prosecuted for every rape, threat, delivery of a controlled substance. All sentences should be consecutive. Perhaps an ongoing criminal enterprise statute should be designed to address this similar to the RICO statutes. These offenders should be included in the sex crimes lifetime sentence program. After serving their prison sentence they will serve the remainder of their life from a work release facility.

The penalties for the johns that use prostitutes should be greatly increased as well. It is the demand that drives the human traffickers and pimps to supply prostitutes. The first offense should include a year of probation, a substantial fine and a substantial amount of community service. The local media should include these offenders in their regular listings of convictions with other crimes. A second conviction should incur a two year work release jail sentence, five additional years of probation, a substantial fine, and a substantial amount of community service. The third conviction should result in a lifetime in the sex offender work release facility after their prison sentence.

The previous paragraph assumes the prostitutes were adults. If the prostitute victim is a minor the penalties should be greatly enhanced. In addition to the previous penalties for johns they should have a statutory rape charge. The second conviction should result in a lifetime in the sex offender work release facility after the prison term. First conviction if it is obvious that the prostitute victim is a minor or there is positive evidence that the offender knew the victim was a minor. Our children need to be protected. They are the most vulnerable to being forced into prostitution. The commercial transaction should void the option of nearness of age or consent as a defense for the offender.

## STD Notice Requirement

Ideally everyone would wait for marriage and only have sex with their spouse but that is not the world we live in. Unfortunately not everyone can even trust their spouse. While everyone has a positive responsibility to protect themselves from harm there still needs to be punishment for those who harm others intentionally, recklessly, or negligently.

More than one million people contract STDs each year in the US. While most of these are not life threatening, they are all damaging. Many can cause a lifetime recurring illness or premature death. People need to be held responsible for not spreading STDs. There should be criminal and civil penalties for failure to inform sexual partners of a STD infection.

Intentionally infecting another person with an STD should be a felony ranging from assault to murder depending upon the circumstances. The infected person should have the burden of proof that notification was provided to sexual partners. This notice should be in writing with the signature of the other person confirming notification. If the person is infected the specific STDs should be listed. If the person has had sex since being tested for STDs they should disclose the date of their last test and the number of partners since being tested. Both parties should keep a copy of these disclosures.

There should not be an absolute requirement to disclose sexual history and testing record. Disclosure is intended as notification proving that there was no criminal intent to cause harm or death. It would be wise if everyone sought disclosure. If a potential partner is resistant to disclosing that raises a red flag that they are infected with something or have had other sexual partners since their last test.

No disclosure should be required from those who are paid for sex. They may be under threat to not disclose any infections so that they can keep earning. Johns should assume that they are infected.

People who become infected should be able to sue for the costs of medical care and other damages. Their estates, insurance providers, and the government should be able to sue to recover costs of care and other damages.

### Convict Labor

Most times inmates in prisons work for very low wages. Sometimes as low as 25 cents per hour. It should be required that prisoners be paid a market wage and benefits for the work that they perform. This will help to keep the system honest. Make sure that convict labor is not unfairly competing with outside labor.

Inmates should also be charged for the cost of room and board. Not the full cost of their incarceration but the average that a one bedroom apartment and typical food budget for someone on the outside. This bill should accrue and follow into their outside life. This bill should have to be paid without the option to bankrupt out of it.

Employers of convicts should provide healthcare coverage comparable to those on the outside. Care would still be sited in prison system approved facilities. This will reduce the cost for taxpayers. The employers should be able to choose their own employees from among the prisoners without knowledge of their medical history. The prison administration and the private employers should both be prevented from cherry-picking which inmates are employed to save on medical costs.

A market wage will help the inmate to pay restitution and child support. These are two constituencies that should have priority. The victims and the children of the inmate should not have to wait for the inmate to get out.

## Repeal the Lautenberg Amendment

The Lautenberg Amendment was passed in the 1990s. It bars firearm possession or ownership by everyone convicted of a domestic violence related misdemeanor or who are under a restraining order for domestic abuse. It occurred during a time when the country was awakening to the problem of domestic violence.

Certainly domestic violence is a problem that we cannot take lightly. Bringing peace to homes is a critical part of solving all the other problems in society. When domestic violence occurs it needs to be addressed as soon as possible to stop it and to minimize the long-term damage that is inflicted. Mandatory arrests are prudent when domestic violence occurs in order to get the people away from each other to let things cool down. There should be deferred prosecution on the first misdemeanor arrest with mandatory individual and couples counseling before the couple can live together again. At least three months of weekly counseling before living together again. During this period there should be a firearms prohibition. These times are full of tension and hot emotions and firearms should not be close at hand. It takes more than a few months to internalize changed behaviors. Whether or not the couple stays together, the counseling and other requirements of the deferred prosecution should be required for at least two years. Although as time goes by counseling could be less frequent than weekly. (Perhaps six months-weekly, six months-biweekly, six months-every three weeks, six months-monthly)

After three years of no law violations the person should get their firearms rights back. This is a constitutional right and should not be removed lightly. Most people who get arrested for domestic violence mature. Anyone who is not later involved in domestic violence, gun violence, or other violence should not continue to be penalized. Under the amendment an estimated six percent of police officers and military service members automatically lost their jobs because they could no longer use firearms. It is likely that a higher percent of the population is currently barred from firearms now because of the increased implementation of mandatory arrest laws. It is not appropriate to take rights away from a large group of people when only a small number of the group will misuse the right. Besides, anyone who wants to get a firearm can easily get one in a private purchase.

Military personnel should still be able to use firearms while on duty as long as they did not use a weapon during their crime and are meeting the other conditions of their deferred prosecution. They should only have use of firearms while under supervision.

Besides being an extreme punishment, the Lautenberg Amendment is usurping the police powers of the states. The issue of punishment for state crimes should be left to the states and not be taken over by the federal government. The federal Lautenberg Amendment should be repealed.

### New Military Pardon/Parole

The United States has been at war for almost fifteen years and the National Guard has played a vital part and will continue to for the foreseeable future. There is a sizeable part of the population that is currently barred from enlisting in the military services due to mistakes made earlier in their lives. Nationally, as much as ten percent of the male population may be felons or restricted from firearms use by the Lautenberg Amendment to the Gun Control Act. This is a proposal to give some of these people a chance to serve and earn full rights of citizenship back again. This is geared toward the National Guard because most law violators have violated state laws but this could be done at the federal level for federal convicts or for state convicts with the cooperation of the states.

It is understandable that the military would be reticent about recruiting people who have violated the law in the past. There is concern about discipline problems and possible future law violations or war crimes that would reflect negatively upon the service and set the mission back. The process that follows should effectively weed out those who could serve honorably from those who may not.

This should be started with veterans. They will be quicker to train and will more fully understand what they are getting themselves into. Because of the time frame of good behavior after conviction the normal enlistment age limits are likely to need to be waived for many of these recruits. Age limits should be waived for these recruits and any other recruits that want to serve in combat and that can meet the physical requirements. If they cannot make it to 20 years before mandatory retirement they should have to signoff that that is acceptable to them.

### Vision

Assign all to infantry companies designated for these new recruits to serve together to hold each other to the highest of standards. Select, preferably volunteer, Officers and NCOs to lead these units. These leaders should be known to be of good, strong character that can offset any actual or perceived limitations in the recruits. This unit would be volunteered for active service on a schedule comparable to active duty units. Preferably the unit would be volunteered for duty in dangerous, austere areas of operation such as the Afghanistan-Pakistan border area or eastern Afghanistan.

It would be understandable that the National Guard would not want this unit to be a part of any current unit out of concern that it may embarrass the unit. This unit should be independent and new for heraldry purposes but could be placed under the authority of current brigades for training and support services.

**Process**

Minimum requirements:

1. All incarceration time is completed.
2. Minimum of five years of time after sentencing and living outside of any institution, halfway house, etc. without a non-traffic law violation.
3. At least two-thirds of probation/parole is completed.
4. All court ordered and Department of Corrections ordered counseling or programs are completed.
5. Must be a U.S. citizen.
6. No convictions outside of primary state that would disqualify the applicant from military service.

**Step 1:** Complete and submit application packet of basic personal and offense information and a personal narrative about the offense(s) and a general release for files to military pardon review board. Packet is reviewed for completeness and meeting of minimum requirements. Military pardon review board subpoenas police, department of corrections, court, counseling, and social service files dealing with the applicant's offenses.

**Step 2:** A military physical is scheduled and completed to determine if applicant meets physical parameters. Failure to pass physical will be without prejudice and applicant will be notified of deficiencies and what needs to be done to correct deficiencies.

**Step 3:** If the military pardon review board requests a psychological evaluation it is completed and the results are submitted to the board and the applicant.

**Step 4:** Platoon sized groups of applicants are required to attend a four week high stress evaluation conducted by Drill Sergeants. Applicants are evaluated during extended periods of high physical, mental, psychological, and emotional stress. The cadre's job is to try to get the applicants to withdraw, act out irrationally, or lose their temper in unacceptable ways. This is to weed out those who break under extreme stress.

**Step 5:** Applicant is notified of the date for appearing before the military pardon review board. The civilian pardon board will attempt to notify victim(s) and prosecutor(s) and give them the opportunity to appear before the board. The applicant will be required to put a public notice of the hearing in the largest newspaper serving the county where each offense was committed for four consecutive weeks prior to the hearing.

**Step 6:** The board interviews the applicant and makes a recommendation to the state Adjutant General. If the Adjutant General approves the applicant then it is submitted to the governor for the military pardon/parole.

**Step 7:** The governor signs the military pardon/parole order. The initial order offers a military pardon conditioned on the completion of the terms of the military parole.

**Step 8:** The military parolees attend training together in platoon or larger units from Basic Combat Training until overseas deployment. Although some may be sent to additional schools for communications, medical, or other specialties needed in infantry companies.

**Step 9:** Applicant completes the conditions of the military parole.

## Military Parole Conditions to Receive Full Military Pardon

General Conditions

1. Firearms use and possession only permitted as required for service. No private possession.
2. No non-traffic law violations—civilian and UCMJ.
3. Not eligible for bonuses.
4. Not promotable beyond E-4 until completion of 12 months in a combat zone or a full pardon is received.

Completion Options to receive a military pardon

1. Serve honorably in the National Guard for four years with at least 24 months in a combat zone in a combat arms military occupational specialty (MOS) or in a field position in a combat arms unit.
2. Killed In Action
3. Wounded In Action and permanently disabled preventing continued service in combat.
4. Becomes a Prisoner of War.
5. Awarded five Purple Hearts.
6. Awarded the Medal of Honor.
7. Awarded two in any combination of Silver Star or greater award.

## Completion of Conditions of Military Parole

Full pardon for all misdemeanor and felony convictions in the state is received and all rights are restored.

## Failure to Complete Conditions of Military Parole

1. No pardon is received.
2. Must complete any uncompleted probation or parole time. Time in service will not count toward probation or parole portion of sentence that was stayed while on military parole.
3. Receive any usual and customary consequences for failure to complete enlistment.
4. May not reapply for military pardon/parole without permission of the military pardon review board.
5. Must wait at least two years to apply for another type of pardon.

## General Pardon

Pardons should be more readily obtainable for criminal offenders who have shown a solid, consistent example of good citizenship. The current process is highly politicized and in many jurisdictions it is nearly impossible to obtain a pardon. Pardons are an incentive for many to reform and be able to be full citizens again. The processes should be fair, consistent, and require a reasonable amount of effort to earn a pardon. This can be a societal indicator of reacceptance that could aid these offenders in better providing for their families. This type of formula will automatically adjust the waiting period to the sentence imposed by the judge.

Part of the requirement is a waiting period without a non-traffic law violation after completion of their sentence.

1. Wait an amount of time equal to any incarceration, plus,
2. Wait an amount of time equal to half of any probation/parole time.
3. Minimum wait of five years.
4. Maximum wait of twenty years.
5. Time is cumulative and starts after completion of last sentence.

In addition, the person needs to be a productive member of society and take responsibility for their crimes.

1. Apologize to their victim(s) in person if the victim consents or in writing or by recording media.
2. Have a job for at least 80 percent of the waiting period sufficient to pay their own bills.
3. Current on any child support.
4. No court ordered payments outstanding other than child support.
5. Actively participate in their children's lives if they have children and are permitted contact by law.

6. Perform 520 hours of community service times the number of years in their waiting period. This is not to say that they have to perform this many hours during the waiting period. If it takes them longer then they simply delay things for themselves. This number is just for calculating how many hours are required. They can start before the waiting period but cannot count any court ordered time.

For those who used a firearm in the commission of their crime there should still be restrictions on their firearm privileges. Their waiting period for the possession or use of firearms should be twice the waiting period for the remainder of the general pardon. This would be a general pardon conditioned on no firearm privileges for a specified period. If their use of a firearm in the commission of a crime resulted in a death then the firearms prohibition is for life. If this condition is violated other than in moments of self-defense or defense of others then the conditional pardon should be revocable by a court.

Ideally the sexual assault reforms described earlier will prohibit these offenders from applying for a general pardon. Any person who earns a general pardon and then is convicted of a felony should not be eligible for another general pardon.

Many people may be of a mind that none of these people should be pardoned or have firearms privileges restored. My belief is that habitual criminals will not be able to meet the conditions listed here. Only people truly striving to become good, peaceable citizens will achieve this status. Employers and others will better be able to differentiate between ex-convicts. It can make it easier for reformed offenders to get better jobs. Society will be the better for it.

# 18 DRUGS, ALCOHOL, AND TOBACCO

**"Some things are easier to legalize than to legitimate."**
**Nicolas Chamfort**

**"Men, in a word, must necessarily be controlled either by a power
within them or by a power without them; either by the Word of God or
by the strong arm of man; either by the Bible or by the bayonet."**
**Robert Winthrop**

## Drugs

The drug war has been going on for several decades with no reduction in
the supply of drugs. Anyone who wants to get drugs can get them. In the
process we have made it possible for criminal gangs to become enormously
wealthy and powerful. We have reduced people's liberty in the fight to stop
the supply of drugs. Not just the liberty of drug dealers and users but of all
people.

Economically, the only way to win the war on drugs is to reduce demand.
When law enforcement reduces the supply of drugs it just makes drug prices
go up. The dealers are able to make great profits even with less product. This
mitigates the risk and incentivizes trying to provide more drugs to the market.
These same drugs in a free market would be low cost, low margin
commodities. There would be no high profits that would warrant the risk of
prison for illegal supply.

Taking the big three of marijuana, cocaine (including crack), and heroin
out of the hands of the cartels, organized crime families, and street gangs will
cut $100 billion dollars of their income. It will drastically reduce their
motivation for murdering each other. It will greatly reduce their ability to
undermine civil society, here and abroad, by buying or intimidating
politicians, police, and judges.

Adding in the prescription narcotics to this program will further undercut
the profits of criminal groups. These drugs are readily available now.

Legalizing their recreational use will not significantly increase their use.

Legalization of these drugs along with strict penalties for human trafficking will reduce the number of foreign criminal gangs operating in the US. A significant reason for their operations in the US is because this is where the money can be made. Taking away their major revenue streams will greatly reduce their operations here.

The problem with drugs is with the users of the drugs. Without self-restraint people will continue to use drugs. The better way to fight drug use is with treatment and sharing the Word of God. That is the only way to truly win this war. Anti-drug peer pressure like has been effective in reducing drinking and smoking will be a better way to address drug use.

But all drugs are not equal. Some are far more devastating and addictive. Drugs should only be sold by licensed dispensaries that may only dispense an amount based on a legally designated maximum daily dose for an individual. Every user should have to make their own purchase and only be able to purchase a maximum number of daily doses at a time. The maximum should be based on the number of daily doses that could pose an overdose danger. This may need to be set in a table based on the weight of the person.

There are some like meth and some designer drugs that should still not be legally available. The speed in which a person can become addicted and the level of destruction should determine which drugs remain illegal. The illegal drug market value of these is small compared to the big three of marijuana, cocaine, and heroin.

### Protection of State's Rights and Employer's Rights

There need to be other limits besides the dosage that need to be in place. First, states need to be allowed to impose greater limits than the federal law imposes. Local people need to be able to decide if they still wish to ban the sale and possession of drugs in their communities. Employers need to be able to weed out impaired workers from their business. They should be able to fire or not hire workers who use drugs.

### Minimum Requirements

The federal law that allows these relaxed drug laws should require a few minimum conditions from states. There must be no tolerance of selling or giving non-prescription drugs to minors. Even parents should be barred from supplying their children. The penalties need to be severe to keep these drugs out of the hands of minors.

Likewise those who continue to trade in drugs illegally should be dealt with severely. The only reason to continue trading illegally would be to supply to restricted groups like children or convicts on probation or parole, or for transshipment to other countries.

There will need to be a registry that all legal vendors consult before selling drugs. They will need to check that their customer has not reached their purchase limit.

## Medicare XXI

When drugs are legalized they will need to be part of the Medicare XXI set aside for HSAs and be revealed to the user's medical insurance company for use in determining premiums. The estimated healthcare cost for each dose of recreational drug use needs to be set aside in the person's HSA just like for alcohol and tobacco purchases.

## Financial Misconceptions

Even though the drug cartels and the whole drug industry supply chain will lose over $100 billion per year in drug revenues that does not mean the new legal industry will be worth that much. Once the risk premium is removed from the cost of the drugs they will likely only be worth ten percent as much. This will not be a source of great tax collections. Marijuana is the least likely to lose substantial value due to the variety of products that can be laced with it. Most likely the set aside for a person's HSA will be a substantial part of the retail cost of these drugs.

## Solution

Drugs are a scourge and it is sheer foolishness to use or experiment with them. But some people use them to escape from reality or have become addicted. The key to solving the problem with drugs, alcohol, and tobacco is peer pressure, treatment, and a personal relationship with Christ. Abuse of these products does great damage to the fabric of society but the overwhelming damage is to the individual and their family. We need to help them to find a new way of life and protect their families and society from the damage as much as possible. Users need to be responsible for the consequences of their actions and for repairing the damage they inflict.

Prison has not been working because it is the wrong tactic. Certainly when people commit other crimes due to their intoxication then incarceration can be appropriate. But we need to use other means to reach users who are primarily harming themselves.

## Protection of Children

There need to be laws against intoxicated parenting. Children deserve the safety and stability of a drug and alcohol free childhood. It is probably too much to bar all drug or alcohol use around children but it is not too much to require that there is at least one responsible adult who remains sober for the care of the children. Someone who must protect the children from anyone who is intoxicated and prevent someone who is intoxicated from driving home with children.

A related matter is making it illegal to smoke in a home where children reside or where children are present. The penalty for this should not result in incarceration. It should result in a hefty fine, most of which should be placed in an HSA for each of the children involved. There should be a fine imposed for each child exposed to the secondhand smoke. This HSA should be invested in an S&P 500 index fund and set aside for when the child is an adult. The parents/guardians should be responsible for a smoke free environment for their children. After a child reaches adulthood they should be able to sue their parents for damages if they had to live in a smoke filled home.

Likewise an adult who supplies drugs or alcohol to a minor should be able to be sued by the minor for the damages related to their health, lost wages, and the cost of treatment for drug abuse. These are natural consequences that will be a larger threat to most people than law enforcement could ever impose. The proceeds of this should have to go in the child's HSA. Similarly insurance companies should be able to join with the child victim in order to recover the costs of treatment for drug, alcohol, and tobacco related conditions.

Giving a minor a sip or a taste of alcohol should not be criminalized or be grounds for a lawsuit. Or even a single drink on special occasions under parental supervision for teens. A more significant level of supply should be necessary.


### Intoxication License

There are some people who should not have access to drugs or alcohol because they have shown themselves to be dangerous or irresponsible when intoxicated. As part of a state ID or driver's license there should be an endorsement or prohibition to the purchase, use, or possession of non-prescription intoxicants.

Every person should automatically be eligible for this endorsement when they reach the age of 18 and graduate high school or earn a GED and do not have an adjudicated bar to the use of intoxicants. As age 18 is the age of majority in this country the 21 year old drinking age should be changed to 18. But it is also appropriate to require a minimum level of maturity as exhibited by successfully earning a high school diploma for the privilege of receiving this endorsement. People on probation or parole or who have committed crimes while intoxicated may have an adjudicated prohibition. This should be a penalty for parents convicted of intoxicated parenting.

Every person making a purchase of intoxicants will need to show their ID.

Every person using or possessing intoxicants will need to have their ID in their possession as well. With the implementation of Medicare XXI, IDs will already be needed for the process of HSA set asides.

### Prescription Reform

There are some reforms needed in the prescription system in the US. There are too many fraudulent narcotics scripts being issued throughout the country. There is also the dangerous practice of unnecessary antibiotic prescriptions. On the other hand there are many things that require a prescription that should be freely available for people to buy.

With a change to legalizing recreational drugs there should be a reduction in medical prescriptions for narcotics. There needs to be a better process for tracking and auditing prescriptions for narcotics. Recreational users need to be steered to those dispensaries so that they have to pay the HSA set aside. In auditing narcotic prescriptions it should be on the prescriber to document the need. Any pain that cannot be attributed to a tangible injury or illness should not be addressed in the prescription system. The patient should have to use the recreational system. If recreational use is not legalized the enforcement should still be improved. Doctors writing unnecessary prescriptions are violating the needs of their patients and need to be weeded out.

The CDC should be auditing doctors prescriptions of antibiotics. In most cases the patient files should have to have a positive bacterial infection test or face a fine. Although there are still times, such as in conjunction with surgery or lengthy hospital stays or depressed immune response when preventative use of antibiotics may be medically recommended. The medical community needs to determine the white, black, and gray areas and the CDC then needs to set and enforce appropriate fines or other penalties for inappropriate uses.

There are numerous medical items that unnecessarily require a prescription. This frequently involves medical devices. An example is a CPAP for people with sleep apnea to help keep their airway open when they sleep. There is no danger to someone without sleep apnea to use a CPAP. To get a prescription requires a sleep study and at least two doctor's appointments. It can take several months and cost thousands of dollars. The actual CPAP can be purchased for about $1,000. Another example is saline or lactated ringer IVs for fluid replacement. People cannot put these in their first aid kits because a prescription is needed. Certainly people need to understand when and how to use these products. But this is not complicated and like most products they can be sold with instructions and warnings. It is proper that an insurance company can require a prescription for payment but there are many things that an individual should otherwise be able to purchase without a prescription. This is a matter of personal liberty and market freedom.

# 19 SECOND AMENDMENT

**"Arms in the hands of individual citizens may be used at individual discretion for the defense of the country, the over-throw of tyranny, or in private self-defense."**
**John Adams**

The Second Amendment is crucial to securing all of our other rights and maintaining our freedom. Throughout history people have been controlled by denying them the right to self-defense and possession of the means of self-defense. Our founding fathers knew this from history and from personal experience.

Contrary to the talking points of many anti-gun activists guns are not primarily about hunting or sport shooting at ranges. Weapons and the purpose of the Second Amendment is all about self-defense. Whether that was on the frontier in the early days, on the streets of today's big cities, or if the government tries to overstep its constitutional bounds in the future.

No level of government should be able to restrict weapon possession except for very limited compelling reasons. Only people with felony convictions, protective orders, and mental illness should have any restrictions imposed by government. Even some of these groups should have a path to regain their weapons possession rights. For felons see the sections about pardons in the Criminal Legal Reforms chapter.

Non-citizens should have to seek permits to possess weapons in the US. Some obvious groups include recognized shooting sports competitors and security staff for foreign officials. Other non-citizens with at least five years of residency in the US without criminal offenses should have the option to possess weapons for self-defense.

I am relatively liberal on the possession of weapons by those who are not violent except in defense of self or others. I am in favor of people even being allowed to own full automatic weapons, crew served weapons, armored vehicles, armed helicopters, and high performance military aircraft. These weapons would have to be stored with and used under the supervision of the

National Guard. The owners would have to pay for the reasonable storage and security costs. The owners would be responsible for rent of training ranges to use these weapons.

Every citizen of a democratic republic needs to be trained to defend it. Every high school student who does not have a criminal or mental health disqualification should go through firearms safety and shooting training.

## Mass Shootings

### School Shootings

There has been an epidemic of school shootings in the past 20 years. Every time they occur the liberals try to stir up support for gun control legislation. This is the opposite of what is needed. We need armed school staff who can respond immediately to an active shooter. The very existence of this trained response team will deter most would-be school shooters. This team should train periodically with the local police to avoid friendly fire incidents when the police arrive and to determine the best procedures to work together.

In addition to firearms there are defensive measures that can be built into schools. These include security cameras, hallway baffles, and secure classrooms. Schools should have video surveillance of entrances and hallways at a minimum. The police should be able to log into both the live and recorded video through the internet. This can give them better situational awareness. Schools frequently have long straight hallways in order to more easily observe the movement of students. These straight hallways can leave many students vulnerable to a shooter who can cover the whole hallway. From inside secure classrooms teachers should be able to crank out baffles that extend about sixty percent of the way across the hallway outside. Several of these from both sides of the hallway will greatly shorten the distance that a shooter can see and target victims. It will give more students shelter as they escape from the shooter. The classrooms should have lockable bullet resistant doors. They should be equipped with a bullet resistant window to identify police when they arrive. The doors should be able to be locked so even a key cannot open it from the outside. All classroom walls and windows should be bullet resistant.

### Other Mass Shootings

Other mass shootings would be better thwarted by more people with concealed carry permits. These shootings happen so quickly that many people can be killed before even a quick police response. Now with the likelihood of ISIS inspired mass shootings in the future there is even more need for many people to have concealed carry permits and to be carrying their handguns.

Unfortunately the large cities that are the most likely to be terrorist targets have some of the more strict gun laws.

It is preferable that these people go through firearm safety, concealed carry law, and combat shooting classes. The first two areas are usually covered in the classes required for concealed carry permits. The combat shooting class cannot be mandated because many jurisdictions would make the testing too difficult for most to pass in order to prevent people from getting permits.

# 20 EMPLOYEE BENEFITS REFORM

**"Labor is the great source from which nearly all, if not all, human
comforts and necessities are drawn."**
**Abraham Lincoln**

### Pension Reform

There has been a running debate about the pros and cons of defined benefit plans and defined contribution plans. Below is a plan that would be a defined contribution plan for employers and a defined benefit plan for employees. The best of both worlds!

The recent economic downturn has highlighted the costs of defined benefit plans. For many years employers, both private and public, have underfunded these plans. Frequently, the projected return of the plan investments is unrealistically high. This allows the employer to put less money in the account and still appear to be putting sufficient money in according to pension protection laws.

In the public sector politicians have pushed the real costs of their promises off on future generations. Later when these promises come due the taxpayers are forced to pay higher taxes without receiving any more services. As has been seen around the country vital government services are being cut in order to pay for promised retirement benefits. The politicians who lied or hid the real costs are either gone or still lying about the problem.

In the private sector, many companies are forced to pay with today's revenues for retirement benefits earned years or even decades before. This has two potential results. The retirees may be shorted in their promised benefits. Or there is a reduction in the profit potential of the company. This reduces the income of current employees and investors. These added costs can force a business to relocate operations overseas to stay profitable.

Another risk to these retirement plans is the bankruptcy of the funding company. This is especially problematic when the plan was already underfunded. In some cases unrealistic pension promises caused the bankruptcy. In other cases poor business decisions, new technology, or bad luck may have forced the bankruptcy. No matter what the reason, a reduced or eliminated pension benefit is a serious blow to the average worker.

On the other hand many workers do not feel capable or prepared to manage their own defined contribution plan. Many also do not accumulate sufficient resources for their retirement in these accounts.

I propose a hybrid that provides more security for employees' retirement while also providing a defined contribution for employers. Instead of one permanent defined benefit retirement plan, each year the employer purchases a defined benefit annuity for each of their employees. Each employee would own their annuity. Traditional defined benefit pension plans are essentially revolving group annuities. Mathematically this new structure should be little different across a large pool of people.

Larger employers could provide employees with multiple annuity options from multiple companies. Annuity options can be reviewed and changed annually providing much more flexibility than a traditional pension plan. Additionally, employers could purchase insurance against bankruptcy or other risks to the annuities. With workers changing employers more frequently these days, they can accumulate a full working lifetime of annuities. They could have a different annuity for each year or each employer they work for. They could continue making contributions into the same annuity from multiple employers or supplemental contributions from their regular wages.

Retirement benefits will likely be proportional to wages so the total retirement will be related to lifetime earnings rather than a few select years. This will reduce the ability to game the system with work rules.

Small employers could be allowed to send an allotment to the annuity of choice of their employees. This would save the employer the administrative costs of providing this retirement benefit. The employer would not need to hire the expertise to assess annuities. The employees could find their own annuity.

Annuities will be especially useful for government employers. There will be a reduced ability of politicians to buy votes by providing a long term benefit when in office that incurs a long-term unfunded liability to taxpayers. There will be no need to set arbitrary years of service and retirement age in contracts. Workers will simply work until they feel they have accumulated enough retirement funds. The cost to taxpayers of double-dipping by getting full retirements from multiple levels of government or from retiring and then working for their past employer will become irrelevant.

Ideally workers would be able to wait until they retire to decide whether to take their benefits as a Life or Joint Life Annuity or Term Certain Annuity. When they decide to start receiving payouts from the annuities they can do so from some without taking payouts from others. Allowing some to continue growing. Flexibility until they elect to start receiving payouts. Each year employees should receive a statement with a table indicating their estimated payout amounts under the different options based on different starting years in the future. It should also inform them how much their benefit could be with certain levels of additional contributions.

Standard annuities tend to have high expenses. An analysis of these expenses should be conducted to determine which would be legitimate for these plans. They should be brought in line with the expenses for a traditional pension plan.

Retirement security for workers while pension benefit liabilities are removed from the company's and the government's books and paid for in the same time period as it is earned. WIN-WIN Deal!

## Employee Trust

Employees are increasingly at the mercy of a changing global economy. Increased automation and offshoring of operations are being used to keep corporations competitive. A true stake in the corporation should be established for the employees who do the work of the company. A benefit that puts them in the same boat with shareholders and management. At the same time the employee trust will reduce the base cost of employee compensation in a competitive market. While corporations are likely to continue to shed jobs, those who remain should benefit from the value of the increased productivity. The workers who lose their jobs will continue to receive some profit sharing for a period of time.

It makes the corporation more flexible in dealing with changing economic conditions and global competition. Companies with higher wages have a competitive disadvantage which needs to be compensated for either by reducing employee compensation, by reducing costs or increasing value in other ways. This method provides the employees, executives, and outside shareholders a common objective by aligning their interests.

Establish a trust of 20 percent of the ownership of the corporation for employees. The proceeds of the trust are distributed to the employees and former employees of the company.

1. Award each wage earner one point per dollar of compensation for the current year.
2. Each wage earner will retain 0.75 points per dollar of compensation from the previous year.
3. Each wage earner will retain 0.50 points per dollar of compensation from two years prior.
4. Each wage earner will retain 0.25 points per dollar of compensation from three years prior.

5. Each wage earner will retain 0.10 points per dollar of compensation from four to twenty years prior.
6. Former employees will receive points for prior years for a period of time equal to one-half of the time that they worked for the company at the same rate as current wage earners.

The corporation's profits must be paid out as dividends regularly. The proceeds of the trust are then distributed to the current and former employees based on the points. The employees will have votes for the Board of Directors of the trust according to their share of the trust. The employees will have votes for the Board of Directors of the corporation according to their share of the trust times the trust's share of the ownership.

For established corporations this trust may need to be established gradually to maintain the financial stability of the corporation. Most likely by foregoing full wage increases for a period of time in exchange for diluting the value of issued stock. Additional provisions will also need to be designed for mergers, spinoff, or dissolution of all or part of the company. Provisions will need to be designed to prevent the allocation of profits to a holding company or a foreign owner that would shift profits away from workers to a select group.

## Value of the Employee Trust

The employee trust allows a company to keep regular wages down while providing a guaranteed share of the profits. It will help to get employee support to make efficiency and waste reduction improvements. Employee support for automation will be easier to obtain. Employees will be motivated to lead reforms and develop solutions to improve processes and policies

In lean economic times the company's base labor costs are lower which will improve its resiliency. There will be less need to negotiate cost reductions with employees or creditors. It will mean less chance that the company will have to lay people off. Less support will be needed by laid off workers from government at a time when tax revenue is depressed. Keeping people employed means a faster turnaround in the economy.

Employees will be better protected from accounting manipulations that occur in connection to traditional profit sharing plans. Employees have an incentive to report discrepancies between company filings and actual observations. The employees own part of the company and receive compensation based on the actual profits. The employees deserve to reap the rewards of their work.

Company executives and sales people should also be a part of this trust. Their direct compensation should count toward points in the trust. Any performance incentive should be from the trust as with the other employees. Only total throughput for the corporation truly increases profits. Bonuses for narrow aspects of the business should be discouraged. These aspects can be the subject of performance reviews but the success of the corporation as a whole should be placed above individual performance. So that executive compensation levels do not overwhelm the trust set a maximum limit per person. No person may receive an annual amount from the trust that exceeds the average for current full-time employees by more than 50X. Voting rights related to participation in the trust are likewise limited to 50X of the average current full-time employee.

Including a period of time of continued compensation for former employees has several benefits. It recognizes the value of their contribution to the company that extends beyond the time that they were directly working. Employees are incentivized to be loyal and motivated right up to the end of employment and after their employment ends.

## Vesting Reform

In the modern labor market employees change jobs more frequently than in the past. Many employers establish a delay before vesting of the employer contribution to 401k plans, pensions, profit sharing, etc. This means that many employees are shorted hundreds or thousands of dollars of benefits. If employers want flexibility with hiring and firing employees then they have to accept the same flexibility from employees who wish to change jobs. Wages and benefits have to be fully vested in the pay period when the labor occurs. ERISA needs to be changed to eliminate this delay. Too many people lose too many years of retirement savings and it will likely become worse in the future as job changes become even more common.

An option if the employer has transaction costs that they feel is significant they can pay out the value of employer contributions to the employee's IRA or other account. Employees are entitled to the money they earn. Game playing to avoid paying some employees cannot be tolerated.

## 21 PULLING IT ALL TOGETHER

**"All the great things are simple, and many can be expressed in a single word: freedom, justice, honor, duty, mercy, hope."**
**Winston Churchill**

The struggle between conservatives and liberals reminds me of the Civil War. The liberals are attempting to protect the slavery of the populace to the government and are rebelling against the newly energized conservative forces attempting to end that slavery and return the country to liberty. The liberals see the end of their way of life as slave masters over the rest of us. Both sides mobilized over the last decade with the liberals gaining ground first, with their biggest victory being Obamacare. The tea partiers and other conservatives mobilized over the last several years and gained ground by taking the US House in the 2010 election and the US Senate in 2014. Much as the South tried to defend the dying institution of slavery the liberals are trying to defend the dying institution of the welfare state which threatens to destroy the country.

Both sides charged into each other during the recurring crises over the raising of the debt ceiling and the federal budget. There are political charges and counterattacks for weeks and in the end there is a stalemate. The liberals are dug in on the hills keeping the conservatives from reaching the two-thirds of each house needed to overcome a Presidential veto. Both sides kept attacking the other but in the end they wound up in the same place—stalemate!

The conflict has generated great uncertainty and fear in the people back home and Republicans started to feel worried about their support. They wavered and cut a deal that was unsatisfying to everyone but allowed each side to step back and regroup.

Much as both sides in the Civil War were surprised by the intensity, the intransigence of their foes and how big the conflict became, both sides in the war between limited government and welfare state were surprised by their foes. Both believed they were right and deserved to win.

I advocated using the debt limit vote as a tool to force the passage of a federal spending limit constitutional amendment since 2009. One of the things I tried to stress was the need to prepare the country for the standoff that would inevitably take place before enough pressure could be brought to bear on enough Democrats to vote for the amendment.

I was wrong to believe that enough Democrats could be convinced. There are too many in solidly Democrat states and districts. Because the liberals are on the defensive all they have to do is not give up or lose decisively to be victorious. For us conservatives we have to win most of the battles or we will lose the war. Eventually if the federal budget and entitlements are not reformed then the American economy will collapse. Great instability usually leads to an erosion of freedom due to people seeking stability. We need to achieve changes before this happens.

We need every state and district to be in play for conservatives. We don't have to win every seat. We have to keep hitting the liberals on the flank. When they turn to meet us we have to shift and hit them on the flank again and again and again. We have to keep tearing away their support on issue after issue. Enough to make them fear the next election. This combined with a hardnosed conservative President who will make a stand against excessive spending can bring fiscal victory. Victory will be passage of a federal spending limit constitutional amendment.

## Lowering the Cost of Doing Business in the US

Many of the proposed solutions in this book are geared toward lowering the cost of doing business in the US. This is vitally important for the creation of jobs. Every expense that a business or a proposed business has to deal with reduces the viability of the business. In order for a business to secure investors or a loan they have to show a high likelihood of covering all the costs and having a sufficient buffer to survive the many risks that a business faces. That buffer will show up as profit. As said earlier, profits are good. They drive economic expansion and new jobs.

The federal spending limit amendment lets business and the world know that there is a limit to the amount of taxes that the US government will take out of the economy. An upper limit on one risk!

Social Security XXI will take most of the cost of Social Security off of the federal books. This reduces the risk of higher FICA taxes and political games over this benefit. It expands the level of investments by the average citizen and helps to create more individual wealth. Every worker and their spouse will have their own account that politicians cannot take away. This will make families more secure and self-sufficient. There is a safety net for those who live long or are unable to earn enough. When someone dies young their contributions will be rolled over to their heirs.

Medicare XXI with HDHPs/HSAs does even more to reduce the costs of healthcare in the US. It takes healthcare off the books of employers and reduces the burden on taxpayers. Economic planning will be easier without having to deal with healthcare cost. At the same time individuals and families will have a better benefit, at a lower cost, and at a lower risk of bankruptcy.

The reforms in the tax rates and structure will make products and services from the US more competitive both here and overseas. The VAT will shift more of the tax burden to the point of purchase from the point of manufacture. The lower corporate taxes will make it less expensive to operate from the US. This will result in more jobs in the US and in more investment income in US citizens' HSAs, Social Security XXI accounts, and other pension plans. This shift will also reduce the cost of filing and collecting income taxes by billions of dollars.

Energy produced here will help to lower the cost of doing business here. Even with most energy prices based on the world market there is benefit due to the inherent reliability in US operations, reduced risk of energy interruptions due to international incidents, reduced transportation costs, and the wealth generated stays here with US investors.

A sound immigration policy will provide enough of the right kinds of legal workers in the US while eliminating the ability of those here illegally to stay here. This will take an unfunded burden off of the healthcare and insurance industries and taxpayers.

The promotion of families in the tax code, welfare reform, and other areas help to reduce poverty and the cost of subsidizing broken families. This will reduce the costs to taxpayers that will keep taxes lower because these costs will be paid for by the recipients of aid when their circumstances improve.

The government reforms to get rid of unnecessary agencies and regulations will save businesses billions of dollars every year. There will be more certainty for business planning, especially in capital projects.

All of these efforts to make business more competitive when operating in the US are good for all of us. Millions more jobs will be generated for US workers. More investment profits help create jobs and produce the money that funds our retirement accounts, pensions, Social Security XXI and HSAs. This is a far better way to reduce income inequality than income redistribution.

## Building Stronger Families

Strong healthy families are the cornerstone of a healthy civil society. Traditionally families were the initial safety net for each of us. Government over the past 75 years has gradually tried to take over this area of responsibility. Unfortunately government can only do a one size fits all program that does not match up with the true needs of people. Government creates dependency. The true needs are stronger relationships with family and friends. By making government the tertiary safety net and returning family and friends to the place of primary and secondary safety nets we will strengthen these relationships.

More individual wealth will be created with the transition to Social Security XXI and Medicare XXI. The tax code is restructured to help all people grow their wealth easier and to reduce the cost burden imposed by the federal government. This includes the ability of families to borrow for education and a home and pay the interest to their own account instead of to the government or a bank. With healthcare costs removed as a lump sum cost for employers they can offer employees more flexibility. It will be easier to afford flexible scheduling for new parents, near retirees, and employees recovering from injury or illness.

Reforms to welfare and the tax structure will encourage the unifying of families. These ideas will help families to become financially stronger and lift millions out of poverty.

## Six Trillion Dollars of New Debt

This is $6 Trillion in President Obama's first term that could have been invested in the private sector if the federal government had not used it to bailout banks, car companies, Fannie Mae, Freddie Mac, AIG, the states and cities. Much of this was to keep the union workers that depend on these organizations from getting laid off. Unfortunately I think that the loss of jobs for these people is a secondary concern for the Democrat leadership. Their primary concern is the loss of union dues that are used to support the Democrat Party and its candidates.

If the federal government had not sucked up all these dollars then the investors would have been looking for other places to invest their money. This could have created millions of jobs in the real economy instead of subsidizing waste. These wasteful deficits must be ended to keep the money in the real economy to grow the economy. Most importantly, it is immoral for us to stick our children and grandchildren with the excessive debt that has been built up over the past years.

## Stop Being Timid

I am conservative and by nature I am against radical changes. There is nothing radical about bringing the federal government back to fiscal restraint and solvency. The government is here to protect the people and the peoples' rights. Government is the servant and not the master. It is time to break up this concentration of power.

One major example I have thought about is the timid positions about reforming Social Security. Public opinion is against all of the options for making Social Security solvent. That is not a surprise. Anytime anyone proposes changes to the program they get trounced on by the rest of the political class and the media. That is why it has acquired the reputation of the "third rail in American politics."

Recently we have had some Presidential candidates brave enough to propose increasing the full retirement age by one year over several decades. This is just too timid for the times and the conditions. Even if such a change could just barely bring Social Security into solvency, Social Security is not the only program in the federal government. We have to look at the full cost of all aspects of the government. When Social Security is paid to people who are able to work then that money is not available for other necessary obligations or for growing the economy. Social Security must return to being part of the safety net. It cannot be the means of support for a substantial part of every person's life. That is not sustainable for the country.

That is the standard by which all spending must be judged. Only necessities and even then there need to be priorities. This is where the federal spending limit amendment comes into play. Forcing the setting of priorities!

While many in the political class will consider many of the ideas presented in this book to be radical they are wrong. It is far more radical to expect that Americans will agree to the decline and fall of the United States. That is the choice that we must make. Courage and national success or timidity and national failure! Which will you choose?

# 22 MAKING CHANGE HAPPEN

**"All that is necessary for the triumph of evil is that good men do nothing."**
**Edmund Burke**

Growing up and as a young adult I had beliefs and values similar to most around me. In those around me there were a variety of political convictions; probably slightly more Democrat than Republican. So I used to consider myself a pragmatic moderate. Lately, to the rest of the world my moderation and the moderation of most around me has been called conservative. Unfortunately many of those around me still call themselves Democrats even though they are conservative on the issues. Talk with your Democrat friends and family. Many who do not pay close attention to politics are likely in the same position.

## WHAT TIME IS IT?

It is time for Tea Partiers and other Conservatives to take over the Republican Party! Especially those of you who like the ideas in this book!

This has to be about promoting values, principles, and ideas! Not about promoting particular individuals. The individuals that lead must represent these values. Within the movement there has to be cooperative competition not cutthroat competition!

## Why?

The combination of the conservative passion and convictions of tea partiers and other conservatives with the structure and resources of the Republican Party will be far stronger than separate organizations. Whether you are a tea partier or other fiscal conservative, right-to-lifer or other social conservative you should take over the local county parties. The issue organizations should be like the militia and the Republican Party like the Army. The national and state parties will provide the structure and the local parties are where all of the people meet and set the agenda, decide on the platform, and stay organized to elect and hold officials accountable.

By taking over the Republican Party, there will be much more influence on the platform and selection of state party and Republican National Committee (RNC) officials. We also have to make sure that the rules for nominations for candidates are not changed in such a way as to make it harder for conservative candidates to win primaries and caucuses.

Most of us have been frustrated by the Republicans in office spending too much, taxing too much, and not crafting sound conservative solutions to national problems. We have seen the RNC and various Republican election committees supporting candidates that do not support core Republican values, core conservative values because they are afraid they cannot get elected in their district. The message of what the Republican Party values has been lost due to these compromises. We in the tea parties have been telling the Republican Party to take a stand and the American people are echoing the call. Now is the time to take over and control the Republican Party from the grassroots.

## How?

The RNC leadership is elected by the voting members of the RNC. The voting members of the RNC are selected in various ways by state party leaders. State party leaders are elected by district party leaders. District party leaders are elected by county party leaders. County party leaders are elected by the dues paying members of the county party. This process usually occurs in the first half of odd years.

In much the same process the platform for the Republican Party is established. Each county party holds an annual caucus in which the dues paying members may discuss, propose changes, and vote for the platform that the majority can agree to. Then they elect members to represent the county at the district level caucus and the state convention. At the district caucus the county platforms are molded into one district platform. The district then elects members to represent it at the state level caucus. This platform is then presented to the delegates to the state convention where it can be approved or amended. The national platform is derived from the state platforms.

By becoming involved at the county level you place yourself in a position to help influence the leadership and platform of the Republican Party. You can help ensure that the Republican Party has conservative values, leaders, and candidates. You put yourself in position to become a delegate at the state and national conventions and have a larger, more effective say on platform and candidates. You will provide the support for conservative candidates to run for office, be nominated, and get elected!

## Getting Started!

Join your county party and bring all of your conservative friends along.

Get a copy of the constitution and bylaws for your state and county party and find out the rules they operate under. Join the committees and volunteer in other ways to learn how things are done and to network to find out who the other conservatives are. Engage in discussions promoting your conservative beliefs. Then usually in the first quarter of the year there is a county caucus. Make sure that you and all the other conservatives are there to submit change motions to the platform, resolutions, constitution, and bylaws and vote on them. Usually in odd years there is an election for new officers for the county party but there may be some vacancies at other times. In many areas the boards of county parties have vacancies that are just waiting for conservative activists to fill. Even if there are no formal vacancies there are likely to be important unofficial positions from which people can exert much influence simply by being there. Take advantage of these opportunities.

## Maintain Unity!

As much as I want only conservatives elected, we all have to commit to maintain unity after decisions are made in primary and caucus votes and join together to vigorously support the nominees. Too often a branch of the party has failed to support a nominee because the person was not good enough for the faction but was still the best of the general election options. The time to promote the best candidate is leading up to the primary or caucus. Help the candidate build sufficient support then. After the primaries and caucuses we must immediately become one again and support our nominees! This must start with the losing candidates congratulating and endorsing the winning candidate! There are few Republican nominees who will be worse than a Democrat nominee.

There is much talk about a schism between the tea parties and the establishment. First, I don't believe that all those called establishment politicians are political moderates or liberals. There are many conservatives in this group. I also don't believe that all of the politicians who court tea party support are truly conservative. (There are certainly opportunists who simply say what they need to get elected in both sets. I do believe that most of our elected officials are not in this category. They are earnest about what they believe.) As I see it the difference lies in perspective and patience. Those who are called establishment believe in gradual incremental change and favor stability. They see the same impending debt and entitlement crises as the tea partiers but believe that we must maintain stability in the process.

The tea parties have lost patience and have strong fears about the future of the country. They have seen excessive spending by a Republican majority in both houses of Congress and a Republican in the White House. They have also seen Democrats propose huge spending and tax levels and the Republicans propose spending and tax cuts. Then when a "compromise" is worked out the Democrats get their huge spending and tax levels. There is great fear about the cost to the country when our entitlement programs and debt levels are exploding and they know it is a ticking time bomb for our economy and way of life. Many think that the compromises that have been made in the name of compromise and stability have caused many in the establishment to lose sight of core Republican values.

I firmly believe that both sides have a common long-term vision for America but have different ideas about how to get there. It is time the establishment get more passionate and effective at making conservative changes happen. It is time that tea partiers show more wisdom and less recklessness in pursuing conservative change.

I think part of the problem is that the party has not done enough to educate the general public about the issues and to organize from the grassroots up for the benefit of all of our candidates. We should not be losing elections based on our core values and beliefs. We are the party of liberty, lower taxes, and common sense.

## Seeing the Vision

*I would like to share this letter sent from the future by a local volunteer and does a very good job in describing the vision I have for developing the party grassroots. It was written shortly after the November 8th, 2016 election.*

Last year another volunteer came to my door asking me to participate in a survey about what was happening at the state capital and Washington. After I completed the survey I was asked to volunteer to help organize my neighborhood for the local Republican Party—to help turn out more conservatives like myself to vote in the upcoming elections. I have to say that I was initially very reluctant to become involved. I had strong beliefs and did not like the direction the country was headed and I liked the changes I was starting to see in the Republican Party and in Republicans in office but I did not want my family to be on the receiving end of bad behavior from any of my neighbors who disagreed with me. Besides, I already had a lot on my plate. I had to think about it for a while.

A little later I was asked to host a get together in my home for other Republicans from the neighborhood and I nervously agreed. The local party helped arrange everything and over 20 people showed up. We talked about what was going on in Washington and the state capital and our frustration about it. But not only that, we talked about our lives, the neighborhood, cars, recipes, sports, and many other things. I made several new friends that night. It reinforced that we were not alone in what we believed and how we felt. The local party also arranged for a couple of local elected officials to stop by and mingle with everyone and answer a few questions. This helped to personalize these officials and I think it made it easier to motivate people to action later. As for action, several local party volunteers were on hand to get everyone connected into one or more issue coalitions and to show them how to stay connected with the local party's website, Facebook page, Twitter account, and e-mail. Also a telephone tree was set up for those who did not have a computer.

Over the next couple of months we doubled in number as a result of everyone inviting other neighbors to join us. Usually it came about when talking with neighbors while walking the dog or the spouse. When people expressed common sentiments they were invited to help out. For the neighbors who were undecided or opposed to what we believed. We arranged for them to receive letters that laid out what and why we believe what we believe and where to find out more information to explore the issue more deeply. Each of the coalitions were getting together every month and keeping us informed about the issues important to us.

Our little neighborhood group became a large neighborhood group as time went by. We got together regularly. Several times were to go door-to-door and make phone calls. But most of the get-togethers were social—someone hosting a barbeque or some other event.

Earlier this year we stepped up our activities in preparation for the local elections. Each week in the month leading up to the election we had about a dozen people who went door-to-door, usually on Saturdays and about the same number who got together to make phone calls. We were contacting those in our neighborhood who we had not identified which party they preferred and which issues were important to them. Our membership grew; we targeted people with information better, and created a call list of supporters to turn out for the election. Most of us only did 1 or 2 of these outreaches in the month leading up to the election. **Many hands make light work!**

Then the last few days before the election most of us volunteered for a three hour shift to help remind other supporters to vote and to make sure they knew who all of the conservative candidates were. Our efforts were very effective! There were more votes cast than ever before in a local election in our district and all of the conservative candidates won our district. That really helped to inspire everyone to do even more.

We also had some healthy discussions with each other about the Presidential primary candidates that were vying for our support. I believe this helped us all better evaluate the candidates. After the Republican Presidential nominee was determined, we quickly rallied behind the candidate. We continued becoming stronger in our own district and helping other districts to organize. Again most of our gatherings were social but we accomplished a lot to support our conservative candidates. The coalitions had matured and were helping us all to stay better informed about the issues.

During the summer our ward took responsibility for filling the office one day each month. By then it was just another get together with friends. When surrounded by friends it was much easier to make phone calls and go up to people's doors and talk with them. Even more fun was joining with so many people from throughout the area in walking in the parades. Our group for the parades was huge.

After Labor Day we started picking up the pace in our activities. These last nine weeks we all started getting excited about the possibility of electing all of our candidates. The polls looked good and we were organized and ready. We had our district ready and we were helping other districts in the county and in other parts of the state. We were fired up! Many of us did a shift every week during this time.

Then these last 4 days most of us worked another shift or two to help remind our friends and neighbors to vote and who the Republican candidates were. **At the election night victory party I was remembering back to times when I did not feel like going out and talking to people or making phone calls. It was at those times I would think about our boys and girls overseas fighting to preserve our freedom and to help others realize their own freedom. Then I would realize that what I had to do here was in no way as difficult as what they had to do but it was just as vital to preserving freedom for us and for future generations. Wow! Looking back I can't believe how much we accomplished. I am glad I stuck with it.**

I would like to thank those who got these neighborhood groups started. They have worked very well. Many of the people I talked with over the past two years did not get involved in politics or did not consider themselves Republicans or conservatives but over time with reasoned friendly discussions they became more involved and many turned out to vote. These new votes were crucial to our wins yesterday. Again, thank you, I look forward to a more hopeful future that I was privileged to be able to fight for.

P.S. Last night the chairman of the local party thanked everyone for their help. He also pledged to keep working on building and maintaining the neighborhood groups and coalitions we built over the past two years. He said we were needed to help keep our Republican representatives supported and hold them to Republican principles so they don't stray and we have a repeat of the last couple decades. That was good to hear because many of us had already decided that on our own. Both to keep the politicians in line and also because we are friends now and we want to continue our association.

*I don't know about all of you but I find it fascinating to hear from the future. Seriously though, my prayer is that every one of us can write a letter similar to this in November 2016.*

## Every Member A Recruiter

Each one of us knows many people, friends and family, who feel the same way as we do about which direction this country needs to go.

> Lower taxes and lower government spending
> Less government intrusion into our daily lives
> Strong national defense
> Protection of family values

Unfortunately they are not party members. This is about more than numbers. While party headcount and dues are important and valuable they are minor compared to the other benefits. It allows us to be more effective on a local level in helping each other stay informed and in mobilizing each other at times of crucial votes in the state capital and Washington, and turning out voters for local elections as well as national elections. Over the past decades we allowed ourselves to be led by our national leaders. Now we need to return leadership to where it belongs, at the local level. Many voices and many hands will make the workload lighter on all of us.

Talk to your family and friends about the issues and then encourage them to follow through on their convictions and join the party and make their voices heard. Together we will rebuild the foundation of freedom beginning with Our County.

## Sharing the Gospel

For all of my Christian brothers and sisters, I believe it is more important to share the Gospel with those around us and to the ends of the earth than any other thing we do. Especially more important than politics! But as citizens of a republic we have a duty to help rule our country, state, and communities. As Christ followers we are ambassadors of Christ and need to strive to represent Him to the best of our ability in everything we do. We need to be open to God carrying us even further than we believe possible. This goes for all aspects of our lives, including politics and public policy. So it is important to be knowledgeable about issues and candidates and involved in voting and running the country.

For far too long we have been lazy about growing the kingdom here on earth. During and after the next election we all need to step up and serve Christ and our thirsting and dying neighbors. The Church needs to take a page out of the Mormon playbook and plan for and expect all of our people to be full-time missionaries for at least a couple years of our adult lives and to actively support the missionaries the rest of our lives. There is so much work to do and too few to do it. The Holy Spirit does the heavy lifting of converting people and changing their lives. We are called to help. There is nothing more valuable for us to do than to show our love by sharing the Gospel and being involved in each other's lives.

Both here and overseas we need to be far more proactive in sharing the Gospel and developing relationships with our worldwide family. The US will not be the sole superpower forever, perhaps no more than another couple decades. We need to engage in the spiritual fight that the government is incapable of fighting. Fostering a culture of love and forgiveness due to personal relationships with Christ will go a long way to bringing peace to the people of the world despite the problems of the world.

As for political change, over the long term the political change will follow the personal spiritual and cultural change. These changes are what will have a better effect on our lives, our relationships, and our society than anything our politicians can do.

# 23 DEALING WITH POLITICAL PHONE CALLS

**"Talkers have always ruled. They will continue to rule. The smart thing is to join them."**
**Bruce Barton**

In politics there are many phone calls being made to you. I have made many thousands of these calls and I have run operations that have made tens of thousands of political phone calls. There are a couple different types of political phone calls. Each type has its own purposes and structure.

**Voter Identification (Voter ID) Survey Calls:** These are to help determine which candidates and party you support and which issues are important to you. The purpose is to identify who should be called at election time to turn out the party's supporters. These are usually made by volunteers although technology now allows for automated surveying.

**Get Out The Vote (GOTV) Calls:** These are made in the final days before an election and on Election Day to remind you to vote and to encourage you to vote for the party's candidates. This is done by a mix of volunteers and recorded "robo-calls."

**Volunteer Recruitment Calls:** These are calls to likely supporters to ask them to help in the campaign. This is done usually by campaign staff, volunteers, and sometimes with "robo-calls."

**Fundraising Calls:** These are done to raise funds for the candidate or party or issue campaign or independent group or other campaign. Whew! Maybe I should have just said everyone! At the national level this is usually done by professional fundraisers. At the state level it is done by a combination of professionals and volunteers. At the local level it is usually done by volunteers unless you are in a large urban district in which case professionals are frequently needed.

**Information and Invitation Calls:** These are done to inform you about upcoming events and activities or to solicit some action such as call about legislation. These are sometimes done with volunteers but are usually done with "robo-calls."

Please take the time to listen to these calls and participate in governing this great country of ours.

I am going to make some suggestions on how to deal with the calls to help who you want to help and hurt those you do not like. I know right now most of you just want to know how to get them to stop. Here is how to stop almost all political phone calls. The basis of most political lists is the state voting lists and past contributors. If you stop voting and stop contributing then you will eventually stop getting called! If not, keep reading!

For calls from Democrats just keep them on the line as long as possible to waste their time and money.

If you like the candidate or party whose campaign is calling stay on point and quickly deal with the call. Most callers do not have a direct line to the candidate or party leaders so don't waste their time with policy discussions or recommendations. Go to their website, office, or write a letter. For surveys please answer the questions. If you do not wish to answer the questions just say you are a supporter but don't want to say anymore and hang up. For GOTV calls as soon as you know who is calling tell them you are a supporter and that you are voting or have voted.

For volunteer recruitment calls please call back and volunteer if at all possible. An incredible amount of volunteer and paid staff time is spent just trying to keep the office filled with volunteers. If everyone who votes Republican did just a single three hour shift per year and two shifts in the final three months before major elections we would be well supported. If you support a candidate or party show it with a few hours of time.

For fundraising calls, if you know you will not be contributing just say that you are a supporter and hang up. Most professionals are required to rebut an initial "no" from one to three times. For all calls time is either money or volunteer time, both of which are valuable. Don't waste it for those you support. Professional fundraising services usually charge a fee of $30-70 per hour for their people to call you. They get paid by the campaign whether you contribute or not. Letting the caller get off the phone with you as soon as possible will allow them to reach people who are going to contribute. An even better solution is to save your favorite candidates and party from having to engage professional fundraisers by supporting them before they need to resort to professional fundraisers.

If each person that votes Republican gave just ten dollars to the national party, state party, county party every year then they would be adequately funded for a Presidential level election. Likewise give five to ten dollars to each of the Republican nominees from US Senator down to local levels each election year. If you can afford more please help more because you know that not everyone will. I suggest joining your county party and helping with double or triple the levels listed above. Together we can restore our lost liberty!

# INDEX

# CONTACT THE AUTHOR

**"I don't measure a man's success by how high he climbs but by how high he bounces when he hits bottom."**
**General George S. Patton**

If you would like to reach out to the Author or help promote the ideas in this book please contact me at:

hugging.the.third.rail@gmail.com
or
https://www.facebook.com/hugging.the.third.rail
or
Follow me on Twitter at http://twitter.com/HugtheThirdRail

Let us relentlessly fight for liberty together!

God Bless You Today and Always,
May God Bless the United States of America,
Let us all look to Almighty God for guidance in all things. Amen